"A bracing narrative that surges with outrag

—*Chicago Tribune*

"A scathing analysis of the political and social aftermath of the storm. Blending interviews with survivors of the disaster with his profound knowledge of Black migration and government policy, he provides the historical framework for the intense debate surrounding the disaster."

—*Ebony*

"It is so weirdly ironic and yet so beautifully simple that, after all the years of demonstrating, debating, legislating and raising our voices 'til they were no longer heard, it took the weather—the weather!—to literally and figuratively rip the facade off America's two biggest taboos: Race and Class. Once again, Michael Eric Dyson lays it all out in a way that none of us can ignore. The lessons of Katrina are not just a moment to feel shame, but an opportunity to give ourselves one last chance to deal—truly deal—with the ongoing tragedy of inequality in America. Dyson thinks we can do it and so do I. Every thinking, caring American should read this book. Should we fail to heed its warnings, the next storm we face will involve more than just wind and rain."

—Michael Moore, Oscar-winning director of *Fahrenheit 9/11* and author of *Will They Ever Trust Us Again?*

"In the wake of Hurricane Katrina, much has been reported, but many newscasts never addressed the glaring social implications. In his new book, *Come Hell or High Water,* Michael Eric Dyson traces America's historical indifference to Black suffering, exposing a dominant culture still rooted in racism and economic injustice."

—*Essence*

"The first major book to be released about Hurricane Katrina. . . . It is certain that not only will Dyson's book be read as criticism of how

America failed Katrina's victims, it will also be looked to as an authoritative chronicle of what happened and when. . . . This best-selling polemicist knows how to rattle society's cage, not least of all by alerting us that the cage is there at all. . . . Writers like Dyson remind us that the system we support, overtly or tacitly, fails entire segments of the population along race and class lines."

—*San Francisco Chronicle*

"If the national forgetfulness now setting in about the Katrina disaster is ever dispelled, it will be because of critics like Michael Eric Dyson. He has done an amazing job of dissecting the perfect storm of indifference, incompetence, and injustice that overwhelmed the least of us in the flooded streets of New Orleans. His history is a sober reminder that you get what you pay for—in this case a do-nothing government that did precious little for the black urban poor. We are long overdue for a conversation about race and poverty that doesn't blame its victims. Dyson's prophetic voice might just help get it started."

—Lawrence N. Powell, professor of history, Tulane University, and author of *Troubled Memory: Anne Levy, the Holocaust, and David Duke's Louisiana*

"Displaying intellectual rigor, political passion and personal empathy, Dyson offers a searing assessment of the carnage caused by both the storm and the political disconnect of the government."

—*Tucson Citizen*

"Dyson offers a compelling analysis of the racial, economic and political disasters that harmed the black poor in the Delta long before Hurricane Katrina struck. Dyson's illuminating narrative of how the government failed the poor is matched by his equally brilliant story of how color, class and religion shaped our response to Katrina. After the storm, the country pledged never to forget the lessons of Katrina, and yet we have already moved on. *Come Hell or High Water* is a searing and eloquent reminder of just what is at stake if we fail to wrestle with the role of poverty and race in our nation's life. This is social history, cultural criticism and political critique at their elegant and rigorous best."

—Marc Morial, former mayor of New Orleans, and president/CEO of the National Urban League

"Dyson offers a second chance for a detailed look at the catastrophe filtered through the prism of race. But trust me, readers of all colors will find enough jaw-dropping information here to disturb any notion of national security they might have had. . . . A thought-provoking perspective on Katrina that collects much of what was reported into one place."

—*Rocky Mountain News*

"Those who think they understand the full story of Katrina's devastation of New Orleans are in for a surprise. In this brilliant and sobering analysis, Michael Eric Dyson dissects the Katrina disaster with a surgeon's scalpel. *Come Hell or High Water* lays bare the racial politics, the ineptitude of Bush functionaries at FEMA, the president's failed leadership amidst crisis, the arrival of vulture capitalists ready to heap up profits on the backs of the dispossessed, and the bizarre religious meanings of the catastrophe as offered by televangelists and conservative opinion-makers. As one of our premier culture critics, Dyson does not simply expose; he also expostulates. Can we respond to his stirring call to the nation for a real discussion about race and inequality in America in the aftermath of Katrina? Will it be said twenty years from now that disaster in American is no longer color-coded?"

—Gary B. Nash, professor of history, UCLA, and author of *The Unknown American Revolution: The Unruly Birth of Democracy and the Struggle to Create America*

"Dyson lays it all out in well-considered arguments that call into question the very fabric of what makes America the so-called leader of the free world, when it so casually dismissed and ignored the needs of its own people."

—*Buffalo News*

"If we are to have a national debate about race and class as a result of the revelations brought by the storm, this book is a fine place to start. It is also a useful platform for a discussion of what citizens have a right to expect from local and federal government. . . . In *Come Hell or High Water*, his forceful analysis of the issues of race and class revealed in Hurricane Katrina's aftermath, "hip-hop intellectual" Michael Eric Dyson recreates in words those powerful visual images of people abandoned in attics, on rooftops, wading through floodwater, suffering in the Superdome. . . . That it was, and that the situation was such an outrage is behind the righteous anger that fuels Dyson's fast-paced narrative. . . . As we begin the painful process of rebuilding, *Come Hell or High Water* provides a stirring exhortation not to fall into the traps of the past."

—Susan Larson, *The Times-Picayune*

"Dyson's volume not only chronicles what happened when, it also argues that the nation's failure to offer timely aid to Katrina's victims indicates deeper problems in race and class relations . . . his contention that Katrina exposed a dominant culture pervaded not so much by 'active malice' toward poor blacks but by a long history of 'passive indifference' to their problems is both powerful and unsettling."

—*Publishers Weekly*

COME HELL OR
HIGH WATER

COME HELL OR HIGH WATER

Hurricane Katrina and the Color of Disaster

Michael Eric Dyson

BASIC
CIVITAS
BOOKS

A Member of the Perseus Books Group
New York

Hardcover edition first published in 2006 by Basic Civitas,
A Member of the Perseus Books Group

Paperback edition first published in 2007 by Basic Civitas

Books published by Basic Civitas are available at special discounts for bulk
purchases in the United States by corporations, institutions, and other
organizations. For more information, please contact the Special Markets
Department at the Perseus Books Group, 2300 Chestnut St., Philadelphia,
PA 19103, or email special.markets@perseusbooksgroup.com

Design by Jane Raese

Cataloging-in-Publication data for this book is available from the
Library of Congress.

Hardcover: ISBN-13: 978-0-465-01761-4; ISBN-10: 0-465-01761-4
Paperback: ISBN-13: 978-0-465-01772-0; ISBN-10: 0-465-01772-X

10 9 8 7 6 5 4 3 2 1

To Three Women Who Love and Help Katrina's Survivors

OPRAH WINFREY
Titan of American Media

"I think we all—this country—owe these people an apology. We still don't know how many of our fellow Americans lost their lives in the Katrina catastrophe. . . . They are not refugees. . . . They are survivors and we, the people, will not let them stand alone. They are Americans."

SUSAN L. TAYLOR
Queen of Black America

"Now more than ever, triage among government, business and communities is needed. We must work through our churches and community organizations to secure our people and help them start a new life. This is the proud tradition of African-Americans."

MARCIA L. DYSON
Conscience of the Clergy

"Even though we are scattered, we must be unified. . . . I've heard so many ministers say they're apolitical. Jesus was a political prisoner. The pulpit is the spot where we transformed our situation. . . . We don't want another Katrina to make us love our people."

And to

JOYCELYN MOSES
Strong Survivor of Katrina

"We were in the Convention Center for five days without food, without water, without help. Only way we got food is we had to go in restaurants and stores where people had looted and vandalized to feed ourselves and give ourselves water. . . . We had nowhere to sleep, we had no security, we had no light. We had to survive in the streets. . . . I think that was the worst nightmare I ever had."

CONTENTS

But that's what's really rich about New Orleans, that we really embrace the simple things about life. It's a very African tradition, that we all extend a hello, we always extend a kiss to people that we know. But my question is, what's going to happen to all the culture that was there, all the music? Boys walking down the street blowing horns. That's what we really enjoyed about our lives. It's more a connection with human beings that we really, really value.

—*Gina Charbonnet, New Orleans native, Katrina volunteer*

PREFACE
Pompeii and 8/29

IN EARLY AUGUST 2005, my wife and I joined our tour group on a bus from the port of Naples to the ancient city of Pompeii. It was a hot summer day, but a gentle breeze stirred the dusty streets of a city excavated from the hardened lava and mud left by the eruption of Mount Vesuvius. The Italian guide led us to spots where grand houses once stood. He led us to the rumbled sites of former horse stables, grand bath houses, and the temples of the goddess Venus and the god Apollo.

We stood shoulder to shoulder in the heat as he told us about the activities that once thrived at the Forum Plaza, Pompeii's center of religious, civil, and economic life. We were amazed at how modern this ancient city was, with its sophisticated water heating and cooling systems in the bath house; its fast-food restaurants situated about the city, where merchants and towns-people could pick up a quick meal of fish, olives, fresh vegetables, and wine; and its paved streets with raised large stones to keep one's feet from getting soaked on a rainy day.

We happened on a large wired pen with plaster casts of the bodies of the unfortunate citizens of Pompeii who were unable to escape the wrath of the hot-headed Vesuvius. Some of the victims were buried with precious items in their hands.

"Who do you think these people were?" our guide queried the group.

After a few wrong answers, my wife raised her hand.

"They were the slaves," she proffered. When her answer was affirmed, the guide quizzed her again.

"And, why do you think they didn't leave the city?"

"The slaves did not own horses or carriages."

I couldn't help but flash on this memory as I watched the unfolding of tragic events during Hurricane Katrina later that month in New Orleans and other parts of the Gulf Coast. The way it was for the poor of Pompeii is the way it was for the poor citizens of New Orleans. They were ensconced in a city rich with culture and yet they couldn't take full advantage of its incredible delights. They served a ruling class and visiting tourists but they were kept from the pleasures they helped to provide. And when the city fell to the fury of nature, they were most vulnerable to the environment's brutal backlash.

The guide also pointed out that many of the slaves were chained to the wheat grinders, mules attached, as selfish and uncaring owners fled the city. The tragic replay in New Orleans on August 29 is unmistakable as city elites and the well to do fled without thought of their poor citizen-servants. And many of the slaves in Pompeii were found with grand and expensive items, things they wouldn't ordinarily possess but that they took nonetheless, knowing they couldn't make use of them during the disaster but wanting to feel what it was like to have nice things, if only for a few fleeting, fatal hours. Like their peers in Pompeii, some of the poor of New Orleans took televisions and other luxury items they had not usually had access to, trinkets of treasure they had been denied by grinding poverty. Perhaps it would blunt for a moment the realization that they had been left behind by their government. But their crime, if it can even be called that, paled in comparison to the criminal negligence that affected their lives long before Katrina.

Of course, unlike Pompeii, New Orleans will be rebuilt. But will it resemble the funky and soulful place that it was made by the percolating gumbo of French, Spanish, and especially African identities? Or will it become a playground for the wealthy, or, perhaps, a zone of integrated pleasures razed of culture's fruits and flaws—Las Vegas in Louisiana? As Tulane University historian Lawrence Powell writes of New Orleans:

> Will its recovery result in one of those "lost cities" that have been restored solely as sites of tourism and myth? Will this quirky and endlessly fascinating place become an X-rated theme park, a Disneyland for adults? Will the gaming industry carpet it with casinos backlit with neon and frosted over with the confection of glitz and garish glamour? Is it fated to be the place where Orlando embraces Las Vegas? That's the American Pompeii I apprehend rising from the toxic sludge deposited by Lake Pontchartrain: an ersatz city, a veritable site of schlock and awe. No less troubling is the possibility that New Orleans will be demographically unrecognizable after its reconstitution: whiter, smaller, and less diverse than when I evacuated two days before Katrina stormed ashore, literally bereft of the African American roots that have seeded so much that is authentic in American popular culture.[1]

But even before such questions are answered, we must ask several more. Why did the black and poor get left behind? What took the government so long to get to the Gulf Coast, especially

New Orleans? What do politicians sold on the idea of limited governance offer to folk who need, and deserve, the government to come to their aid? Why is it that the poor of New Orleans, and, really, the poor of the nation, are hidden from us, made invisible by our disinterest in their lives? Why was it a surprise that they are in as bad shape as the storm revealed? Has the administration's hostility to science matters like global warming made us even more vulnerable to natural disaster? Has the war in Iraq diverted critical social attention from pressing domestic issues and depleted our emergency resources? Has the war on terror made us forget the urgent need for emergency management and mitigation? Does George Bush care about black people? Do well-off black people care about poor black people? Did God cause Katrina? Can we really afford to proceed as a nation without addressing how race, poverty, and class gang up on too many of our citizens and snatch from them their futures? Unless we answer these questions, we are in jeopardy of becoming a morally and politically lost nation bled dry of our humanity by disasters of nature and soul.

COME HELL OR
HIGH WATER

It's a community with many economic challenges—chronic and systemic poverty in a core group. And because of the roots, the fact that mama and grandmamma and daughters all live in the same neighborhood, there's a real connectivity of home and family. There's a diversity of income, but the greater portion [face] the challenge of poverty, and the elderly population primarily have fixed incomes.

—*Cynthia Willard-Lewis, Councilwoman, District E*
(including the Lower 9th Ward)

CHAPTER 1

UNNATURAL DISASTERS
Race and Poverty

THE BARRAGE OF IMAGES in newspapers and on television tested the nation's collective sense of reality. There were men and women wading chest-deep in water—when they weren't floating or drowning in the toxic whirlpool the streets of New Orleans had become. When the waters subsided, there were dead bodies strewn on curbsides and wrapped in blankets by fellow sufferers, who provided the perished their only dignity. There were unseemly collages of people silently dying from hunger and thirst—and of folk writhing in pain, or quickly collapsing under the weight of missed medicine for diabetes, high blood pressure, or heart trouble. Photo snaps and film shots captured legions of men and women huddling in groups or hugging corners, crying in wild-eyed desperation for help, for any help, from somebody, anybody, who would listen to their unanswered pleas. The filth and squalor of their confinement—defecating where they stood or sat, or, more likely, dropped, bathed in a brutal wash of dredge and sickening pollutants that choked the air with ungodly stench—grieved the camera lenses that recorded their plight.

Men, women, and children tore through deserted streets lined with empty stores, hunting for food and water and clothing for their bodies. They were hurried along by the steadily diminishing prospect of rescue by the government, by *their* government, whose only visible representatives were the police who came after them for looting. There were wailing infants clasping crying mothers who mouthed prayers for someone to please just save their babies. There were folk stuffed in attics pleading for the cavalry to come. Many colors were present in this multicultural stew of suffering, but the dominant color was black. From the sight of it, this was the third world—a misnomer, to be sure, since people of color are two-thirds of the world's population. The suffering on screen created cognitive dissonance; it suggested that this must be somewhere in India, or the outskirts of Biafra. This surely couldn't be the United States of America— and how cruelly that term seemed to mock those poor citizens who felt disunited and disconnected and just plain dissed by their government. This couldn't be the richest and most powerful nation on the globe, leaving behind some of its poorest citizens to fend for themselves.

And yet it was. It was bad enough to witness the government's failure to respond to desperate cries of help scrawled on the tattered roofs of flooded homes. But Hurricane Katrina's violent winds and killing waters swept into the mainstream a stark realization: the poor had been abandoned by society and its institutions, and sometimes by their well-off brothers and sisters, long before the storm. We are immediately confronted with another unsavory truth: it is the exposure of the extremes, not their existence, that stumps our national sense of decency. We can abide the ugly presence of poverty so long as it doesn't interrupt the natural flow of things, doesn't rudely impinge on our daily lives or awareness. As long as poverty is a latent reality, a solemn social fact suppressed from prominence on our moral compass, we can find our bearings without fretting too much about its awkward persistence.

It's not as if it was news to most folk that poverty exists in the United States. Still, there was no shortage of eureka moments glistening with discovery and surprise in the aftermath of Katrina. Poverty's grinding malevolence is fed in part by social choices and public policy decisions that directly impact how many people are poor and how long they remain that way. To acknowledge that is to own up to our role in the misery of the poor—be it the politicians we vote for who cut programs aimed at helping the economically vulnerable; the narrative of bootstrap individualism we invoke to deflect the relevance of the considerable benefits we've received while bitterly complaining of the few breaks the poor might get; the religious myths we circulate that bring shame on the poor by chiding them for lacking the appropriate hunger to be prosperous; and the resentment of the alleged pathology of poor blacks—fueled more by stereotypes than by empirical support—that gives us license to dismiss or demonize them.

Our being surprised, and disgusted, by the poverty that Katrina revealed is a way of remaining deliberately naive about the poor while dodging the responsibility that knowledge of their lives would entail. We remain blissfully ignorant of their circumstances to avoid the brutal indictment of our consciences. When a disaster like Katrina strikes—a *natural* disaster not directly caused by human failure—it frees us to be aware of, and angered by, the catastrophe. After all, it doesn't directly implicate us; it was an act of God. Even when human hands get involved, our fingerprints are nowhere to be found. We're not responsible for the poor and black being left behind; the local, state, or federal government is at fault.

We are thus able to decry the circumstances of the poor while assuring ourselves that we had nothing to do with their plight. We can even take special delight in lambasting the source of their suffering—a source that is safely external to us. We are fine as long as we place time limits on the origins of the poor's plight—the moments we all spied on television after the storm, but not the numbing years during which we all looked the other way. Thus we fail to confront our complicity in their long-term suffering. By being outraged, we appear compassionate. This permits us to continue to ignore the true roots of their condition, roots that branch into our worlds and are nourished on our political and religious beliefs.

There are 37 million people in poverty in our nation, 1.1 million of whom fell below the poverty line in 2004.[1] Some of the poorest folk in the nation, people in the Delta, have been largely ignored, rendered invisible, officially forgotten. FEMA left them dangling precipitously on rooftops and in attics because of bureaucratic bumbling. Homeland Security failed miserably in mobilizing resources to rescue Katrina survivors without food, water, or shelter. President Bush lighted on New Orleans only after Mayor Ray Nagin's profanity-laced radio-show diatribe blasting the federal government for its lethal inertia. Because the government took its time getting into New Orleans, Katrina took many lives. Hundreds of folk, especially the elderly, died while waiting for help. But the government and society had been failing to pay attention to the poor since long before one of the worst natural disasters in the nation's history swallowed the poor and spit them back up. The world saw just how much we hadn't seen; it witnessed our negligence up close in frightfully full color.

The hardest-hit regions in the Gulf States had already been drowning in extreme poverty: Mississippi is the poorest state in the nation, with Louisiana just behind it.[2] More than 90,000 people in each of the areas stormed by Katrina in Louisiana, Mississippi, and Alabama made less than $10,000 a year. Black folk in these areas were strapped by incomes that were 40 percent less than those earned by whites. Before the storm, New Orleans, with a 67.9 percent black population, had more than 103,000 poor people. That means the Crescent City had a poverty rate of 23 percent, 76 percent higher than the national average of 13.1 percent.[3] New Orleans's poverty rate ranked it seventh out of 290 large U.S. counties.[4]

Although black folk make up 31.5 percent of Louisiana's population, their offspring account for 69 percent of the children in poverty. Though the national average for elders with disabilities is 39.6 percent, New Orleans hovers near 57 percent. The New Orleans median household income is $31,369, far beneath the national median of $44,684.[5] A full 9 percent of households in New Orleans didn't own or have access to a vehicle.[6] That means that nearly one in four citizens in New Orleans, and one in seven in the greater New Orleans metropolitan area, had no access to a car.[7]

In fact, New Orleans ranks fourth out of 297 metropolitan areas in the country in the proportion of households lacking access to cars.[8] The top three metropolitan spots are in the greater New York area, which has the most extensive public transportation system in the country. New Orleans ranks ninth among 140 big cities for the same category, a far higher ranking than cities with similar demographic profiles such as Detroit and Memphis.[9] Black households nationwide generally have far less access to cars than white households, a trend mirrored in New Orleans, where only 5 percent of non-Latino whites were without car access, while 27 percent of blacks in New Orleans were without cars.[10] Nationwide, 19 percent of blacks lack access to cars.[11]

And children and elderly folk are even more likely to live in households without access to cars. Children and the elderly made up 38 percent of the population in New Orleans, but they accounted for 48 percent of the households without access to cars in the city.[12] The poor and the near-poor made up the vast majority of those without car access in New Orleans, accounting for nearly 80 percent of the city's car-less population.[13] These facts make it painfully clear just why so many folk could not evacuate before Katrina struck. They weren't shiftless, stupid, or stubborn, as some have suggested (FEMA's Michael Brown blamed the poor for staying behind and drowning while discounting or ignoring the many obstacles to their successful exodus). They simply couldn't muster the resources to escape destruction, and, for many, death.

The most glaring feature of their circumstance suggests that Katrina's survivors lived in concentrated poverty—they lived in poor neighborhoods, attended poor schools, and had poorly paying jobs that reflected and reinforced a distressing pattern of rigid segregation.[14] Nearly 50,000 poor folk in New Orleans lived in areas where the poverty rate approached 40 percent. In fact, among the nation's fifty largest cities with poor black families jammed into extremely poor neighborhoods, New Orleans ranked second. Those households living in concentrated poverty often earn barely more than $20,000 a year. In neighborhoods with concentrated poverty, only one in twelve adults has a college degree, most children are reared in single-parent families, and four in ten working-age adults, many of whom are disabled, have no jobs.[15] Nearly every major American city has several neighborhoods that are desperately poor and severely segregated. Cities like Cleveland, New York, Atlanta, and Los Angeles have economically distressed neighborhoods where more than 30 percent of their population's poor blacks live.[16]

Concentrated poverty is the product of decades of public policies and political measures that isolate black households in neighborhoods plagued by severe segregation and economic hardship. For instance, the federal government's decision to concentrate public housing in segregated inner-city neighborhoods fueled metropolitan expansion. It also cut the poor off from decent housing and educational and economic opportunities by keeping affordable housing for poor minorities out of surrounding suburbs. The effects of concentrated poverty have been amply documented: reduced private-sector investment and local job opportunities; higher prices for the poor in inner-city businesses; increased levels of crime; negative consequences on the mental and physical health of the poor; and the spatial dislocation of the poor spurred by the "black track" of middle-class households to the suburbs.[17]

In the antebellum and post–Civil War south, New Orleans brought together slaves, former slaves, free blacks, Creoles of color, and Cajuns and other whites in an ethnically diverse mélange that reflected the city's Spanish, French, and African roots and influences. Despite the bustling ethnic and racial interactions—driven in part by the unique "backyard" patterns, where blacks and whites lived near each other, a practice that had its roots in slavery—the city endured increasing segregation as suburbanization made New Orleans blacker in the latter half of the twentieth century.[18] In the case of New Orleans, patterns of extreme exodus from urban centers to suburban communities followed a national trend. As the city got blacker, it got poorer.

In 1960, New Orleans was 37 percent black; in 1970, it was 43 percent black; by 1980, it was 55 percent black. In 1990 the city was 62 percent black, and by 2000 it was more than 67 percent black. As whites fled New Orleans, they turned to Jefferson Parish, which is 69.8 percent white and only 22.9 percent black; to St. Bernard Parish, which is 88.29 percent white with a paltry 7.62 percent black population; and to St. Tammany Parish, which is 87.02 percent white and 9.90 percent black. The black middle class sought refuge in Gentilly and New Orleans East, intensifying the suffering of a largely black and poor inner city.[19]

Perhaps most damaging for the young, concentrated poverty stifles the academic success of black children. A child's socio-economic status, along with other influential factors like teacher/pupil ratio, teacher quality, curriculum materials, expenditures per student, and the age of the school building, greatly affects her academic success. Wealthier parents are able to send their children to better public schools and higher-quality private schools, which, in turn, clear the path for admission to prestigious colleges and universities.[20] New Orleans has a 40 percent illiteracy rate; over 50 percent of black ninth graders won't graduate in four years. Louisiana expends an average of $4,724 per student and has the third-lowest rank for teacher salaries in the nation.[21] The black dropout rates are high and nearly 50,000 students cut class every day.

When they are done with school, many young black males end up at Angola Prison, a correctional facility located on a former plantation where inmates still perform manual farm labor, and where 90 percent of them eventually die.[22] New Orleans's employment picture is equally gloomy, since industry long ago deserted the city, leaving in its place a service economy that caters to tourists and that thrives on low-paying, transient, and unstable jobs.[23]

If President Bush is serious about what he said in his first speech on national television in Katrina's aftermath, that the "deep, persistent poverty" of the Gulf Coast "has roots in a history of racial discrimination, which has cut off generations from the opportunity of America," and that we must "rise above the legacy of inequality," then he must foster public policy and legislation that help the poor to escape their plight.[24] But can a self-proclaimed antigovernment president develop policy that actually improves people's lives? Bush would have to change his mind about slashing $35 billion from Medicaid, food stamps, and other social programs that help the poor combat such a vile legacy. The federal government also owes the black poor better schools. Bush's No Child Left Behind act of 2001 promised to bolster the nation's crumbling educational infrastructure, but conservative politics have only exacerbated the problems: underperforming schools, low reading levels, and wide racial and class disparities. The schools that need money the most—those whose students are up against challenges like outdated curriculum materials and poor teacher/pupil ratios—have their funding cut when their test scores don't measure up. Oddly enough, Bush has also failed to sufficiently fund his own mandate, reinforcing class and educational inequality.

Bush also owes it to the poor to use the bully pulpit of the presidency to address the health crisis in black America. When Katrina swept waves of mostly poor and black folk into global view, it also graphically uncovered their poor health. More than 83,000 citizens, or 18.8 percent of the population in New Orleans, lacked health insurance (the national average is 15.5 percent); the numbers for black women doubled those for white women.[25] Nationally, there are nearly 40 million folk without health insurance, many of them black and poor. They resort to the emergency ward for health maintenance. Their survival is compromised because serious diseases are spotted later than need be. If President Bush is the compassionate conservative he says he is, then he must help fix a health care system that favors the wealthy and the solidly employed.

Concentrated poverty does more than undermine academic success and good health; since there is a strong relationship between education and employment, and quality of life, it keeps the poor from better-paying jobs that might interrupt a vicious cycle of poverty. In New Orleans, severe underemployment and unemployment, and unstable employment, gang up on the black poor. This circumstance is made worse by the densely populated communities and housing in which they live, the sheer social misery of much of postindustrial urban Southern life, and their dreadful infant-mortality and homicide rates—the disenfranchised turn more readily and violently on each other rather than striking against the inequality that puts them at each other's throats.

The Lower Ninth Ward is a perfectly bleak example of the concentrated poverty the city's poor black residents confront. The Lower Ninth Ward, also known as the Lower 9, is symptomatic of the geographical isolation on which concentrated poverty feeds. The Lower 9 "crouches behind a pile of dirt, separated by a big bend in America's biggest river and a thick canal and eons of tradition from the 'high-class people' up on the high ground over in the French Quarter."[26] The Lower Ninth was one of the last neighborhoods in the city to be developed. To its west lies the Industrial Canal; to the north are the Southern Railway railroad and Florida Avenue Canal; to the east lies the parish line; and the river traces its southern border.[27] The Lower 9 grew so slowly because it was isolated from the rest of the city and because it lacked adequate drainage systems.[28] The Lower 9 evolved from a cypress swamp to a series of plantations that extended from the river to the lake. Poor black folk in search of affordable housing—and Irish, German, and Italian immigrant workers too—fled to the area although risking disease and natural disaster.

The Lower 9's growth was so delayed that by 1950 half of it remained undeveloped. The dry docks of the Industrial Canal were the center of development at the time, while some activity trickled out to residential areas in the neighborhood's northern section. By the end of the decade, the second bridge between the city and the Lower 9, the Claiborne Avenue Bridge, was built across Industrial Canal at Claiborne Avenue.[29] During this time, retail development along St. Claude Avenue took off and corner stores became popular. By 1965, industrial and commercial enterprise thrived on the strip that ran along the Industrial Canal between Claiborne and Florida Avenues.[30]

In September of 1965, Hurricane Betsy visited its deadly fury on New Orleans, killing eighty-one people and covering 80 percent of the Lower 9 in water. The storm's surge rose to ten feet, overwhelming the eight-foot levee. As with Katrina, survivors waded through waist-deep water holding babies to escape Betsy's aftermath. Other victims awaited rescue from their rooftops. Critics maintain that Betsy's carnage fueled the decline of the Lower 9, especially since many residents didn't receive adequate loans or other financial aid to help rebuild the neighborhood. Many longtime residents fled, and several commercial and industrial businesses soon followed.

The area received assistance in the late sixties and early seventies from a federal program that targeted blighted neighborhoods to spark metropolitan development and revitalization—leading to the Lower Ninth Ward Neighborhood Council, Total Community Action's Lower Ninth Ward Head Start Program, the Lower Ninth Ward Housing Development Corporation, and the Lower

Ninth Ward Health Clinic. The Lower 9 has many small businesses, barber and beauty shops, corner grocery stores called "superettes," eating spots, gasoline stations, day care centers, churches, and Laundromats called "washeterias."[31] Despite its rich cultural and racial pedigree—the Lower 9 is home to famed entertainer Fats Domino and features during Carnival some of the most exciting "second-line" parades, characterized by churning rhythms and kinetic, high-stepping funk grooves—the area has continued to struggle with persistent and concentrated poverty.[32]

Before Katrina, the Lower 9 was peopled with poor blacks who were the maids, bellhops, and busboys who looked after tourists on pleasure hunts and thrill quests in New Orleans. They are now the clerks, cops, and carpenters who are helping to revive and rebuild the city, along with the sculptors, painters, and musicians who are staples of the local scene.[33] The vast majority of the Lower 9's 20,000 residents were black, and more than a third of them, 36 percent, lived beneath the poverty line, nearly double the statewide poverty rate.[34] The Lower 9's residents were often victims of the complicated racial dynamics in New Orleans, where police brutality and retail and business profiling dogged them from outside their neighborhood, and where bigotry against poorer, often darker, blacks echoed within many African American communities. The faces of the Lower 9's residents—though forgotten by their government and overlooked by their fellow citizens—looked out from their watery wasteland and for a moment focused the eyes of the world on their desperate plight.

But it was not merely that we forgot to see or know the poor that forged the searing image of our national neglect and American amnesia. And neither was it the fact that Katrina exposed, to our horror and amazement, the bitter outlines of concentrated poverty that we have reason to be ashamed. It is not all about what we saw—which, after all, may be a perverse narcissism that makes *their* plight ultimately about *our* failure and what *we* must learn at their great expense. It is also about what *they*, the poor, saw in us, or didn't see there, especially the government that didn't find or feed them until it was late—too late for thousands of them. It is their surprise, not ours, that should most concern and inform us. Perhaps it is their anger, too, that is inspiring, since the outrage of the black survivors proved their tenacious loyalty to a country that hasn't often earned it.

As Michael Ignatieff argues, the poor blacks struggling to survive Katrina's backlash saw more clearly than most others "what the contract of American citizenship entails."[35] For Ignatieff, a contract of citizenship "defines the duties of care that public officials owe to the people of a democratic society." Ignatieff says that the "Constitution defines some parts of this contract, and statutes define other parts, but much of it is a tacit understanding that citizens have about what to expect from their government." Ignatieff contends that the contract's "basic term is protection: helping citizens to protect their families and possessions from forces beyond their control."[36] According to Ignatieff, when a woman at the convention center proclaimed "We are American," it was "she—not the governor, not the mayor, not the president—[who] understood that the catastrophe was a test of the bonds of citizenship and that the government had failed the test." Ignatieff explores the racial backdrop to the government's disregard of the poor while clarifying the demand of the poor that we honor a contract by which we claim to abide:

It may be astonishing that American citizens should have had to remind their fellow Americans of this, but let us not pretend we do not know the reason. They were black, and for all that poor blacks have experienced and endured in this country, they had good reason to be surprised that they were treated not as citizens but as garbage. . . . Let us not be sentimental. The poor and dispossessed of New Orleans cannot afford to be sentimental. They know they live in an unjust and unfair society. . . . So it is not—as some commentators claimed—that the catastrophe laid bare the deep inequalities of American society. These inequalities may have been news to some, but they were not news to the displaced people in the convention center and elsewhere. What was bitter news to them was that their claims of citizenship mattered so little to the institutions charged with their protection.[37]

In his lucid explanation of the compelling bonds of citizenship, Ignatieff outlines detriments to the social contract that make us all less than what we ought to be. Ignatieff calls attention to the role of race in coloring perceptions on either side of the cultural and political divide about how we should have met our moral and civic obligations to the poor. The deeper we dig into the story of Katrina, the more we must accept culpability for the fact that the black citizens of the Big Easy—a tag given New Orleans by black musicians who easily found work in a city that looms large in the collective American imagination as the home of jazz, jambalaya, and Mardi Gras—were treated by the rest of us as garbage.

Bush has not shown that he cares for civil rights or cares for the interests of black people.

—*Jesse Jackson, civil rights leader and Katrina volunteer*

My cousin hollered, "You're shot." I got up and tried to jump over the tree stumps in the street, and as soon as I got in mid-air another blast hit me in my back. And I fell on the ground again. Somehow, it was a miracle, I got up again, and I began to run. I heard [the white guys] saying, "Nigger, you gotta run." I ran around a corner and I saw this black guy sitting on the porch, and I said "Man, help me." And he said, "Come on," but he was in the house with some white people. When I went to the back of the house, this white lady said "I can't help you. You gotta get out of here." So I ran away from their house. And I ran up to this truck with two white guys, and I said, "Please, please, please help me." I felt like I was going to die. And the older white guy said, "Get away from my truck. We can't help you. We're liable to shoot you ourselves." And they pulled off and called me a nigger. It's like [white people] were using the opportunity to do something they've been waiting to do. And I'm thinking about racism and all that's running in my head. I'm like, "I can't believe this." After everything we've gone through, and everything I've been through, I would have never imagined this happening to me.

—*Darnell Herrington, Katrina survivor*

CHAPTER 2

DOES GEORGE W. BUSH CARE ABOUT BLACK PEOPLE?

WHEN PRESIDENT BUSH and the federal government tragically failed to respond in a timely and life-saving manner to the disaster on the Gulf Coast, they made themselves vulnerable to the charge that race was the obvious reason for their delay. And that charge was vigorously pursued—in media and entertainment camps, in black and poor communities across the nation, by many of the nation's distinguished intellectuals and political critics, and, indeed, by observers around the world.[1] Many claimed that had there been mostly white people trapped by Katrina's vengeance, the government would have gotten into town a lot quicker. "If it was a bunch of white people on roofs in the Hamptons," actor Colin Farrell colorfully stated on television's *Access Hollywood*, "I don't have any f****** doubt there would have been every single helicopter, every plane, every single means that the government has to help these people."[2]

Perhaps social commentator and humorist Nancy Giles captured the feelings of many when she more diplomatically, but with no less outrage, framed the issue on CBS's *Sunday Morning:*

> After meeting with Louisiana officials last week, Rev. Jesse Jackson said, "Many black people feel that their race, their property conditions and their voting patterns have been a factor in the response." He continued, "I'm not saying that myself." Then I'll say it: If the majority of the hardest hit victims of Hurricane Katrina in New Orleans were white people, they would not have gone for days without food and water, forcing many to steal for mere survival. Their bodies would not have been left to float in putrid water. . . . We've repeatedly given tax cuts to the wealthiest and left our most vulnerable American citizens to basically fend for themselves. . . . The President has put himself at risk by visiting the troops in Iraq, but didn't venture anywhere near the Superdome or the convention center, where thousands of victims, mostly black and poor, needed to see that he gave a damn.[3]

Would Bush and the federal government have moved faster to secure the lives of the hurricane victims if they had been white? The question must be partnered with a second one that permits us to tally a few of the myriad injuries of the racial contract that has bound American citizens together: did the largely black and poor citizens in the Gulf Coast get left behind because they were black and poor?

It is clear that President Bush and officials of the federal government, like the rest of us, have been shaped by racial forces that have continually changed our society since its founding. The tragic reign of slavery for 250 years, the colossal efforts of the government and the legal system to extend white supremacy through Jim Crow law, and the monumental effort of black folk to resist these forces while redefining black identity have formed the rhythms, relations, and rules of race. The rhythms of race have largely to do with customs and cultural practices that feed on differences between racial groups. The relations of race have mostly to do with the conditions that foster or frustrate interactions between racial groups. The rules of race have to do with norms and behavior that reflect or resist formal barriers to social equality.

The rhythms, relations, and rules of race have both defined the forces against which progress must be made and provided a measure of the progress achieved. They help us understand that even when fundamental changes in law and practice occur—say, the Fourteenth Amendment, the *Brown v. Board of Education* Supreme Court decision, or the Civil Rights Act of 1964—there is the matter of racial vision and imagination to consider. They help us see that racial terror has bled through the boundaries of law as surely as harmful racial customs and beliefs persist in the deep pockets of a formally changed society.

This framework must be kept in mind as we answer the question of whether race played a role in how the federal government responded to Katrina's victims. But as I've made clear, the question shouldn't be whether race played a role, but what role it played. How can race possibly be quarantined from a consideration of Katrina when it so thoroughly pervades our culture—the choices we make, the laws we adopt and discard, and the social practices that are polluted by its pestering ubiquity? Of course race colored the response to Katrina, although it may not mean that explicit racial prejudice fueled the decision to leave poor black folk defenseless before the fury of nature.

After all, one need not have conscious or intentional racist beliefs to act out a script written long before specific actors come on the political stage to play. We take our cues from different parts of the culture that have vastly opposed ways of viewing the same racial event. Our conscious decisions are drawn from the reservoir of beliefs, attitudes, and dispositions that form our group's collective racial unconscious. When we gear up for response to a particular event, when we dissect or process a specific item of information, we pull from these resources, which have shaped our understanding of what can and should be done. The collective racial unconscious, and the rhythms, relations, and rules of race, together constitute the framework for making decisions, even those that apparently have nothing to do with race. Thus, one can reasonably say that race was the farthest thing from one's mind even as its subtle propositions lure one forward into territory invisibly bounded by racial criteria. And one can scrupulously proclaim, and mean it, that race does not affect one's calculus of desert, of how resources should be shared, while appealing to ancient racial understandings that shape just who is seen as meriting a particular sort of treatment.

It should also be clear that although one may not have racial intent, one's actions may nonetheless have racial consequence. In discussing the charge that racism was at the heart of the response to Hurricane Katrina, Senator Barack Obama said, "I've said publicly that I do not subscribe to the notion that the painfully slow response of FEMA and the Department of Homeland Security was racially-based. The ineptitude was colorblind."[4] Obama went on to say that "I see no evidence of active malice, but I see a continuation of passive indifference on the part of our government towards the least of these."[5] However, one may agree with Obama that there was no racial intent, no "active malice," in the response to Katrina, and yet hold the view that there were nonetheless racial consequences that flowed from the "passive indifference" of the government to poor blacks. Active malice and passive indifference are but flip

sides of the same racial coin, different modalities of racial men-
ace that flare according to the contexts and purposes at hand. In
a sense, if one conceives of racism as a cell phone, then active
malice is the ring tone at its highest volume, while passive indifference is the ring tone on vibrate. In either case, whether
loudly or silently, the consequence is the same: a call is transmit-
ted, a racial meaning is communicated.

When it comes to the federal government's response to the
victims of Hurricane Katrina, the specific elements at play must
be examined. There were poor blacks, mostly from Louisiana,
drowning in twenty-five-foot floods, stranded in their homes, or
crammed into makeshift shelters, awaiting help from a Texas-
bred president and an Oklahoma-born head of FEMA. At its
core, this was a Southern racial narrative being performed before a national and global audience. If Southern whites have
been relatively demonized within the realms of whiteness—
when compared to their Northern peers, they are viewed as
slower, less liberal, more bigoted, and thoroughly "country"—
then Southern blacks are even more the victims of social stigma
from every quarter of the culture, including Northern and
Southern whites, and even among other blacks outside the
region.

Southern blacks, especially poor ones, are viewed as the worst
possible combination of troubled elements—region, race, and
class—that on their own make life difficult enough. They are
stereotyped as being backward, belligerently opposed to enlightenment, and tethered to self-defeating cultural habits that
undermine their upward thrust from a life of penury and ignorance. Their woes are considered so entrenched that they cannot
be overcome by social programs or political intervention. Not
even a change of geography is seen as completely successful;
when transposed to Northern terrain, poor Southern blacks are

believed to be victims of a time warp of anachronistic values that work against absorption into the middle class and instead drive them to carve enclaves of urban horror from their rural roots.

When they were not being painted in unflattering terms on the canvas of social history, the lives of poor Southern blacks have stirred the colorful fantasies of whites across their native region and beyond. The exotic Southern black supposedly had more soul, was closer to nature as a semiliterate savage, could sing and dance well, was more innately spiritual, was oblivious to the caste system that kept her in poverty, and, hence, was happy to be the white Southerner's slave, servant, or entertainer. The art created by poor blacks was rarely recognized by whites unless it confirmed crude stereotypes of black sensual longing and intellectual emptiness. The complex and demanding creations of poor blacks, whether sophisticated blues lyrics or visual art of high quality, was either dismissed, ignored, or, at best, seen as exceptional to the inferior work of other black artists. In fact, white culture was burdened by bigoted beliefs in the inherent inferiority of black humanity, intelligence, and culture. Such beliefs die hard. Even when the customs that ushered them into prominence fade, those Southern whites who inherit from their ancestors and predecessors the rhythms, rules, and relations of race—and the collective racial unconscious—find it difficult to defeat or betray their racial orientation to the world.

To be sure, caricatures of black identity have been swept away in many white Southern quarters and replaced with far more sophisticated and nuanced ideas about black folk. But such progress runs hard into another wall constructed out of racial history: the structural inequities that support the inferior social position of poor blacks. While one may point to enlightened ideas about black folk as proof of racial progressivism, the per-

sistence of, and investment in, complicated legacies of social inequality by the very whites who wear their racial bona fides on
their sleeves are equally confusing and troubling.

For instance, Bill Clinton, who garnered wide black political
support, and continues to enjoy wide black affection, is as enlightened a Southern white man as has come into politics. He in-
tuitively sways to the rhythms of black life; he stands on the
transformed racial relations that the civil rights movement inaugurated; and he helped to forge a modest defense of affirmative
action, a significant racial rule. Despite his racial charisma, or
perhaps because of it, he was able to do considerable damage to
black interests, especially those of poor blacks, by signing a
crime bill that viciously targeted them, and a welfare reform bill
that heaped stigma, but no help, on the backs of the vulnerable.

If George Bush lacks Clinton's racial charisma, he also lacks
Clinton's grasp of the need to play the racial game at a high, if ultimately manipulative, level. Clinton proved every bit a victim
of the collective racial unconscious of his Southern white heritage, except the lesson he learned was that one must survive by
appearing to support black interests while exploiting them.
Thus, Clinton forged political survival in a racial climate still
suspicious of black intelligence and humanity by signaling support for the white mainstream through his embrace of conservative policies that hurt the black poor. Clinton criticized Bush for
his leadership in the federal government's response to Katrina,
noting the disproportionate burden borne by the black poor.[6]
Yet, because some of Clinton's presidential decisions hurt poor
blacks, neoliberal neglect is sometimes just as large a factor in
their suffering as conservative assault. It may have been Bush's
hands stretching forth to rebuke the interests of poor blacks in
Katrina's aftermath, but the misery of the black poor has been
indelibly marked by Clinton's fingerprints.

Still, Bush's racial approach does not benefit black folk. Not only does Bush lack Clinton's mix of advantages and deficits, but he lacks as well the instincts and policies that might push, or play to, racial progress in our epoch. His racial etiquette has been shaped in an ethos of hard conservative forces that fought racial progress when it was unfolding and roadblocks its path today. Not only is Bush devoid of the devout, if devious, racial grammar deployed by Clinton. He lacks as well a suitable language of political empathy and moral suasion that resonates with the rhythms of black culture—or an appreciation for the structural and institutional matters that might revive poor black life.

It is safe to say that race played a major role in the failure of the federal government—especially for Bush and FEMA head Michael Brown—to respond in a timely manner to the poor black folk of Louisiana because black grief and pain have been ignored throughout the nation's history. Bush and Brown simply updated the practice. Southern black suffering in particular has been overlooked by Southern whites—those in power and ordinary citizens as well. In discussing the profound differences between white and black Southern historical memory, historian W. Fitzhugh Brundage captures how whites ignored black success and suffering, while blacks sought to overcome the segregated conscience of white society to emphasize a unified national memory and purpose.

Southern white historical memory exalted white civilization, legitimated white power, and virtually excluded any admission of meaningful black agency in the region's past. White accounts seemed to insulate blacks from history. There was, in white history, no acknowledgment of true suffering or real accomplishments among blacks. They were without personal ancestry, their lives were small, and there was a great void in their past. And if southern whites grudgingly acknowledged the restoration of the union, they still embraced a willfully sectional historical identity. This jealous defense of sectional honor that was at the heart of the white southern memory had no parallel in black memory. Rather, most southern blacks, in rhapsodically nationalist terms, imagined a biracial America in which they would assume their place as equal and full citizens. To the same extent that white southerners insisted on their sectional identity, southern African Americans exalted their national ties. Likewise, blacks recounted a past in which black participation figured decisively in all of the nation's defining moments.[7]

The black poor of the Delta lacked social standing, racial status, and the apparent and unconscious identifiers that might evoke a dramatic empathy in Bush and Brown. Had these factors been present, it might have spurred Bush and Brown to identify *with* the black poor, indeed, see themselves *as* the black poor. Since their agency and angst had been minimized in the Southern historical memory, the black poor simply didn't register as large, or count as much, as they might have had they been white. If they had been white, a history of identification—supported by structures of care, sentiments of empathy, and an elevated racial standing—would have immediately kicked in. That might have boosted considerably their chances of survival because the federal government, including Bush and Brown, would have seen their kind, perhaps their kin, and hence themselves, floating in a flood of death in the Delta.

The undeniable incompetence of the federal disaster relief infrastructure still might have hampered the chances of even white folk surviving Katrina. But their relatively higher social and racial standing might have prompted a quicker attempt to respond, and thus to work out the problems. It also might have made Bush and Brown more adventurous, more daring, more willing to suspend rules, more determined to accept help from whatever quarters it came (they turned down offers of help from several countries), and more open to deferring procedural correctness in the interest of saving lives. The irony is that poor blacks were pained by their erasure from the historical record—both in the past and with Katrina—because, as Ignatieff argues, they uphold, and expect in return, the social contract. And, as Brundage writes, they are fully invested in a democratic and multiracial accounting of the nation's history.

Ignatieff's and Brundage's arguments about race and memory and political obligation can help to decipher Kanye West's controversial television appearance in which he charged President Bush with indifference to the plight of the black poor. On September 2, 2005, the rapper appeared on an NBC telethon in support of the American Red Cross disaster relief efforts in the Gulf Coast. After Harry Connick, Jr., played piano as he longingly, achingly sang "Do You Know What It Means to Miss New Orleans?" accompanied by Wynton Marsalis's crisp but mournful trumpet wails, the cameras turned to comedian Mike Myers and West. Both of them were to read from a script. Myers was faithful to the task. "With the breach of three levees protecting New Orleans," Myers said in clipped speech that was nearly perfunctory, "the landscape of the city was changed dramatically, tragically and perhaps irreversibly. There is now over 25 feet of water where there was once city streets and thriving neighborhoods."[8] Myers half-turned to the obviously nervous West, who cleared his throat before he spoke.

"I hate the way they portray us in the media," West intoned. "If you see a black family, it says, 'They're looting.' You see a white family, it says, 'They're looking for food.' And, you know, it's been five days [waiting for the government to arrive] because most of the people are black. And even for me to complain about it, I would be a hypocrite because I've tried to turn away from the TV because it's too hard to watch. I've even been shopping before even giving a donation. So now I'm calling my business manager right now to see what is the biggest amount I can give. And just to imagine if I was down there, and those are my people down there. So anybody out there that wants to do anything that we can help—with the way America is set up to help the poor, the black people, the less well-off, as slow as possible. I mean, the Red Cross is doing everything they can. We already realize a lot of people that could help are at war right now, fighting another way. And they've given them permission to go down and shoot us!"[9]

West's nervy chiding of the federal government froze Myers's face in disbelief and small panic. But he soldiered on and stuck to the script, rushing his words as if he wanted to quickly as possible banish the anxious feelings that fluttered in his eyes. "And subtle, but in many ways even more profoundly devastating, is the lasting damage to the survivors' will to rebuild and remain in the area. The destruction of the spirit of the people of Southern Louisiana and Mississippi may end up being the most tragic loss of all." Once again, Myers turned to West, this time with a bit of trepidation creasing his brow. West let out his final off-script pronouncement with as sure a statement as he had made during his brief and amiable diatribe. "George Bush doesn't care about black people."[10] With that, just as Myers mouthed the beginning of his plea for viewers to phone in— "Please call . . ."—someone in the NBC control room, working with a seven-second delay aimed at blocking profanity, finally understood West's tack and ordered the camera to turn unceremoniously away from the duo and cut to comedian Chris Tucker, who picked up his cue and tried to roll past West's punches.

Kanye West simply made Ignatieff's and Brundage's arguments into a polemic. West was suggesting that the government had callously broken its compact with its poor black citizens, and that it had forgotten them because it had not taken their pain to heart. West's claim that "George Bush doesn't care about black people" was a claim not about Bush's personal life, but rather his professional life. Bush's wife and father understandably jumped to his defense. "I think all of those remarks were disgusting," Laura Bush said in an interview with American Urban Radio Networks. "I mean I am the person who lives with him. I know what he is like, and I know what he thinks, and I know he cares about people."[11] On CNN's *Larry King Live* talk show, former president George H.W. Bush defended his son against the "particularly vicious comment that the president didn't care, was insensitive on ethnicity. . . . Insensitive about race. Now that one hurt because I know this president and I know he does care . . . that's what's in his heart."[12]

Unlike Bush's wife and father, West was not referring to the president's personal sentiments about black people, which he probably had no way of knowing. Neither was West addressing Bush's personal concern for black people. West was speaking of George Bush as the face of the government. In fact, our understanding of West's comments depends on our making distinctions in three categories. First, one must address the question of *personae*—is one referring to a *private* persona that is, relatively speaking, autonomous and independent, or is one referring to a *public* persona that is representational and functional? Second, one must address the question of *identities*—is one referring to an *individual* identity that primarily concerns one's self, an *institutional* identity that is concerned with one's role in relation to a particular institution, or a *social* identity that is concerned with one's role in society? Third, one must address the question of *care*—is one speaking of *personal* care, an area of interest limited to, or rooted in, one's own life; *moral* care, an area of interest shaped by consideration of ethical effects on self and others; or *political* care, an area of interest shaped by the consideration of political concern and consequences in society?

With these distinctions in mind, it is clear that when West declared that Bush doesn't care about black people, he was referring to Bush's public persona, not his private one, since what was at stake was his function as a representative public figure; that he was referring to Bush's institutional and social identities, as the face of the federal government and in his role as president of the United States; and that he was speaking of Bush's political care in his role as chief symbol of the nation's political organization. West was thus calling into question—and in my opinion rightly so—the apparent lack of political concern by a public figure whose duty it is to direct the resources of the nation to those areas that cry out for address. When West claimed that Bush doesn't care about black people, it was a critical judgment about the failure of the government, which George Bush represents, to take care of, in a timely fashion, those citizens under his watch. When Bush conceded that the response of the government was "unacceptable"—and when he later took full responsibility for the failure of the government to adequately do its job—he was partially acknowledging the legitimacy of West's criticism. In the political realm, care is measured, in part, by the satisfaction of legitimate claims with effective action that fulfills the duties and obligations of one's office.

Perhaps one of the reasons President Bush cares so little about the black poor is that he has not found political favor among them, or, for that matter, among most blacks. Poor blacks are neither economically stable nor vote rich; they matter very little in the president's political philosophy. In 2000, Bush got 8 percent of the black vote; in 2004, he got 11 percent, extending a trend begun in the 1930s of blacks voting heavily Democratic. Of course, black freedom struggles, especially the civil rights movement, destroyed, then reshaped, the Democratic Party in the South, driving whites into the party of Richard Nixon, and later Ronald Reagan. Over time, the racist Southern Democrats of the Jim Crow era gave way to the liberal Democrats of the civil rights era. As a result, Republicans have largely spurned the black vote for the last forty years and courted conservative white constituencies that were hostile to black interests and people.[13] This may help explain why Bush didn't rush to Democratic-dominated territory in Louisiana nearly as quickly as he did to Republican-friendly ground in Mississippi after Katrina struck. As critic Jacob Weisberg says, "it's a demonstrable matter of fact that Bush doesn't care much about black votes," and that, "in the end, [it] may amount to the same thing" as not caring about black people.[14]

Weisberg argues that because "they don't see blacks as a current or potential constituency, Bush and his fellow Republicans do not respond out of the instinct of self-interest when dealing with their concerns." Rendering assistance to low-income blacks is a "matter of charity to them, not necessity."[15] Their condescending attitude is magnified in New Orleans, "which is 67 percent black and largely irrelevant to GOP political ambitions." Only at election time are cities in swing states with large black populations important to Republicans—and in the immediate past, to Bush and his aides. Since Louisiana's paltry nine electoral votes are not presently up for grabs in an election cycle, the state doesn't show up much on the conservative political radar. "If Bush and Rove didn't experience the spontaneous political reflex to help New Orleans," Weisberg writes, "it may be because they don't think of New Orleans as a place that helps them."[16] Weisberg detects the president's lack of political care for black folk in his delayed and lackluster response to Katrina, while Hurricanes Charley and Frances, which affected the Republican stronghold of Florida, prompted the president and the federal government to greater urgency and generosity.

> Had the residents of New Orleans been white Republicans in a state that mattered politically, instead of poor blacks in a city that didn't, Bush's response surely would have been different. Compare what happened when hurricanes Charley and Frances hit Florida in 2004. Though the damage from those storms was negligible in relation to Katrina's, the reaction from the White House was instinctive, rapid, and generous to the point of profligacy. Bush visited hurricane victims four times in six weeks and delivered relief checks personally. Michael Brown of FEMA, now widely regarded as an incompetent political hack, was so responsive that local officials praised the agency's performance. The kind of constituency politics that results in a big life-preserver for whites in Florida and a tiny one for blacks in Louisiana may not be racist by design or intent. But the inevitable result is clear racial discrimination.[17]

Bush's claim that race played no role in the recovery efforts betrayed a simplistic understanding of how a complex force like race operates in the culture. "My attitude is this: The storm didn't discriminate and neither will the recovery effort," Bush said. "When those Coast Guard choppers . . . were pulling people off roofs, they didn't check the color of a person's skin. They wanted to save lives."[18] Katrina's fury may have been race neutral, but not its effect: 80 percent of New Orleans's minority households lived in the flooded area, while the same was true for only 54 percent of the city's white population. The average household income of those in the flooded area trailed those who lived on New Orleans's higher ground by $17,000.[19] Concentrated poverty rendered poor blacks much more vulnerable to the effects of natural disaster. Before Katrina, these blacks had been hit by hurricanes of social and economic devastation. Such a fact never seems to register with the president. Nor does it prod him into deep reflection about the unintended, but certainly foreseen, racial consequences of catastrophe and mayhem.

The proof of Bush's lack of political care for blacks before Katrina is equally distressing: under his presidency black poverty has increased, black unemployment has risen, and affirmative action has been viciously assaulted. The Bush administration has disseminated what the Government Accountability Office called "covert propaganda" by paying conservative black commentator Armstrong Williams to say good things about educational policies that hurt black folk.[20] By giving tax breaks to the wealthy, and by freezing the minimum wage at $5.15 an hour, Bush has undermined the fragile prospects of the working poor and the black working class. By seeking to cut the food stamp budget by $1.1 billion over the next decade, Bush will douse even further the fortunes of the black poor.

Nearly forty years ago, Muhammad Ali's single line captured the reason for his conscientious objection to the Vietnam War while summing up millions of black people's feelings—"Ain't no Viet Cong ever called me 'nigger.'"[21] Now, Kanye West's simple sentence brilliantly condensed an analysis that millions of other blacks have made about an uncaring Bush regime. As a public figure who is the ultimate representative of the American government, George Bush doesn't care about black people—no matter how many black folks like Condoleezza Rice (who defended the president against West's charge as well) he puts in vaunted places.[22] He may have promoted some blacks, but as for the rest of us, he has left us far behind. Bush's slow response to black suffering by wind and water was but a symptom of a larger, equally dangerous political neglect.

Indeed, what Katrina's gale forces have uncovered, yet again, is the strong disagreement between blacks and whites over the role that race plays in who gets what and when in our society—and what group most often gets left out, and behind, in the social contract. Polls taken immediately after Katrina prove the racial divide. A CNN/*USA Today*/Gallup poll found that 60 percent of blacks believed that race caused the government's delay in rescuing folk, leaving many of them to starve or drown, while only 12 percent of whites agreed.[23] The racial divide was similar when taking class into consideration: 63 percent of blacks blamed poverty for the slow rescue, while 21 percent of whites held that view. Until many white and well-off folk feel the full force of black pain, and open their eyes to see racial and class suffering, that divide will only widen. And the black poor will continue to be left behind long after Katrina recovery efforts are over.

If race played a role in who lived and died, how did it affect the federal government's response to Katrina? To answer that question, we must understand the federal government's role in disaster relief—a prospect that will clarify how incompetence and antigovernment philosophy, among other factors, made a bad situation even worse.

Disasters happen in New Orleans. I've been here for 64 years. I think the hurricane played a major role [in the suffering of the people]. But I also believe that [it is] because of the injustice that exists in Louisiana. . . . And even referring to the levees that were supposed to be fixed to protect this city and [weren't], there were people like the Army Corps of Engineers who were aware of this. God does His will, but there's also some inefficiency because of politics.

—*Ronald Chisom, Executive Director, People's Institute, Katrina survivor*

CHAPTER 3

THE POLITICS OF DISASTER

AT THE 2000 REPUBLICAN CONVENTION in Philadelphia, presidential nominee George W. Bush struck a strangely dulcet tone when he denounced "the soft bigotry of low expectations."[1] This melodic phrase conjured Bush's disdain for racial circumstances where preference got the better part of merit—and signified his desire to end social promotion of black children in standards-starved segregated schools. The phrase has since served as a credo for the Bush administration's approach to race and educational policy. But as with many political slogans that titillate before they taunt, Bush's mantra has come back to bite his administration in its vulnerable parts. If Hurricane Katrina's lethal fury unleashed unforgettable images of suffering in its wake, the Bush administration answered one of the nation's worse natural disasters ever with a political maelstrom fed by ineptitude, inexperience, and ignorance.

The Bush administration's response to Katrina was further stymied by chronic cronyism. Even more than other presidents,

Bush has relied on loyalty and friendship rather than competence in choosing who gets in.[2] There has also been a diversion of attention and resources (such as the National Guard) from domestic affairs to the "war on terror," especially in Iraq. To throw salt water in the faces of a population already drowned by race, poverty, and storm surges, the federal government offered reconstruction contracts to huge companies in a glaring example of "disaster capitalism."[3] The Bush administration's problems were also philosophical and ideological: they harbor hostility for the public sector, and for the active role of the government in aiding its most vulnerable citizens. At the heart of the administration's response to Katrina was the grossly inefficient FEMA—Federal Emergency Management Agency. Their botching of the response to Katrina led, arguably, to the loss of hundreds, perhaps thousands, of lives.

To understand FEMA's role in disaster relief, one must understand the history of how emergencies have been managed, and the role the government has come to play in such efforts. In fact, the federal government has not always been responsible for responding to natural disasters. There were American natural disasters before the nation was even founded. In 1755, Boston was rocked by a major earthquake, and a hurricane tore through Yorktown at the end of the Revolutionary War, forcing British troops to surrender and helping American colonists to victory.[4] Although the nation's first disaster legislation was enacted in 1803—offering financial aid to a New Hampshire town razed by fire—the United States lacked a coherent and unified federal strategy for addressing natural and man-made disasters for the first 160 years of its history.[5]

Horrific events like the New Madrid, Missouri, earthquakes of 1811–1812; the Chicago fire of 1873; the Johnstown flood in 1889; the Galveston hurricane of 1900; the San Francisco earthquake and fire of 1906; the Miami hurricane of 1926; the Great Mississippi flood of 1927; and the New England hurricane of 1938 imposed enormous structural damage and financial ruin, but were largely unmet by federal assistance.[6] Even though Congress passed 128 acts between 1803 and 1947 avowing sympathy for the toll of natural disasters, there was little in these gestures besides occasional token financial assistance to ease the burden.[7] The response to catastrophes was local and humanitarian; cities, states, and churches and other charitable organizations outside the disaster zone pitched in as well.[8]

The American Red Cross was founded by Clara Barton in 1881 as the American branch of an international effort to provide assistance to civilian and combat victims of war. It became the nation's first organization devoted to disaster relief when it coordinated the distribution of food and other supplies after an 1881 forest fire ravaged large parts of Port Huron and Bad Axe, Michigan.[9] In 1905, Congress incorporated the Red Cross and officially sanctioned it as the first disaster relief agency in the United States.[10] By granting the Red Cross a charter, Congress authorized the organization to work nationally and internationally to relieve suffering from pestilence, famine, fires, floods, and other catastrophes.[11] Although the Red Cross was the primary source of relief for disaster victims from its founding until the 1960s, it has historically received limited funds from the federal government. The same is true today.

If the duty to respond to, rescue, repair, and reconstruct communities in the wake of disasters was local, and heavily dependent on charitable efforts, there were signs of a shift toward federal responsibility in the early 1900s. Such change didn't occur without tremendous political and ideological struggle. The progressive reform movement opposed the prevailing laissez-faire philosophy, which held that government shouldn't tinker with the private market economy. Laissez-faire ideology wove easily into fatalistic strands of American theology that preached that disasters were "acts of God" that no government could foresee or prevent. Providence and private capital seemed to be yoked in the belief that "What will be, will be," equal parts Billy Sunday and Doris Day. Laissez-faire appeals to the provenance of the market held in check challenges to corporate power and building codes, even when greed and negligence were clearly the source of disaster.[12]

The market also impinged on municipal decisions about the use of private land in the aftermath of catastrophe. For instance, after the 1906 San Francisco earthquake and fire, the city expanded a limited water supply that was to blame for its uncontrolled inferno. The federal government approved of San Francisco's damming the Hetch Hetchy River in Yosemite National Park and building an aqueduct to direct water from the Sierra Nevada 150 miles away to the city. But in their rush to quickly rebuild San Francisco, city leaders gave in to the wishes of a well-financed and well-insured private business community, which sparked the city's quick recovery from disaster.[13]

The business community ignored redevelopment plans that took into account the city's precarious site. Instead, they followed the original patterns of streets and land use. Daniel H. Burnham's "City Beautiful" plan had been presented before the fire, and was overlooked after the flames felled the city. As historians Gordon Thomas and Max Morgan Witt argued in 1971, San Francisco chose to "build at a rate and manner which made the city not only less beautiful than was possible, but more dangerous." They also prophesied that because the "rubble of the 1906 disaster was pushed into the Bay" and "buildings were built on it," those buildings "will be among the most vulnerable when the next earthquake comes."[14] In 1989, their words rang true: San Francisco's Marina District, resting on the rubble from 1906, was severely damaged in the Loma Prieta earthquake.

Reformers like Robert La Follette, Jane Addams, Lillian Wald, Hazen Pingree, Samuel Jones, James Phelan, Lincoln Steffens, Jacob Riis, and Theodore Roosevelt countered the logic of laissez-faire with resistance to corporate monopolies, wasted natural resources, and horrible factory conditions. They promoted stricter tenement housing codes, municipal ownership of public utilities, enhanced city services, state banking control reforms, hiked corporate taxes, workers' compensation, child labor laws, minimum wages, and widows' pensions.[15] Muckraking journalists colorfully exposed unprincipled business practices. With their pens, cameras, stump speeches, policies, programs, and political manifestos, progressive reformers helped to establish the reasonable expectation of corporate responsibility and the need for public action to protect citizens from corporate misbehavior. Despite a conservative Senate, Roosevelt aggressively promoted corporate regulation and social welfare legislation. During Roosevelt's administration, Congress passed the Elkins Act in 1903 and the Hepburn Act in 1906, both aimed at regulating railroads. In 1906, Congress also passed the Pure Food and Drug Act and the Meat Inspection Act to regulate the food industry.[16]

Later, two disasters sparked even further calls for corporate regulation and business reform: the Triangle Shirtwaist Factory fire in New York City, which killed 146 young women in 1911, and the sinking of the *Titanic* in 1912. The Triangle Shirtwaist Factory fire instigated advocacy for fire safety laws and limits on building heights.[17] The *Titanic* catastrophe raised awareness in the industrialized world about the need to limit excessive corporate ambition—the White Star line that built the ship sought to break the speed record across the North Atlantic despite ice

warnings. It also highlighted the class chasms and divergent social privileges that are often reinforced by corporate behavior:
the ship only had enough lifeboats and rafts for 1,100 people,
less than half of the number of folk on board. Predictably, the
greatest percentage of those who died were lower-class passengers. The *Titanic* disaster hastened the call for international
standards for safety at sea, and cleared the path for the government to oversee other hazardous activities.[18]

Judicial progressivism in American courts also played a role in
protecting the public welfare from private enterprise. As technology advanced, urban society grew—the 1920 census indi-
cated that for the first time in U.S. history more folk lived in
urban areas than rural ones. In light of these changes, judicial
progressives argued that the nation had to recast ill-suited laws
derived from medieval England aimed at defending the public
interest. Judicial progressives believed that the country must
promote stronger government regulation of private industry.[19]

The signal legal decision that flowed from such efforts came in
the 1926 case *Ambler Realty v. Village of Euclid*, which, in light
of increased urbanization, upheld the zoning of urban land use.
"Euclidean zoning," as it became known among planners, was
widely adopted across the nation to prevent "discordant" patterns of urban land use. It was used to keep single-family neighborhoods free of apartment buildings, and to keep adult
bookstores away from elementary schools.[20] Euclidean zoning,
however, was rarely applied to building in hazardous areas, especially those areas vulnerable to flooding.

Since floods have caused the greatest disasters in the nation's
history, Congress, beginning in 1917, has intermittently enacted
flood control legislation and disaster relief acts designed to protect private property.[21] After several floods in the 1920s and
1930s, and the 1933 Long Beach, California, earthquake, Con-

gress looked beyond disaster relief in tentative efforts to provide aid to homeowners in rebuilding their homes.[22] Franklin Roosevelt's New Deal politics led to social legislation that broadened the role of government in stimulating the economy and guarding the public trust. In the 1930s, the Reconstruction Finance Corporation and the Bureau of Public Roads were authorized to make disaster loans to repair and reconstruct public facilities damaged by disaster.[23] The Tennessee Valley Authority came into being, in part, to reduce flooding in the area. The Flood Control Act of 1934 granted greater authority to the U.S. Army Corps of Engineers to design and craft flood-control projects.[24] But it wasn't until 1950 that Congress threw the weight of the federal government behind efforts to respond to natural disasters.[25]

Although Public Law 81-875, the Disaster Relief Act of 1950, institutionalized federal disaster relief, the bill was severely limited. It offered victims little aid (the Red Cross and other private charities were expected to address their needs). There was a meager overall appropriation of $5 million for the repair of public facilities with presidential approval. Still, the law set the pattern for the development of subsequent federal legislation aimed at assisting private citizens and businesses.[26] Several hurricanes in the 1950s sparked congressional disaster relief legislation. In 1954 Hurricane Hazel struck Virginia and North Carolina. In 1955 Hurricane Diane struck numerous mid-Atlantic and northeastern states. And in 1957, Hurricane Audrey caused the most damage of the three storms when it struck Louisiana and North Texas.[27]

In the thirty years after the 1950 Disaster Relief Act, disaster relief legislation added specific provisions in the evolving federal response to natural catastrophes. For instance, the Midwest flood in Kansas, Oklahoma, and Missouri in 1951 prompted legislation to provide for emergency housing. A 1962 bill added grants to repair state facilities. In 1966, Congress passed legislation to make rural communities eligible for relief, while also providing funding for damage to higher education facilities and for the repair of public facilities under construction. In 1969, a bill added funding for debris removal from private property, the distribution of food coupons, and unemployment compensation for disaster victims.

A year later, legislation added grants to individuals for temporary housing and relocation, funding for legal services, and community payments for tax loss. In 1974, legislation distinguished "major disasters" from "emergencies," and authorized funding for mental health counseling, recovery planning councils, community loans, state disaster planning, and repairs to parks and recreation facilities. Other legislation was disaster specific: three bills in 1964 and 1965 addressed, in turn, an Alaskan earthquake, Pacific Northwest floods, and Hurricane Betsy, which struck Florida, Louisiana, and Mississippi.[28]

Federal disaster legislation was accompanied by a burgeoning, though splintered, emergency management bureaucracy. At least six agencies have been responsible for federal disasters since the 1950 federal Disaster Relief Act.[29] First, from 1951 to 1952, the Housing and Home Finance Agency (HHFA) was in charge of federal disaster relief, quickly followed by the Federal Civil Defense Administration (FCDA), which handled disaster relief from 1953 to 1958. FCDA had little staff and few resources; it primarily offered technical assistance. Given the prevailing Cold War mind-set, the national emphasis in emergency management was on the possibility of nuclear disaster. There were a flurry of bomb shelters built by local citizens and communities to defend against the threat of nuclear holocaust. Local and state directors of civil defense programs were widely viewed as the front line of emergency management.

The Department of Defense (DOD) established the Office of Defense Mobilization to focus on emergency preparedness, including gathering and organizing crucial materials in case of war. In 1958, the two offices merged and became the Office of Civil Defense Mobilization (OCDM), which handled disaster relief until 1962, when the Office of Emergency Planning (OEP) took charge. In 1974, the U.S. Department of Housing and Urban Development's Federal Disaster Assistance Administration (FDAA) began to manage natural disasters.[30] The picture grew even more complicated in the 1970s because various functions of emergency management were divvied up among several more federal departments and agencies. Weather, warning, and fire protection were handled by the Department of Commerce, while the General Services Administration addressed continuity of government, stockpiling, and federal preparedness. The Treasury Department was responsible for import investigation, while the Nuclear Regulatory Commission oversaw power plants. And the Department of Housing and Urban Development (HUD) was in charge of flood insurance and disaster relief.[31]

FEMA was formed in 1979 when President Jimmy Carter sought to consolidate the fragmented federal emergency management community.[32] The first person to head FEMA was John Macy, a Carter cabinet member who was the head of the Office of Personnel Management. (Before Macy's appointment in August, Gordon Vickery and Thomas Casey both served the agency as acting directors in 1979.) Macy's task was to bring coherence and unity to a fledgling agency that was both physically and philosophically divided. FEMA in the early days was spread over five buildings and focused on everything from nuclear war preparations to environmental concerns and floodplain management. Macy developed the idea called Integrated Emergency Management System (IEMS), which organized under one conceptual umbrella a plan of preparation to meet all hazards, from small disturbances to nuclear attack.[33]

When Ronald Reagan swept into office, he appointed, in quick succession, Bernhard Gallagher and John W. McConnell as acting heads of the agency in 1981. Later that year, Reagan selected Louis O. Guiffrida to head FEMA. Guiffrida, a friend of Ed Meese, one of Reagan's closest advisers, had a state government background in training and terrorism preparedness. He focused on getting the country ready for a nuclear attack. Ironically enough, however, he failed to envision a role for states in national security, ostracizing the very state directors who had pushed for FEMA's creation. Moreover, the state directors' authority and funding declined under Guiffrida. Questions about FEMA's operations—and Guiffrida's authoritarian style—sparked congressional hearings and Department of Justice investigations, leading to Guiffrida's resignation. Robert H. Morris was acting director for two months until a successor was found in November of 1985.

Guiffrida was replaced by Julius Becton, a retired military general who had been director of the Office of Foreign Disaster Assistance in the State Department.[34] Becton continued down the policy path of his predecessor at FEMA but brought back a sense of integrity. He spearheaded the expansion of FEMA's duties when the Department of Defense requested that he oversee the off-site cleanup of chemical stockpiles at the department's bases. FEMA's umbrella included over twenty programs, but Becton ranked natural hazards programs that addressed earthquakes, floods, and hurricanes near the bottom in level of importance. The former general perpetuated the view that natural hazards programs were a stepchild to emergency management's parent organization.[35]

At the end of the 1980s FEMA was clearly in trouble—Robert H. Morris returned as acting director in 1989 for a year, succeeded in that capacity by Jerry D. Jennings for an even shorter stay, while Wallace E. Stickney served from 1990 to 1993, all under George H.W. Bush. FEMA's wobbly position under the elder Bush was underscored by two major natural disasters in 1989: Hurricane Hugo struck the Carolinas, leaving eighty-five dead and $15 billion in damage, and less than a month later, the Loma Prieta earthquake shattered Northern California's Bay Area. In both instances, FEMA proved dangerously tentative. FEMA was slow to respond to Hugo, relying on the two states' governors to take the lead. FEMA's focus on nuclear attack planning rendered the organization of little use in the Bay. Fortunately, state leaders in emergency management saved the day and performed far better than their federal counterparts.

Although FEMA had been lucky with the Loma Prieta quake (there were great costs but little loss of life), its weaknesses were exposed in 1992. That's when Hurricane Andrew clobbered Florida and Louisiana and, a few months later, Hurricane Iniki struck Hawaii. Neither the parent organization nor its state partners were prepared for the crisis, a failure that was widely dissected in the media. President George H.W. Bush had to send Secretary of Transportation Andrew Card and the military to clean up the political and structural mess.[36] Hurricanes Hugo, Andrew, and Iniki revealed the flaws in FEMA's system and process of responding to emergencies. But for the first time in the nation's history, FEMA leveraged its national security assets in a natural disaster during Hurricane Andrew. The gesture proved largely ineffective because it came too late. FEMA was a national disgrace, if not disaster, and the agency withstood cries for its abolition.[37]

If one former Southern governor gave birth to FEMA, another gave it new life. When Arkansas governor Bill Clinton gained the presidency, FEMA gained a vital advocate.[38] Clinton shored up the failing agency's standing by appointing as its director James Lee Witt, a former state director for Emergency Management in Arkansas. Witt changed the organizational culture of FEMA by striking cordial relations with employees and establishing customer service training. Witt ramped up the agency's technological capacity in delivering disaster relief services. He also expanded the philosophy of the agency to match post-disaster efforts—rescue and relief—with pre-emergency hazard mitigation and risk avoidance.[39] It is the difference between seeking medical treatment for an illness after disease strikes, and adopting preventive measures to keep it from coming at all—or at least to lessen its blow when it strikes.

When a series of natural disasters flared to test Witt's philosophy of disaster management—including the Midwest floods of 1993, which caused major disasters in nine states, and the Northridge, California, earthquake in 1994—FEMA responded successfully. Witt's focus on mitigation and avoidance affected the agency's post-disaster recovery plans as well. After the Midwest floods, FEMA inaugurated the biggest voluntary buyout and relocation program ever. The program removed folk from the floodplain that left them vulnerable to hazard. Over the next several years, as FEMA battled deadly tornadoes, ice storms, hurricanes, floods, wildfires, and drought, the agency and its state branches enhanced their reputation for technologically sophisticated and efficient response to natural disaster. Clinton signaled the importance of FEMA and boosted the fortunes of the agency even further when he made Witt a member of his cabinet.[40]

The advent of terror, with the first bombing of the World Trade Center in New York City in 1992, followed by the Oklahoma City bombing in 1995, forced FEMA to contend with preparation for terrorist threats. Several factors affected FEMA's fate in regard to this newest and potentially most deadly plague. There was Senate legislation that didn't specify what agency would take the lead in the national response to terror. Also, FEMA failed to step up and deploy its experience in hazard management to lead the response to terror. And then there was the scramble by several departments and agencies to seize leadership in the terror sweepstakes.[41] Nevertheless, FEMA sharpened its focus on hazard mitigation by forming Project Impact: Building Disaster-Resistant Communities, an effort to embrace communities across the country in exercising emergency management and preparedness.

Project Impact encouraged communities to integrate principles of hazard mitigation and risk avoidance into the normal fabric of local decision making. FEMA's visibility, and its reputation for strong leadership in risk avoidance and hazard mitigation, spawned at least two positive results. First, it inspired the development of disaster relief professionals whose skills, rather than political connections alone, won them governmental and private positions. Second, it sparked the institutionalization of emergency management in higher education through degree programs in more than sixty-five colleges and universities.[42]

It would be easy to say that FEMA was thrust into the fierce winds of mediocrity and flooded by inexperienced and incompetent leaders when George W. Bush seized the presidency—but it wouldn't be wrong. The agency was almost immediately sacked by "the soft bigotry of low expectations." Bush's choice to lead FEMA was Joseph Allbaugh, his former chief of staff when Bush was Texas governor and his campaign manager for the 2000 election. During his confirmation hearings, no mention was made of Allbaugh's dreadful lack of emergency management

skills or disaster relief background.[43] One of Allbaugh's first decisions was to ax funding for Project Impact, signaling an end to
community-based emergency management that thrived on tying
local threads of hazard mitigation into the larger quilt of disaster
relief.

Shortly afterward, Seattle, Washington, was rocked by the
Nisqually Earthquake. Since Seattle had successfully imple-
mented the principles of Project Impact, its mayor went on national television to praise the program for minimizing damage
from the quake. Although Vice President Dick Cheney defended
the elimination of Project Impact because of its alleged ineffectiveness later that evening, Congress eventually put funds back
into the initiative.[44] Still, Allbaugh's attitude toward disaster
management reflected the Bush administration's goal of privatiz-
ing a great deal of FEMA's work. Allbaugh captured his boss's
dislike of government's active role in public spheres when he argued that many "are concerned that federal disaster assistance
may have evolved into . . . an oversized entitlement program."
He argued that "expectations of when the federal government
should be involved and the degree of involvement may have bal-
looned beyond what is an appropriate level."[45]

In 2001, Allbaugh established the Office of National Preparedness, re-creating an office first opened in FEMA under
Guiffrida's watch (but closed by Witt) to focus on nuclear holocaust.[46] Instead of nuclear threats, Allbaugh concentrated on the
rise of terrorism. In an eerie foreshadowing of the tragic events
of September 11, 2001, Allbaugh gave a speech the day before
terror struck declaring that FEMA would focus on firefighting,
disaster mitigation, and preparation for catastrophe.[47] When the
tragedy of September 11 exploded, FEMA abided by the Federal
Response Plan. New York and Virginia operations ran smoothly,
proving the strength of a system created under Witt's leader-

ship. Earlier in the year, Allbaugh had testified before a joint hearing of three Senate committees that the Office of National Preparedness would coordinate the terrorist response efforts of more than forty federal agencies even as Vice President Cheney would oversee the development of a plan to respond to terrorist attacks.[48]

The plan was for FEMA to take up the role previously played by the FBI's National Domestic Preparedness Office, which worked with local police, fire, and emergency management agencies.[49] Bush's choice of FEMA to handle these duties side-stepped the creation of a high-level coordinating council in the White House that was stipulated in congressional legislation. Bush's action also undercut the recommendation of a commission charged by Congress to establish a new National Homeland Security Agency that would combine the duties of the Coast Guard, the Customs Service, the Border Patrol, and FEMA. Bush's resistance to the congressional commission's recommendation melted in the fires of September 11, 2001. A year later, the Department of Homeland Security was formed.

When Bush signed the Homeland Security Act on November 25, 2002, it called for the largest reorganization of the U.S. government since the Departments of War and Navy were combined into the Department of Defense in 1947.[50] More than twenty-two agencies and departments were gathered under Homeland Security's bailiwick, including FEMA. By now the agency's focus had shifted from tornadoes to terror. Allbaugh timed his resignation to take effect on March 1, 2003, the date that FEMA would be downgraded from a cabinet level agency and folded into the Department of Homeland Security.[51] He immediately set up a consulting firm to advise companies doing business in Iraq. Allbaugh was succeeded by his former college pal and FEMA deputy Michael Brown, who, like his boss, had no previous experience in disaster relief and emergency management. Brown served for a decade as commissioner of the International Arabian Horse Association before coming to FEMA in 2001 as its general counsel.[52] That didn't keep Allbaugh from proclaiming, when Bush nominated his old classmate to head FEMA, that "the President couldn't have chosen a better man to help . . . prepare and lead the nation."[53]

But Brown's mediocrity, even for a crony, was unmistakable. He padded his résumé to make it appear that he had oversight of emergency services in an early job, when in truth he was little more than an intern in the emergency services division of the city of Edmond, Oklahoma.[54] An online profile of Brown also claimed that he was an "Outstanding Political Science Professor [at] Central State University," but that, too, appears to be false. According to university officials, Brown was a student, not a professor (though he may have been an adjunct professor, which is vastly different in academe). And his claims to have made the dean's list or to have been an "Outstanding Political Science Senior" can't be confirmed.[55] Brown also falsely claimed to be the director of the Oklahoma Christian Home in Edmond from 1983 to the present. (A FEMA official says he claimed only to be on the board of directors of the nursing home, which, as it turns out, seems untrue as well, at least according to a veteran employee of the center.) Stephen Jones, the well-known defense attorney who represented Oklahoma City bomber Timothy McVeigh, and for whom Brown worked in the early 1980s, may have also captured Brown's work at FEMA when he said of his former charge that there "was a feeling that he was not serious and somewhat shallow."[56]

Brown was woefully underprepared for emergency management. By the time he arrived, FEMA had a greatly diminished status in an administration obsessed with fighting terror. The combination charted an untenable, even dangerous, path for an agency that was still responsible for addressing natural disasters. An already precarious situation was exacerbated in 2003 when FEMA's preparation and planning functions were reassigned to a newly opened Office of Preparedness and Response. The change shifted the agency's focus to response and recovery—not mitigation and avoidance.[57] FEMA's decline made it a "bureaucratic backwater."[58] To its detriment, the agency has been politicized and packed with patronage appointments.

Of FEMA's top eight officials, five joined the agency with virtually no experience in disaster management.[59] FEMA's top three leaders—Brown, Chief of Staff Patrick J. Rhode, and Deputy Chief of Staff Brooks D. Altshuler—were plucked from Bush's 2000 campaign or the White House advance operation.[60] Scott R. Morris, Altshuler's predecessor and now director of the agency's Long-Term Recovery Office for Florida, worked as a media strategist for Bush's 2000 presidential campaign. David I. Maurstad, a senior official at FEMA's headquarters, was the Republican lieutenant governor of Nebraska before joining the agency.[61] Among FEMA's top fifteen jobs in D.C., the only folk who have experience or a single permanent assignment—some FEMA employees pull double duty—are the agency's top lawyer, its equal rights director, its technology chief, and its inner-agency planning chief.[62] None of these figures are directly responsible for disaster response or preparations.

This scenario lowered the agency's morale even further and left it dangerously devoid of experience and competence at the top. The ranks of skilled personnel thinned as dedicated professionals bolted when they learned that emergency management, hazard mitigation, and risk avoidance for natural disasters are simply not a priority in the Bush administration. Skilled veterans like Eric Tolbert, a hurricane specialist who led the agency's office of response, Laurence W. Zensinger, a World Trade Center disaster manager who led the office of recovery, and Bruce P. Baughman, a World Trade Center disaster manager who headed the office of preparedness, are all casualties of the agency's politicization and patronage.[63] The high rate of turnover means that three of the five FEMA heads of natural disaster–related operations, and nine of ten regional directors, are serving in an acting capacity. The agency has also suffered deep budget cuts.

The picture is gloomy for FEMA. It has been undercut by a combination of cronyism, politicization, inexperience, and incompetence. It has been hampered as well by the Bush administration's hostility to government's helping the public domain and its view of FEMA as an overwrought public entitlement. The administration's desire to privatize FEMA's work has been harmful to its mission. And FEMA's reorganization under Homeland Security means that it has failed to adequately pay attention to emergency management. All of these factors eventually exacted a high toll, none more costly than the unnecessary loss of lives in the Gulf Coast. As Katrina built, the local and state governments hesitated, and the federal government seemed to fiddle while Rome was burning.

It pained and angered me as I watched it. I believe one of the critical errors that was made was that the city waited too long before ordering a mandatory evacuation.

—*Marc Morial, former Mayor of New Orleans,*
President/CEO, National Urban League

CHAPTER 4

HURRICANE AND HESITATION

WHEN IT APPEARED, Hurricane Katrina was the eleventh named tropical storm, the third major hurricane (out of four hurricanes), and the first Category 5 hurricane of 2005, making the year one of the most active Atlantic hurricane seasons ever. On Tuesday, August 23, 2005, the United States National Hurricane Center (NHC) reported at 5:00 P.M. EDT that tropical depression 12 had taken shape over the southeastern Bahamas. It was quickly upgraded to Tropical Storm Katrina by 11:00 A.M. on Wednesday, August 24.[1] By the time Katrina made landfall at 7:00 P.M. on Thursday, August 25, on the east coast of Florida, it had become a minor hurricane. It registered a Category 1 on the Saffir-Simpson hurricane scale, with eighty-mile-per-hour winds, killing nine people and causing power loss for a million residents.[2] On Friday, August 26, Katrina underwent a dangerously rapid expansion. At 11:30 A.M. it was upgraded to a Category 2 hurricane, and by 5:00 P.M. CDT it was announced that it would soon reach Category 3 intensity.[3]

At 5:00 P.M. Louisiana governor Kathleen Blanco declared a state of emergency in Louisiana, while on Saturday, August 27, Governor Haley Barbour followed suit in Mississippi.[4] On Friday, the governors of the Gulf States requested the presence of National Guard troops from the Pentagon, a contingent that would be colorfully and efficiently led by Army Lieutenant Russel Honore, commander of Joint Task Force Katrina.[5] Judging by the number of troops Barbour and Blanco requested—Barbour, on Friday night, requested 1,000 troops, with 600 on standby, while Blanco summoned 4,000 troops, a number that would eventually swell to more than 30,000—they didn't truly comprehend the magnitude of the storm heading their way.[6] Of the 4,000 Louisiana troops activated, 2,800 were sent to New Orleans. Of course, the number of troops available to Blanco—6,000 in total—had been severely diminished by the war in Iraq, where 35 to 40 percent of Louisiana's National Guard is on active duty. Besides governmental regulations and procedural snafus, the deployment of troops in Iraq may help explain why 12,000 more troops weren't scheduled to arrive in Louisiana until Friday, September 2.[7]

On Saturday, Governor Blanco asked Bush to declare a state of emergency in Louisiana. She wrote that "I have determined that this incident is of such severity and magnitude that effective response is beyond the capabilities of the State and affected local governments, and that supplementary Federal assistance is necessary to save lives, protect property, public health, and safety, or to lessen or avert the threat of a disaster."[8] President Bush declared a state of emergency for Louisiana on Saturday, August 27—and for Mississippi and Alabama on Sunday, August 28, while declaring a major disaster in Florida the same day. However, a clerical error in the federal emergency declaration left off twenty-four parishes (the equivalent of counties), including Orleans and Jefferson, which would most likely be hardest hit.[9] Though the mistake had no material effect, it was portentous nonetheless, foreshadowing how New Orleans—and its poor, mostly black citizens—would be overlooked by the federal government.[10]

In his August 27 Louisiana emergency declaration (and, subsequently, in those for Mississippi and Alabama), Bush authorized DHS and FEMA to manage the disaster and provide relief, though it didn't spur either the department or agency to action. Perhaps they were mimicking their boss's casual approach in responding to disaster. Earlier in the day, Bush hadn't mentioned Katrina at all in his weekly radio address.[11] At her news conference on Saturday morning, Blanco admitted that "Louisiana appears to be in a direct path of the hurricane."[12] By 4:00 P.M. CDT Governor Blanco ordered contra-flow—the reversal of traffic on inbound interstates that turns superhighways one-way out of the coastal areas to speed evacuation. Barbour did the same for Mississippi. Throughout the two states local officials issued voluntary and mandatory evacuation orders. With predictions that Katrina would make landfall on Monday, August 29, New Orleans Mayor Ray Nagin finally issued a voluntary evacuation at 5:00 P.M. on Saturday. Nagin hesitated to make the order mandatory because of the city's potential legal liability for closing hotels and other businesses. Still, Nagin warned that "come the first break of light in the morning, you may have the first mandatory evacuation of New Orleans."[13]

Although Nagin's hesitancy hemmed his city further in, his office's refusal of an offer of help from Amtrak proved costly as well. The last regularly scheduled train out of New Orleans had departed several hours earlier, but Amtrak decided to run a "dead-head" train later in the evening to transport equipment out of town.[14] The train's destination was Macomb, Mississippi, which was far above sea level and much safer ground than New Orleans. Amtrak says it had room for several hundred passengers. "We offered the city the opportunity to take evacuees out of harm's way," lamented Amtrak spokesman Cliff Black. "The city declined." At 8:30 P.M., the ghost train left New Orleans without a single passenger on board.[15]

National Hurricane Center director Max Mayfield phoned Nagin at home—Mayfield also called Blanco and Barbour—to impress on him the severity of what was about to occur, and to satisfy his conscience that he had exhausted all means to save as many lives as possible.[16] "I just wanted to be able to go to sleep that night knowing that I did all I could do," Mayfield said.[17] Nagin was having supper with his wife and six-year-old daughter when Mayfield informed him that Katrina—not yet a Category 4, but quickly building up to it—was the worst hurricane he had ever seen and that officials should do all they could to move folk out of danger. "It scared the crap out of me," Nagin told a reporter. "I immediately said, 'My God, I have to call a mandatory evacuation.'"[18]

Remarkably, Nagin still hesitated in following through. At stake were the lives of the 130,000 New Orleans citizens who suffered below the poverty line. Nagin knew he lacked both adequate shelter space and public transportation to squire his impoverished charges to safety. The state of Louisiana's hurricane evacuation plan calls for the use of "school and municipal buses, government-owned vehicles and vehicles provided by volunteer agencies" to assist folk who "lack transportation and require assistance in evacuating."[19] In an ideal world, successful evacuation was a matter of arithmetic: if New Orleans had 134,000 folk without transportation, and 550 municipal buses and 254 working school buses (70 of the city's 324 school buses weren't functioning), that adds up to 804 buses with 60 seats each, space enough for 48,240 folks. It would take three trips to get every-one to safety.[20]

From the time Nagin declared a voluntary evacuation on Sat-urday, August 27, until Katrina made landfall two days later, a great many more evacuees may have made it to safety on buses that were famously shown on television drowning with the city. (Officials in New Orleans were later pleased that 80 percent of its population safely evacuated before the storm hit, but that is lit-tle consolation to the poorest citizens in Louisiana and Missis-sippi who lacked the resources to get out of harm's way.)[21] Nagin also worried whether the city's hospitals should be exempt from a mandatory evacuation order. Nagin and the city's lawyers grappled with these issues all night.

Finally, at 10:00 A.M. on Sunday morning, flanked by Gover-nor Blanco, Nagin held a televised press conference. He con-fessed that "we're facing the storm most of us have feared . . . [t]his is going to be an unprecedented event," and announced a mandatory evacuation order—*after* Katrina had climbed dan-gerously to a Category 4 at 1:00 A.M. and then escalated to a Category 5, the highest possible rating, with lethal 161 mile-per-hour winds, at 8:00 A.M.[22] Governor Blanco said that President Bush had phoned her before the press conference began to ex-press his concern about the storm's impact and to urge Blanco and Nagin to order the evacuation.[23] Nagin suggested that the 134,000 citizens who didn't own cars should hitch rides with friends, family, neighbors, and church members.[24] For those who couldn't, the mayor suggested they make it to the Superdome as quickly as possible. Later, Mayfield personally briefed Bush on Katrina during a video teleconference with the president and federal and state emergency management organizations at his ranch in Crawford, Texas, where Bush was vacationing.[25]

More than 25,000 people took Nagin's advice and headed by

bus and foot to the Superdome. The Louisiana National Guard had delivered three truckloads of water (90,000 liters) and seven truckloads of MREs (43,776 "meals ready to eat") before the storm.[26] Still, thousands couldn't even make it to the Superdome, especially the elderly, the feeble, the sick, and the desperately poor. The Superdome was clearly a place that state and city officials had not planned to stock with food and water. The supplies they had would only feed 15,000 people for three days, or, given the number of people gathered, enough to last a day and a half. Authorities viewed the Superdome as the "shelter of last resort," not a place where people would stay for any length of time. But Katrina's fast and furious approach scuttled all plans— plans for evacuation that surely would have to be rethought in the aftermath of the storm. New Mexico governor Bill Richardson offered Blanco the assistance of his state's National Guard. Blanco accepted, but the paperwork needed to set the troops in motion was delayed from Washington for four days until Thursday, September 2. It was a sign of things to come—or, as it were, *not* to come, at least from the federal government.

What *did* come on early Monday morning were waves of water crashing over the Lake Pontchartrain levee. And then, a 5:00 A.M. phone call to the Army Corps of Engineers headquarters near Tulane University in central New Orleans, announcing a breach in the 17th Street Canal levee, which traces the boundary between Orleans and East Jefferson parishes.[27] (A National Guard timeline suggests the breach occurred at 3:00 A.M.)[28] This news was particularly devastating because the weakened levees of New Orleans were the reason that astute observers argued that a Category 4 or 5 hurricane in the Gulf was one of the nation's greatest, and foreseeable, catastrophes. It was envisioned as a blow that would do the city in, or, more likely, take it under, since New Orleans is a bowl-shaped city largely below sea level that would fill once the levees broke. At 6:10 A.M. CDT, Katrina made lethal landfall as a Category 4 storm south of Buras, Louisiana, along the Mississippi Delta.[29] The eye of the storm brushed the eastern outskirts of New Orleans around 9:00 A.M. as six to eight feet of water covered the Lower Ninth Ward, among the city's poorest and most vulnerable communities. The Army Corps of Engineers believe that as a storm surge sent water over the Industrial Canal, a barge broke free and crashed into the floodwall, gashing a breach that accelerated the flooding of the Lower Ninth Ward and St. Bernard Parish. The storm's furious lashing made it impossible to get to the levee, much less repair it. At a 1:00 P.M. press conference, Mayor Nagin focused more on a burst water main than on the 17th Street Canal levee—confidently suggesting that things would be normal again soon.

When the storm let up enough for the Army Corps engineers to test the waters and see if they could confirm the breach, they were met with nearly fifteen feet of water where Interstate 10 meets Interstate 610. The Corps' district commander Colonel Wagenaar said he knew immediately that something was gravely wrong and that he could assume the breach had indeed occurred.[30] City officials confirmed the breach at 2:00 P.M. Wagenaar returned to his office and informed his superiors at the Corps' Vicksburg headquarters that the levee had breached, and then emailed them a formal situation report, the status or whereabouts of which remains unclear.[31] Nor is it clear what Mayor Nagin did with the information passed on to him by Marty Bahamonde, a FEMA spokesman who spent the day at the Superdome. Bahamonde told Nagin that from a Coast Guard helicopter, he had seen a water surge that was "surprising in its intensity."[32] Nagin was "devastated"; the realization that New Orleans's resources, and preparation for disaster, were no match for the mighty storm that mugged his city was finally palpable and overwhelming.

Bahamonde phoned the same information in to the FEMA team in Baton Rouge, and their response was equally unclear. It *is* clear that several agencies and officials knew by 6:00 P.M. that the levee had breached, but none made a desperate cry for help during the daytime, a plea that might have sparked a rescue effort to spare the lives of people who needlessly died in the Lower Ninth Ward.[33] "What's very obvious is that the powers that be either didn't recognize how bad the flooding would be from breached levees, or totally misunderstood what the impacts would be," said Ivor van Heerden, head of the Louisiana State University Hurricane Center.[34] As several other crumbled or overtopped levees were visible by Tuesday morning, city officials couldn't help but understand the devastating impact, and the symbolic significance, of that first levee's breach. Tragically, by the time the federal government understood, more than a thousand lives would be lost.

THERE IS LITTLE DOUBT that state and local officials made many mistakes in responding to Katrina, some of them fateful. New Orleans City Council president Oliver Thomas admitted as much, but offered a sobering view of his city's severely overstrained and quickly depleted resources. Thomas deemed it "ludicrous" that "in the richest nation in the world, people really expected a little town with less than 500,000 people to handle a disaster" like Katrina. If state and local responses to the disaster were at times horrible, the federal government's dangerously delayed reaction verged on the criminal.[35]

That didn't stop Blanco from initially praising Brown and Bush. "Director Brown," Blanco said at a press conference in Baton Rouge, where FEMA's chief had repaired on Sunday to ride out the storm, "I hope you will tell President Bush how much we appreciated—these are the times that really count—to know that our federal government will step in and give us the kind of assistance we need."[36] Louisiana Senator Mary L. Landrieu glowed as well. "We are indeed fortunate to have an able and experienced director of FEMA who has been with us on the ground for some time." And Brown returned the praise. "What I've seen here today is a team that is very tight-knit, working closely together, being very professional doing it, and in my humble opinion, making the right calls."[37] Within days, Blanco would be battling Bush for control of the evacuation; Landrieu would be criticizing, and then threatening, Bush; and Brown would be blaming his woes on the Louisiana officials he had just praised.[38]

In the meantime, Michael Brown inexplicably waited until five hours *after* Katrina hit to request in a memo to DHS chief Michael Chertoff that 1,000 Homeland Security employees be dispatched to the Gulf Coast.[39] Apart from calling Katrina a "near catastrophic event," his tone was decidedly unhurried, almost casual, as Brown asked that the employees be given forty-eight hours to arrive. Brown seems to have been overly concerned with PR, as he described one of the roles of the personnel as conveying "a positive image of disaster operations to government officials, community organizations and the general public."[40] That Brown was more concerned about public relations than disaster relief would soon be apparent.

After Bush made his disaster emergency declarations for Louisiana, Mississippi, and Alabama to free up federal funds, and got an update on Katrina from Brown, he flew Air Force One from Texas to Arizona, calling DHS Secretary Michael Chertoff en route to discuss illegal immigration—but not Katrina.[41]

Bush's staff also participated in a video teleconference on Katrina with state and federal officials. In the meantime, Katrina ripped two holes in the curved roof of the Superdome and let rain pour on thousands of evacuees inside.[42] After Bush landed, he joined in a birthday cake photo op with Arizona Senator John McCain, which means, symbolically at least, that while New Orleans flooded, the president ate cake.[43] If the image literally inverts the logic of Marie Antoinette's apocryphal "let them eat cake"—hers was a heartless if ironic retort to the complaint that the peasants had no bread—it manages to shine a light on a group the Antoinette story was invented to scold: an indifferent aristocracy.

Despite having at least three days' warning that Katrina would do serious damage to the Gulf States, and despite waiting until several hours after the deadly hurricane made landfall to ask for help, FEMA's Brown on Monday suddenly became a stickler for process—a process involving elements of preparation and mitigation that he had systematically ignored in the past, and a process that, if competently executed, demanded urgent response and rescue in the present. Instead, Brown urged fire and emergency services personnel *not* to respond to counties and states hurt by Katrina unless they were requested and lawfully dispatched by state and local authorities. "The response to Hurricane Katrina must be well coordinated between federal, state and local officials to most effectively protect life and property," Brown said. "We appreciate the willingness and generosity of our Nation's first responders to deploy during disasters. But such efforts must be coordinated so that fire-rescue efforts are the most effective possible."[44]

Although due process is critical to effectively managing emergencies, its value is compromised when there is a crisis of authority, direction, and execution in the agency charged with relieving disaster. Over the next few days, it would become apparent just how extensive the crisis was. While abrogating its responsibilities and curtailing other relief efforts through procedural correctness—and thus costing precious time and lives—FEMA gladly welcomed the Red Cross's announcement that it was "launching the largest mobilization of resources in its history for a single natural disaster."[45] Ironically, the Red Cross would be seen by critics as a roadblock to recovery for the hundreds of thousands of black evacuees exiled in their own land.

As if to underscore the carefree attitude of top administration officials to the crisis in New Orleans, Pentagon chief Donald Rumsfeld—who was later criticized for not rushing the military in earlier to help with rescue efforts—took in a San Diego Padres baseball game on Monday night, nearly twenty-four hours after Katrina hit.[46] The military didn't even set up a task force to respond to Katrina until Wednesday, August 31, two days *after* the storm made landfall, when Katrina had slowed to a rainstorm over Ohio.[47] Bush—as prickly in private as he is personable in public—heard, but refused, Blanco's urgent plea for help on Monday night at 8:00 P.M. "Mr. President, we need your help," Blanco begged Bush. "We need everything you've got."[48] But Bush was vague and noncommittal. Besides he had, to his way of thinking, a more pressing crisis to address. Bush was in San Diego to give a speech on the war in Iraq the next day. He left Blanco, and the Gulf Coast, drowning in their helplessness, and went to bed.[49] After all, he was still on the longest presidential vacation in thirty-six years.

The next morning, at 11:00 A.M. CDT, Bush went on with business as usual and delivered his speech on Iraq at the sixtieth anniversary of V-J Day at Naval Air Station North Island in San Diego. Bush began his remarks by briefly addressing Katrina, assuring his audience that "our priority is on saving lives, and we are still in the midst of search and rescue operations." He also claimed that "federal, state and local governments are working side-by-side to do all we can to help people get back on their feet."[50] Beyond the hyperbole common to politicians of all stripes, Bush's statement was especially disingenuous for its denial of the facts as he knew them, in fact, as he helped to shape them by his chilling inaction the night before.

Bush also knew that neither DHS nor FEMA had yet to devote their full resources to rescuing the Gulf Coast and its citizens from their deadly plight. Where Bush had placed the full resources of the federal government was obvious as he quickly turned in his speech to the war on terror and linked aid to the battered South by the government with "our troops [who] are defending all our citizens from threats abroad."[51] To a nation that would soon witness the tragedy in the Gulf Coast on their televisions, and the horrible mismanagement of the disaster by their government, Bush's questionable assertions about his administration's efforts in the South must surely have raised suspicion about his claims of effective action in Iraq.

By 11:24 A.M. CDT, the White House announced that Bush would cut his vacation short by two days and return to Washington, D.C., to help monitor federal efforts to help Katrina victims. He would vacate his leisure on Wednesday, August 31, instead of Friday as originally planned.[52] As Bush wrapped up his vacation, the Superdome and the New Orleans Convention Center were swollen beyond capacity as nearly 100,000 people in the city awaited evacuation. It was finally on midday Tuesday, DHS chief Chertoff later confessed, that "I became aware of the fact that there was no possibility of plugging the gap and that essentially the lake was going to start to drain into the city."[53] As dead bodies piled up and floated aimlessly in toxic water, federal, state, and local officials toured the devastation by helicopter before huddling with Nagin for a briefing at the Superdome. The mayor said that the effort to rescue victims and repair two breached levees was his top priority.

Later, the officials reflected the nearly indescribable tragedy in their comments at a press conference in Baton Rouge at 3:30 P.M. CDT. "The magnitude of the situation is untenable," said a tired and teary Blanco. "It's just heartbreaking."[54] (Nagin said elsewhere that the situation was so bad that rescue boats were not even "dealing with dead bodies. They're just pushing them on the side.")[55] FEMA's Bill Lokey, who was coordinating federal assistance, concluded that Katrina might be "the most significant disaster ever to visit the United States." But even as a 300-foot-wide breach in the Orleans side of the 17th Street Canal levee unleashed Lake Pontchartrain onto the low-lying areas of the northwestern part of the city near the Lakefront area, and as the Lower Ninth Ward and St. Bernard Parish were under water, the latter caused by a breach in the St. Bernard side of the Industrial Canal, Senator David Witter pointed out that "I don't want to alarm everybody that, you know, New Orleans is filling up like a bowl. That's simply not happening."[56] Of course, more than 80 percent of New Orleans was under water. If Witter's point was to calm fears that New Orleans was completely sunk—"The French Quarter was dry," he said, an assertion backed up by Blanco—it only reinforced the renewed perception of profound structural inequality in New Orleans, whether it resulted from geographical fortune (the French Quarter is not as low as poorer areas in New Orleans), or, as some conspiracy-minded critics later alleged, from the action of nebulously identified forces that deliberately dynamited the levees near the Lower Ninth Ward to protect whiter, richer areas in the city.[57]

In Mississippi, the official death toll stood at fifty-five, while 900,000 people were without power. In Alabama, there were two confirmed deaths, and a half-million power outages. In Louisiana, two were confirmed dead, with the expectation that it could easily top a few thousand, while thousands were jammed into the Superdome and convention center. Eight hundred thousand people in the state were without power. Military resources seemed scarce as well. For instance, Alabama sent Mississippi 800 National Guardsmen to join their contingent of 1,600. The Pentagon insisted, however, that the Gulf States had sufficient forces to handle Katrina's aftermath, with at least 60 percent of the National Guard available in each state (6,500 troops in Louisiana, 7,000 troops in Mississippi, nearly 10,000 in Alabama, and about 8,200 in Florida).[58] This was a preemptive strike by the Pentagon to deflect criticism about the diversion of National Guard resources from domestic disasters to the war in Iraq.

There were reports of widespread looting (although such reports would later prove to be grossly exaggerated) as people were drowning or waiting on rooftops to be rescued. While the folk of the Gulf States suffered, the president played guitar with country singer Mark Willis in San Diego. It was a gesture that, however unintentional, underscored Bush's cheerful indifference to their cruel misfortune.[59] As he returned to his ranch in Crawford for the last night of his shortened vacation, the image of Bush partying while his people plunged to watery graves couldn't be erased by his sacrifice of two more nights of pointless pleasure. Doing only the least he could do made his act hollow and self-serving.

Finally Chertoff declared Katrina an "Incident of National Significance"—after Nagin announced that efforts to sandbag the 17th Street Canal levee breach had failed because National Guard Blackhawk helicopters were diverted to rescue people trapped in a church. That magical phrase would unlock the federal government's resources for natural disaster as specified under its National Response Plan.[60] The National Response Plan is a conceptual and organizational map of how agencies address natural disasters and terrorist attacks. Chertoff's announcement had unintended negative consequences for the administration: it highlighted the White House's failure to assign a staff member responsibility to monitor federal actions; it reinforced the lack of a senior-level official's being assigned oversight responsibilities; and it proved that the administration had not followed the very emergency plan it put in place to handle national and natural disasters.

Chertoff's memo made it painfully clear that he, not Michael Brown, was responsible from the get-go for the federal response to a natural disaster, as the National Response Plan states.[61] Additionally, an order issued by Bush in 2003 assigned the homeland security director the responsibility to respond to catastrophe.[62] The memo from Chertoff establishes that it wasn't until late on August 30, thirty-six hours after Katrina struck the Gulf Coast, that he designated Brown as the Principal Federal Official (PFO), the official in charge of managing the response and recovery operations for the federal government.[63] Chertoff's memo, addressed to fellow cabinet members, suggests that he, and perhaps the president, were confused about the chain of command in responding to the disaster. Chertoff states that Bush had established the "White House Task Force on Hurricane Katrina Response" to hold its first meeting on Wednesday, August 31.[64]

After he declared Hurricane Katrina an "Incident of National Significance"—a necessary designation to facilitate federal coordination—Chertoff shifted power to Brown. But if Bush was familiar with the National Response Plan, why would he convene a task force, essentially duplicating the work of DHS? If Chertoff was familiar with the plan, why wouldn't he alert the president to the proper flow of authority outlined in the plan? If Brown was familiar with the plan, why didn't he ask Chertoff in his memo for the authority to be the point person for the federal response and recovery operations, since FEMA was ostensibly best suited to handle a disaster? True enough, this was the first time the National Response Plan was used since being put into effect in December 2004. But there can be little excuse for such broad-based federal failure to follow its details since its purpose is to provide clear guidance during catastrophe. The apparent confusion of Bush, Chertoff, and Brown is foreboding since the National Response Plan outlines the chain of authority for the federal response to terrorist attacks, and suggests that an equally inept, and deadly, result may be in the offing. Armed with a political philosophy that has no faith in government, these leaders proved that their beliefs undercut effective governance. As the ideological children of Ronald Reagan, Bush and his administration have thrived on tax cuts, downsizing, the neglect of civic infrastructure, the shredding of the safety net, the will to privatization, the degrading of the public sector, and advocating Reagan's idea that government is the enemy of the people. The Bush administration's incompetence in Katrina was the most devastating indictment of such a philosophy.

On Wednesday morning, Bush held a video teleconference from his ranch in Crawford, gathering Deputy Chief of Staff Karl Rove and Deputy National Security Adviser J.D. Crouch (both in Crawford), Chief of Staff Andrew Card in Maine, Vice President Cheney in Wyoming, Chertoff and Deputy Secretary Michael Jackson, both in the White House, and Homeland Security Adviser Fran Townsend and Domestic Policy Council head Claude Allen, who was overseeing the Task Force, both in D.C. Brown phoned in from the Gulf Coast.[65] Brown updated the group about efforts in the region, about the flooding and efforts to fix the breaches, as the participants discussed martial law being imposed in Louisiana and Mississippi. They also discussed the National Guard's role enforcing it, and the coordination of the federal response effort—making it clear that Chertoff was in charge of overseeing operations from Washington, D.C., while Brown was in charge of overseeing operations from the region, and that the task force was "really a coordinating body . . . not an operational body."[66]

As Bush flew back to Washington later in the day, he might have stopped in New Orleans or another troubled spot along the Gulf Coast to show that he was an engaged commander in chief, an on-the-ground leader prepared to take in the suffering of his fellow Americans firsthand. Instead, he directed Air Force One to swoop down from the clouds so that he could have a bird's-eye view of the devastation several thousand feet below. "It's devastating," Bush told his aides. "It's got to be doubly devastating on the ground. It's totally wiped out."[67] The next day, in the Rose Garden, Bush continued to revel in his aerial anthropology—his airnography—oblivious to the callous symbolism of his distance-keeping gesture. His self-described "flyover" was another symptom of his tone-deaf empathy for the vulnerable.[68]

Bush may have remained at a safe distance from the furious aftermath of Katrina, but tens of thousands of poor citizens in New Orleans were thrust into chaos and calamity in shelters of last resort inside the Superdome and convention center.[69] The same chaos and abandonment occurred in parts of Mississippi. Filth and feces, stench and urine, hunger and hopelessness, anarchy and anxiety, and darkness and death polluted the air as the stranded, largely black poor exiles were crammed into unforgiving spaces that reeked of unrelieved horror for up to five days. Their government had forsaken them; they weren't citizens but castoffs, evacuees turned effortlessly, in language and life, into refugees. Blanco issued an executive order commandeering buses for evacuation and relief efforts.[70] She followed the next day with an executive order of emergency occupation of hotel and motel rooms by evacuees already in place who could afford to continue paying, or who could guarantee payment through insurance coverage or the assistance of FEMA.[71]

Jefferson Parish emergency services director Walter Maestri pleaded tearfully for help at 1:05 P.M., saying that there was no food or water left for the evacuees. Emergency workers had "seized" food, water, and other drinks—Maestri apparently refuses in this instance to view such life-sustaining activity as looting—from Wal-Mart, Sam's Club, and other grocery stores. Maestri said that evacuees were "upset and harried" and that "FEMA and national agencies are not delivering the help nearly as fast as it is needed."[72] Former New Orleans mayor Sidney Barthelemy reinforced Maestri's plea, estimating that there were 80,000 folk marooned in the city—30,000 alone stranded at the Superdome, and another 3,000 at the convention center, without nourishment or instructions for evacuation—while urging Bush to send more troops.[73]

The evacuees' plight was symbolized by the death of ninety-one-year-old evacuee Booker Harris, who died in the back of a Ryder panel truck on Wednesday as he and his ninety-three-year-old wife Allie were being shuttled to safety from eastern New Orleans. The driver of the truck plumped Allie and her husband's body in front of the convention center, where he remained, a casualty of triage that gave priority to rescuing the living, even though that task proved daunting enough. When National Guardsmen caught sight of Allie feebly feeding on crackers, she was scooped up and whisked away in a truck with other elderly survivors, her husband's solitary body left behind, propped up on a lawn chair and covered with a yellow quilt. Fellow exile John Murray summed up the incredible prospect of such a scene happening in contemporary America. "This is 2005," Murray protested as he stood near Harris's abandoned corpse. "It should not be like this for no catastrophe. This is pathetic."[74]

As the natural course of disease unfolded after a natural disaster—cholera, typhoid, hepatitis, and mosquito-borne illnesses are common in the aftermath of catastrophe—Health and Human Services secretary Michael Leavitt declared a public health emergency for the Gulf Coast.[75] Medical experts from the Centers for Disease Control and Prevention set out for the Gulf Coast as well.[76] Bush's press conference in the Rose Garden at 5:11 P.M. EDT outlined his strategy in the region in a presentation that an editorial in the *New York Times* the next day called "one of the worst speeches of his life," arguing that "nothing about the president's demeanor yesterday—which seemed casual to the point of carelessness—suggested that he understood the depth of the current crisis."[77] Bush's threefold strategy consisted of saving lives through search and rescue operations; sustaining lives through distributing adequate food, water, shelter, and medical supplies for "dislocated citizens" (Bush's slip of the tongue had him say "dedicated citizens" before he corrected himself, which they were indeed); and executing a comprehensive recovery effort.[78]

Blanco had already ordered the complete evacuation of New Orleans after efforts by the Army Corps of Engineers to clog the gaping wound in the levee systems failed, flooding the already besieged city even more.[79] "The challenge is an engineering nightmare," Blanco said on national television. "The National Guard has been dropping sandbags into it, but it's like dropping it into a black hole."[80] Later that day, a caravan of buses left the Superdome heading for Houston's Astrodome, jumpstarting the mass exodus of evacuees out of the city.[81] Nagin ordered his beleaguered and dwindled 1,500-member police force to abandon search and rescue operations and, instead, to stem the tide of looting as he cried out for federal assistance.[82]

Blanco had called the White House earlier in the day with the same plea, but she met with a stonewalling that would have worked miracles for New Orleans levees. Finally Blanco got through to Homeland Security Adviser Townsend, whose vague assurances didn't work. Blanco called back later in the day, when she was able to collar Bush and ask for 40,000 troops. "I just pulled the number out of the sky," Blanco said of her desperate arithmetic.[83] A week *after* the storm, the military had mobilized 70,000 troops and hundreds of helicopters to the area, but it typically took several days to get them into position, as Blanco and Nagin were to quickly find out.[84] (The original complement of 4,000 troops dispatched to Louisiana was already stationed nearby.)

When New Mexico governor Bill Richardson made his offer of troops to Blanco on Sunday, August 28, both governors became quickly snagged in the fabric of governmental and legal technicalities. Richardson couldn't send his troops until he received approval from the National Guard's Washington bureau. But that couldn't be granted until Blanco made a formal request, which she did on Tuesday, when New Orleans was completely drowned. Finally, on Tuesday, Washington authorized the transfer, but by then, it had been four days since Katrina had sent its ugly deluge.[85]

If Washington's bureaucratic guidelines fatefully slowed the delivery of vital services to the Gulf Coast, administration elites effectively escaped work—and dodged obvious distress over hundreds of thousands of waterlogged citizens in Mississippi, Louisiana, and Alabama. Not to be outdone by Rumsfeld or Bush in blithe disentanglement from the suffering at hand, Secretary of State Condoleezza Rice was booed on Broadway by audience members attending a Wednesday night performance of the Monty Python musical *Spamalot* after the houselights identified her familiar frame at the play's close.[86]

A day later, Rice hit Fifth Avenue for some shopping, gliding into the tony leather-goods boutique Ferragamo to buy several thousand dollars' worth of shoes. Another shopper quickly disapproved of what she felt was Rice's callous indifference to suffering citizens in the Gulf. "How dare you shop for shoes while thousands are dying and homeless," she bellowed. Of course, even if the shopper were asked the same question—instead of purchasing goods, she might have sent the money she was spending to victims of Katrina—she wasn't an internationally recognized Bush administration official who at that moment was the face of the government. The ad hoc protester was immediately removed from the premises. After hitting balls with former tennis champ Monica Seles at the Indoor Tennis Club in Grand Central Station, Rice headed back to D.C. the next day to be briefed on the Gulf Coast situation.[87] After all, the globe's most powerful woman couldn't appear to be more interested in Broadway, Blahniks, and balls than the misery of her black brothers and sisters drowning on television for the world to see. As the administration quickly sought to make Rice's faux pas seem like water under the bridge, a much bigger problem arose—water over the levees.

We didn't think it was going to be that bad. So we waited it out. But then when we heard those boom-banging explosions throughout the city, [we said] "They've blown up the levees." They exploded them with dynamite to protect the CBD—the central business district. Concrete don't make a "boom" sound when it breaks. Only something that's exploding—[it] ignites from something. They blew it up. That's why we're all here [in a Houston shelter].

—*Girard Walker, Katrina survivor*

CHAPTER 5

LEVEES AND LIES

IF THE LEVEES IN NEW ORLEANS had been fatally breached, a hole the size of Texas opened in the administration's stories about what they knew and when they knew it. On Wednesday night, August 31, Brown told CNN's Larry King, "I must say, this storm is much bigger than anyone expected."[1] On Thursday morning, as signs of "Help, come get me" were etched in desperation on rooftops, and as folk waved furiously for assistance from attics, Bush told journalist Diane Sawyer, in a rare live national television interview, "I don't think anybody anticipated the breach of the levees."[2] Both proclamations of being ambushed by the unexpected are pitifully wrong.[3]

On Sunday, August 28, the National Weather Service warned that Katrina would make southeast Louisiana "uninhabitable for weeks, perhaps longer," and that there would be "human suffering incredible by modern standards."[4] The agency also warned in capital letters: "SOME LEVEES IN THE GREATER NEW ORLEANS AREA COULD BE OVERTOPPED."[5] Bush and Brown should have been aware of this warning that came from one of the few federal agencies that performed well during the crisis. And a local newspaper on the same day announced a grim prophecy that was nationally discussed: forecasters feared that the levees might give way under the punishing waters whipped up by the ferocious storm.[6]

Bush and Brown had no excuse for not knowing the severity of the storm or the likelihood of breached levees. Their willful ignorance, however, is characteristic of the Bush administration's "see no evil, hear no evil" approach to uncomfortable facts and inconvenient truths. Bush's presidential style seems to take as its motto a song from the Broadway play *The Wiz*, a musical adaptation of L. Frank Baum's classic tale *Wizard of Oz*, where Evilene, the Wicked Witch of the West, sings, "Don't Nobody Bring Me No Bad News."[7] Journalist Evan Thomas writes that it's "a standing joke among the president's top aides: who gets to deliver the bad news? Warm and hearty in public, Bush can be cold and snappish in private, and aides sometimes cringe before the displeasure of the president of the United States, or, as he is known in West Wing jargon, POTUS."[8]

Bush's and Brown's negligence formed a sizable knot in the tapestry of denial that cloaked the administration's view of New Orleans's keen vulnerability to a massive hurricane and levee failure. In 2001, a FEMA report concluded that a catastrophic hurricane in New Orleans was "among the three likeliest . . . disasters facing this country."[9] The other two were a terrorist attack on New York City and a major earthquake in San Francisco. Also in 2001, *Popular Mechanics* published a feature, "New Orleans Is Sinking," warning that emergency planners "believe that it is a foregone conclusion that the Big Easy someday will be hit by a scouring storm surge," and that "given the tremendous amount of coastal-area development, this watery 'big one' will produce a staggering amount of damage."[10] In 2001, *Scientific American* said that a "major hurricane could swamp New Orleans under twenty feet of water, killing thousands," that "only massive reengineering of southeastern Louisiana can save the city," and that "New Orleans is a disaster waiting to happen" because a "direct hit is inevitable."[11]

In December of that year, the *Houston Chronicle* ran a story titled "Keeping Its Head Above Water: New Orleans Faces Doomsday Scenario." The article argued that a severe hurricane would "strand 250,000 people or more, and probably kill one of 10 left behind as the city drowned under 20 feet of water." It accurately predicted that "thousands of refugees could land in Houston."[12] In June of 2002, the *Times-Picayune* of New Orleans published a heralded five-part series, *Washing Away*, which predicted that it was "only a matter of time before South Louisiana takes a direct hit from a major hurricane." One article concluded that "hundreds of thousands would be left homeless," that it "would take months to dry out the area and begin to make it livable," and that "there wouldn't be much for residents to come home to."[13] In 2004, *National Geographic* published an article entitled "Gone with the Water" that opened with a hypothetical storm—the writer said it was "the worst natural disaster in the history of the United States"—that was chillingly premonitory, describing a fury that was eerily similar to Katrina.[14]

In early 2005, the PBS science show *Nova* featured an episode that addressed the threat of a major hurricane in New Orleans.[15] And the liberal journal *American Prospect* ran an online article that proved prescient in portraying the aftermath of a major hurricane in New Orleans: "Soon the geographical 'bowl' of the Crescent City would fill up with the waters of the lake, leaving those unable to evacuate with little option but to cluster on rooftops—terrain they would have to share with hungry rats, fire ants, nutria, snakes, and perhaps alligators. The water itself would become a festering stew of sewage, gasoline, refinery chemicals, and debris."[16] Although Bush doesn't read the papers, or, presumably, academic or popular journals, he still may have been exposed to the possibility of a catastrophic New Orleans hurricane if he tuned in to the June 2005 FX Network docudrama *Oil Storm*. The show portrayed a Category 4 hurricane battering New Orleans and forcing evacuation to the Superdome, and speculated about the economic consequences of a severely depleted oil supply.[17]

Bush's ignorance of the precarious state of levees in New Orleans is ironic since his administration was responsible for severe budget cuts in the Army Corps of Engineers programs that may have literally stemmed the tides of Katrina. (As a group of journalists observed, for years "engineers up and down the Mississippi River have talked about the disaster that would result if New Orleans' bulwark of levees and flood walls were hit by a hurricane like Katrina," but "when it was time to find money to strengthen them, the city's defenses ended up far down the federal government's priority list.")[18] For the last ten years, the Army Corps of Engineers has been commissioned by Congress to steer the Southeast Louisiana Urban Flood Control Project (SELA). SELA was authorized by Congress after flooding from a huge rainstorm in May 1995 killed six people.[19] Since that time, the Army Corps of Engineers has spent $430 million on strengthening the levees and building pumping stations. However, federal funds for another $250 million worth of projects aimed at strengthening levees eroded or sunken by hurricane activity in the Atlantic basin have all but dried up.[20] The culprit: the war in Iraq, which not only stymied the response of the National Guard to Katrina, but which diverted critical resources from the Army Corps of Engineers as well.

For instance, in 2004, the $750-million Lake Pontchartrain and Vicinity Hurricane Protection project, a huge Corps undertaking aimed at building up levees and protecting pumping stations on the east bank of the Mississippi River in Orleans, St. Bernard, St. Charles, and Jefferson parishes, endured proposed budget slashes by Bush as the cost of the war in Iraq escalated. The president sought to spend less than 20 percent of what the Corps estimated it would take to complete the project, which remains 20 percent incomplete because of insufficient funds.[21] In Bush's 2005 budget, the Lake Pontchartrain project was to receive $3.9 million, a shortfall of more than $18 million according to Corps projections.[22] As emergency management chief Walter Maestri said in 2004, it "appears that the money has been moved in the president's budget to handle homeland security and the war in Iraq, and I suppose that's the price we pay. Nobody locally is happy that the levees can't be finished, and we are doing everything we can to make the case that this is a security issue for us."[23] Bush's cuts, the deepest in hurricane and flood control spending in New Orleans history, were even more remarkable considering that the 2004 hurricane season was by far the most severe in decades.[24]

Of course, Bush and Brown should have at least known about the deadly levee situation after FEMA hired a private company, IEM Inc. of Baton Rouge, to run an eight-day emergency response drill in 2004 for a fictional killer hurricane.[25] City officials and local scientists joined the exercise, which featured computer models simulating the effect of a Category 4 hurricane on New Orleans. The fictitious storm was dubbed Hurricane Pam, and it proved to be deadly, tracking through New Orleans with winds up to 130 miles per hour and overwhelming the levees and flood walls that guard the city, much like Katrina did.[26] Hurricane Pam forced a fictitious evacuation of a million people who needed shelter for months. Thousands more needed rescue. Nearly 600,000 buildings were destroyed.[27] It also featured a helicopter evacuation of the Superdome and 15-foot flooding in sections of the city.[28] Unfortunately, the company didn't get the chance to finish the second part of its commission—to design a plan to address unresolved problems like evacuating sick and injured folk and providing housing for thousands of citizens—because their funding was cut.[29]

Bush and Brown would have known about the levees if they had listened to Alfred C. Naomi, a thirty-year veteran and senior project manager of the Corps. Naomi repeatedly raised his voice to protest budget cuts that undercut his efforts to strengthen the levees of a city built on slowly sinking mud, surrounded by water, and vulnerable to vicious winds.[30] Naomi was especially disappointed in 2005 by a $71-million cut in funds for the New Orleans district just as the Gulf Coast was projected to endure a volatile hurricane season.[31] The slash meant that the Corps wouldn't have sufficient resources to address the already strapped 17th Street levee, which was composed of an aging system of barriers and pumps. When the 17th Street levee gave way during Katrina, it was hardly a surprise to anyone even remotely familiar with the city's levees and the budget cutbacks that left an already untenable system of protection even weaker.[32] In fact, over the last five years, Congress has steadily increased funding for New Orleans's levees above Bush's relatively meager requests.[33]

Surely Bush's advisers who distill the news for him picked up on headlines that trumpeted the travail of the levees. The *AP* said on August 5, 2002, "Louisiana Sinking: One State's Environmental Nightmare Could Become Common Problem." *CBS Evening News* on October 2, 2002, explored "damage that a major hurricane could do to New Orleans." The *Times-Picayune* on

October 10, 2002, said, "La. Needs New Plan to Survive Big Storms; Put Politics Aside, Army Corps Warns." The *Lafayette Daily Advertiser* on October 14, 2002, said in a headline, "Hurricane Levees Talked About for Decades." The *New York Times* on July 4, 2003, featured "New Orleans's Hurricane Problem." The *Times-Picayune* on April 13, 2004, read "Levee Money Falling Short; Corps Says Millions Needed to Close Gaps." The *Times-Picayune* on June 8, 2004, warned, "Shifting Federal Budget Erodes Protection from Levees; Because of Cuts, Hurricane Risk Grows." The paper said three days later, "Flood-Project Firm Left High, Dry; Federal Dollars Are Tapped Out."

On September 15, 2004, the *Houston Chronicle* read "Hurricane Ivan; Direct Hit Could Spell Doom for New Orleans; Residents Fleeing Deluge." The *Times-Picayune* noted on October 6, 2004, that "Taxes Will Rise to Pay for Levee Work; Feds No Longer Paying for It." On December 3, 2004, the *Times-Picayune* said, "Levees Don't Measure Up, Corps Warns; Many Not as High as Previously Thought." The paper announced on May 28, 2005, that "As federal aid wanes, local leaders are trying to find ways—including movable barriers to ward off storm surge—to protect the metro area from the fiercest hurricanes." And the *New Orleans CityBusiness* sounded the budget shortfall on June 6, 2005: "New Orleans District of the U.S. Army Corps of Engineers Faces $71.2M in Federal Cuts." Even if Bush's advisers ignored FEMA and the Army Corps of Engineers, they couldn't have pleaded ignorance about the levees if they kept up at all with the papers.

On October 17, 2000, a headline from the *Philadelphia Inquirer* warned of "New Orleans' Growing Danger; Wetlands Loss Leaves City a Hurricane Hit Away from Disaster." This underscores one of the direct consequences to New Orleans of Bush's failed environmental policies. Wetlands, including bayous, marshes, and barrier islands, are critical buffers to storm surges and remove some of the fury from a hurricane's wind. *National Geographic* says that "research after Hurricane Andrew showed that every linear mile of wetland cut the height of the surge by three inches."[34] A 1998 report by the Louisiana Coastal Conservation and Restoration Task Force, which included federal, state, and local officials, concluded that the "rate of coastal land loss in Louisiana has reached catastrophic proportions," and that "within the last 50 years, land loss rates have exceeded 40 square miles per year, and in the 1990's the rate has been estimated to be between 25 and 35 square miles each year," representing "80% of the coastal wetland loss in the entire continental United States."[35] Coastal Louisiana comprises two huge wetland areas, the Deltaic Plain of the Mississippi River and the Chenier Plain, both influenced by the Mississippi River and both undergoing profound shrinking and deterioration as a result of natural changes and human activities.[36]

As for natural changes, there has been serious coastal erosion since the 1890s, a process that reached its peak in the 1950s and 1960s, resulting in the loss and deterioration of marshes and barrier islands.[37] Hurricanes are the greatest single factor in the erosion of wetlands.[38] But there are other factors, too. "Delta soils naturally compact and sink over time, eventually giving way to open water unless fresh layers of sediment offset the subsidence," writes Joel K. Bourne, Jr., in *National Geographic*.[39] "The Mississippi's spring floods once maintained that balance, but the annual deluges were often disastrous."

To set things in order, especially after the Great Flood of 1927, "levees were raised along the river and lined with concrete, effectively funneling the marsh-building sediments to the deep waters of the Gulf." Human activity has exacted a toll; levees intended to prevent flooding also erode wetlands because they prevent the natural dispersal of sediment to the marshes.[40] "Since the 1950s engineers have also cut more than 8,000 miles (13,000 kilometers) of canals through the marsh for petroleum exploration and ship traffic. These new ditches sliced the wetlands into a giant jigsaw puzzle, increasing erosion and allowing lethal doses of salt water to infiltrate brackish and freshwater marshes."[41] The conversion of wetland areas—in particular, swamps and marshes—into fastlands for agricultural, residential, and industrial use have had an immensely negative effect. Although regulating dredge and fill activities in wetlands (for petroleum exploration, pipelines, canal developments, and logging industry) is an effort to put an end to such conversion, it contributes significantly to marsh destruction and threatens coastal integrity.[42]

Each new storm leaves the region's oil and gas pipelines and facilities, which supply a quarter of the nation's energy needs, far more vulnerable. Oil and gas activities, plus the federal government's attempts to control the Mississippi River for navigation and flood control, contribute significantly to massive coastal erosion. But the energy policies of Bush and his predecessors—including his father—are especially friendly to the energy companies invested in exploiting natural resources for commercial gain. Bush has been anything but helpful in restoring the wetlands and enhancing coastal health. Right before Katrina hit, Bush had urged Congress to increase Louisiana's share in the proposed Water Resources Development Act from 35 to 50 percent. Bush's failure to restore wetlands grows from his antipathy to science and the notion of global warming, and a caustic environmental philosophy.[43]

In fact, after Governor Blanco returned from an early 2004 trip to Iraq, she wrote a letter to the *New York Times*, applauding the paper for urging the restoration of Iraqi wetlands but pointing out the lack of federal support for her state. "Ironically," Blanco wrote, "the Bush administration and the Republican-led Senate will not demand the same urgency of action to save coastal wetlands at home." After she noted the annual loss in Louisiana of twenty-five to thirty-five square miles of coastal marsh, "largely because of federal activities," Blanco argued that "in their rewrite of the energy bill, Senate Republicans killed spending provisions addressing Louisiana's coastal loss, while our residents have done just the opposite—dedicating state dollars to a federal-state restoration effort." The spending provision Blanco referred to would have given Louisiana a share of profits from lucrative offshore oil drilling, adding an estimated $1 billion to the state's coffers and allowing Louisiana to subsidize natural barriers against a devastating hurricane like Katrina.[44] The failure to do so will now cost more than $25 billion to rebuild the region.[45] Blanco acknowledged that Congress "has begun restoring the Chesapeake Bay and the Florida Everglades, and now we're restoring Iraq's wetlands. National leaders should address an environmental and economic crisis more significant than any of these: the loss of 'America's Wetland' in coastal Louisiana."[46] If the Bush administration failed to heed warnings of approaching doom, it failed even more miserably to address the clear and present danger of Katrina.

First of all, neither charity nor justice was in any of the design that had to do with why the helicopters were [in the Gulf Coast rescuing people]. The helicopters went there because the realm was seriously weakened by the moment. Clearly, Bush faltered deeply. His arrogance was really quite key to that, and the arrogance of others who are in his service.

—**Harry Belafonte, humanitarian, entertainer, Katrina charity participant**

CHAPTER 6

FOLLOW THE LEADER?

IF BUSH'S AND BROWN'S IGNORANCE of impending disaster was clear, so was their failure to follow through in the storm's aftermath. Terry Ebert, head of Homeland Security for New Orleans, bluntly captured the federal government's incompetence. "This is a national emergency," Ebert declared. "This is a national disgrace. FEMA has been here three days, yet there is no command and control. We can send massive amounts of aid to tsunami victims, but we can't bail out the city of New Orleans."[1] Mayor Nagin was equally emphatic, pleading with whoever would listen. "This is a desperate SOS," he said on CNN as police clashed with angry crowds, the dead bodies began to pile up, and it remained painfully clear that the American government was disinclined or incapable—and perhaps it was both—of responding to desperate screams for help let out by a sunken black metropolis that had become a floating signifier of neglect and abandonment.[2] "Right now we are out of resources at the Convention Center and don't anticipate enough buses. We need buses. Currently the Convention Center is unsanitary and unsafe and we're running out of supplies."[3]

Brown's ignorance was exposed again when he confessed on national television that it wasn't until Thursday morning—more than twenty-four hours after the news had been all over the media—that he learned of the folk suffering in the Superdome and convention center. (Bush didn't learn that there were people in the convention center, or that some were dying while others had already died, until Thursday when an aide delivered a news agency report from New Orleans to the Oval Office for Bush to see. Bush was particularly peeved because he had been briefed Thursday morning by Chertoff, whose source of information was Brown. Neither of them was aware of the conditions in the convention center, leaving the president vulnerable when he appeared that morning on *Good Morning America*.)[4]

In an interview with CNN on Friday morning, anchor Soledad O'Brien, after citing the chaos in the streets, demanded to know, "What are you doing to protect these people right now?" Brown replied, "Well, that's why we're trying to get additional boots on the ground, because we have to protect them. And, Soledad, I want the American people to know that we understand how dire this situation is." Brown then made his startling admission. "And we're going to do everything we can to get that aid down to that individual level. You know, we're feeding stuff into the Superdome. When we found out about the Convention Center yesterday, we started diverting supplies to get them fed, too. And now we're finding literally as we do evacuations that more and more people are beginning to manifest and show themselves in areas that we didn't [know] that they were there, and so we're doing everything we can to get to them." O'Brien pressed Brown. "You were unaware of the situation at the Convention Center until yesterday? When yesterday did you become aware?" His matter-of-fact retort revealed just how strangely isolated Brown and FEMA were from the brutal realities on the ground. "I think it was yesterday morning when we first found out about it," he said. "We were just as surprised as everybody else."[5] O'Brien's conspicuous disbelief mirrored the nation's response to Brown's nearly unbelievable comments.

In the wee hours of Thursday morning, around 2:00 A.M., buses began rolling up to Houston's 50,000-seat Astrodome to deposit America's newly exiled and perhaps weariest citizens.[6] By mid-morning, there were reports that the evacuations that had just begun from the New Orleans Superdome were suspended because of escalating unrest outside the arena, especially reports of gunfire at rescue helicopters. But National Guard officials in Louisiana who were on the ground at the time later said that no helicopters had been attacked, and that no evacuations had been stopped because of gunfire.[7] There would be many more unfounded allegations circulated in the media, testimony to the strange brew of selective paranoia and stereotyping that floated in the toxic waters of New Orleans and the mainstream press.

Later that day, Bush lunched with Federal Reserve chairman Alan Greenspan to discuss the economic impact of Katrina, and asked his father and former President Clinton to raise private funds for Katrina victims as they had for victims of the tsunami.[8] News reports began circulating that Speaker of the House Dennis Hastert, in response to a journalist's question of whether it made "sense to spend billions and billions and billions of dollars rebuilding a city" that was seven feet below sea level, suggested it "doesn't make sense to me . . . it looks like a lot of the place could be bulldozed."[9]

Meanwhile, DHS chief Chertoff did his best Michael Brown imitation when he told NPR anchor Robert Siegel that "I have not heard a report of thousands of people in the convention center who don't have food and water," despite Siegel's insistence that reporters had just witnessed that very sight.[10] In a press conference earlier in the day, Chertoff had been similarly obstinate, arguing that the "fact of the matter is, the Superdome is secure" when it was obviously a seething pot of pain and suffering.[11] Instead of acknowledging the federal government's miscues, Chertoff seized on the condition of the evacuees to express a compassion that seemed to indirectly blame them, not for their condition, but for their response to it. Chertoff said the evacuees were "anxious, they're impatient, they're hot, they're tired, they want to get someplace else. That is more than understandable."

By concentrating on the evacuees' "understandable" reactions, Chertoff let the federal government off the hook. He implied that if the evacuees were less anxious and more patient—obscuring the government's inefficiency and ineffectiveness, factors that Chertoff might have noted were reasonable spurs to anxiety and impatience—then things might have gone a bit better. To bring full circle the federal government's tragic and bizarre response to Katrina, Brown reprised his earlier exchange with O'Brien for *Nightline's* Ted Koppel, who, like O'Brien, pelted the FEMA chief with tough questions that further exposed his incompetence.[12] "Don't you guys watch television?" Koppel asked incredulously. "Don't you guys listen to the radio? Our reporters have been reporting about it for more than just today." Brown could only muster a weak-kneed appeal to empirical data in his defense. "We learned about it factually today that that's what existed," he responded.

But the most explosive media appearance of the day belonged neither to Brown nor to Chertoff—nor, for that matter, to Blanco, who blasted Hastert for the "unthinkable" act of "kick[ing] us when we're down"—but to Nagin, who lashed out with obscenity on radio station WWL-AM at the failure of federal and state powers to rescue his sunken city.[13] In an interview with Garland Robinette, Nagin said he chided Bush for flying over New Orleans instead of getting on the ground. Nagin clipped Bush and federal authorities for responding quickly to other American cities and world crises while neglecting New Orleans.[14] "We authorized $8 billion to go to Iraq, lickety-quick, to take care of New York and other places," Nagin complained. "Now you mean to tell me that a place where most of your oil is coming through, a place that is so unique—when you mention New Orleans anywhere around the world, everybody's eyes light up—you mean to tell me that a place where you probably have thousands of people that have died, and thousand more that are dying every day, that we can't figure out a way to authorize the resources that we need? Come on, man." In response to presidential press conferences and the governor's promise that 40,000 troops were on the way to Louisiana, Nagin went ballistic. "I don't want to see anybody do anymore goddamn press conferences," the mayor bellowed. "Put a moratorium on press conferences. Don't do another press conference until the resources are in this city. And then come down to this city and stand with us when there are military trucks and troops that we can't even count. Don't tell me 40,000 people are coming here. They're not here. It's too doggone late. Now get off your asses and do something, and let's fix the biggest goddamn crisis in the history of this country."[15]

The already-beleaguered survivors of Katrina who remained in New Orleans were greeted the next morning with an unpleasant reminder of their fragile existence in a toxic environment. At 4:35 A.M., an explosion at a chemical storage facility east of the French Quarter near the Mississippi River forced yet another evacuation of citizens in the area because of possible toxic exposure from the gray smoke that filled the sky.[16] The blast was soon followed by a series of railcar explosions and a huge fire in an old retail building in a dry section of Canal Street.[17] The aftereffects of the explosions shook the city as far away as downtown.[18]

The same morning, Bush prepared to take his first trip to the Gulf Coast to tour the devastation firsthand.[19] As he fielded questions from reporters on the south lawn of the White House, Bush admitted that the results of his administration's efforts were "not acceptable."[20] This was a rare public acknowledgment of error by a president who finds it difficult to concede he made a mistake. Several of his aides admitted that the depth of the horror in New Orleans didn't strike Bush until Thursday night.[21] Because Bush doesn't regularly watch the news, and hardly ever reads it, his communications director Dan Bartlett prepared a DVD of the television broadcasts out of New Orleans that Bush could watch on the ride down to get a sense of the suffering in Mississippi, Alabama, and Louisiana.[22]

Bush's itinerary called for a six-hour jaunt to several spots along the Gulf Coast, joined by fifty firemen, who were to serve as props for the president's photo ops in the area.[23] At the Mobile Regional Airport in Mobile, Alabama, Bush infamously, and inexplicably, praised his FEMA chief, saying "Brownie, you're doing a heck of a job."[24] Bush displayed yet again his awkward attempts at public compassion when he singled out Senator Trent Lott as a victim of Katrina, and not the thousands of poor folk who lost everything. Bush's use of Lott as an example of Katrina's damaging effect reinforced the perception that the loss and grief of common folk only matters when the rich and well placed are victimized as well. "The good news is—and it's hard for some to see it now—that out of this chaos is going to come a fantastic Gulf Coast, like it was before. Out of the rubbles of Trent Lott's house—he's lost his entire house—there's going to be a fantastic house. And I'm looking forward to sitting on the porch." Bush recovered long enough to pledge that "if it's not going exactly right, we're going to make it go exactly right. If there's problems, we're going to address the problems. And that's what I've come down to assure people of."[25] Before long, however, Bush backslid into old habits of denial and twisted his admission of "not acceptable" into an awkward attempt to have it both ways—to split hairs and say at once that things were acceptable and unacceptable. "I am satisfied with the response," Bush said at a stop in Biloxi, Mississippi. "I'm not satisfied with all the results."[26]

As Bush continued his tour of the Gulf Coast, the airline industry launched "Operation Air Care" to provide emergency airlift services for 25,000 citizens stranded in New Orleans.[27] FEMA claimed that it would oversee the evacuation, sending the first evacuees to San Antonio's Lackland Air Force Base. Congress passed a $10.5 billion bill for emergency rescue and relief of the Gulf Coast right after noon, but State Representative Karen Carter, whose district includes the French Quarter, argued that in the short run transportation was more important than cash. "Don't give me your money," Carter pleaded. "Don't send me $10 million today. Give me buses and gas. Buses and gas. Buses and gas. If you have to commandeer Greyhound, commandeer Greyhound. . . . If you don't get a bus, if we don't get them out of there, they will die."

Near midday, four days after Katrina struck, the National Guard arrived in New Orleans in full force, bringing food, water, and weapons as they convoyed in trucks through floodwaters with orders to secure the streets and relieve suffering.[28] At the convention center, some of the more than 20,000 evacuees greeted the Guard with great joy. "Thank you, Jesus," they cried, their arms flung heavenward as camouflage-green trucks and hundreds of soldiers poured in. "Lord, I thank you for getting us out of here," Leschia Radford exclaimed.[29] But evacuee Michael Levy withheld blessings and instead bestowed a curse on the arriving cavalry and the city of New Orleans. "Hell, no, I'm not glad to see them," Levy bitterly declared. "They should have been here days ago. I ain't glad to see 'em. I'll be glad when 100 buses show up," Levy stated as folk around him yelled "Hell, yeah! Hell, yeah!" Levy added to his pained homily by stating that "we've been sleeping on the . . . ground like rats. I say burn this whole . . . city down."[30] The Guard began to evacuate folk from the Superdome as well, where one mother, in the midst of knee-deep trash and blacked-out bathrooms, said, "This was the worst night of my life."[31]

As if to underscore how color and class rank drenched the city before the flood, the evacuation of the Superdome was interrupted to permit 700 guests and employees from the far less damaged and chaotic Hyatt Hotel—where Nagin had established makeshift headquarters because it was across the street from city hall—to move to the head of the line after their caravan of school buses arrived. When Howard Blue, who had been trapped in the Superdome, tried to protest the unjust gesture by joining their line—"How does this work?" he said. "They [are] clean, they are dry, they get out ahead of us?"—he was, according to a reporter, blocked by the National Guard "as other guardsmen helped the well-dressed guests with their luggage."[32] National Guard captain John Pollard later conceded that it was a "very poor" decision to allow the Hyatt guests to cut the line.[33] More than 600 people, including 110 patients, were evacuated from Louisiana State University Hospital, while 2,220 folk, including 363 patients, were evacuated from Charity Hospital, although terminally ill patients died in the process. Staff and patients at three other New Orleans hospitals—Tulane University, Methodist, and Kindred—were evacuated as well.[34]

As evacuees were drained from the Superdome and convention center, Houston's Astrodome filled to capacity with 15,000 people, and, initially at least, 1,750 evacuees on 35 buses were turned away.[35] Bill White, Houston's mayor, quickly announced that the Reliant Center nearby would be opened to accommodate the overflow. Obviously facing the same legal concerns that vexed New Orleans mayor Nagin as he pondered a mandatory evacuation of the city, White cast such concerns to the wind. "We want this exhibition hall open right now," the mayor insisted. "If it entails someone suing us, then OK. Then [they can] explain to the American public why."[36] Besides the evacuees in the Astrodome, and the 3,000 who were being processed for the 11,000-capacity Reliant Center, 4,000 others were dispersed in local shelters. In a visit to a shelter set up at the Cajundome in Lafayette, Louisiana, First Lady Laura Bush conceded, "This response is not an adequate response," that this "is not the kind of response the federal government wants" and that we "know we can do it better, and that we can get it better."[37]

At a press conference sponsored on the same day by the Congressional Black Caucus, the National Urban League, the Black Leadership Forum, the National Council of Negro Women, and the NAACP, black leaders were far more critical of the federal government's slow response to the suffering in the Gulf Coast. U.S. Representative Carolyn Kilpatrick, from Michigan, said that she was "ashamed of America and . . . of our government. I am outraged by the lack of response by the federal government."[38] U.S. Rep. Elijah Cummings, from Maryland, said that "poverty, age and skin color" played a role in who lived and died in the Gulf Coast. Quoting a passage of scripture where Jesus admonishes his followers to do justice to the "least of these," Cummings scolded Bush and told him that "God cannot be pleased with our response."[39] As for the charge of looting leveled against the mostly poor and black survivors of Katrina, U.S. Representative Diane Watson from California argued that "desperate people do desperate things," while Illinois U.S. Representative Jesse Jackson, Jr., suggested a more compassionate view of their plight. "Who are we to say what law and order should be in this unspeakable environment?"[40]

When Bush made it to New Orleans, with Louisiana senator Mary Landrieu in tow, he stopped at the breached 17th Street levee in New Orleans, but not at the more problematic Superdome or convention center. After all, he wanted to avoid being seen on television with the mostly black victims who might spoil his photo-op journey with an outburst of genuine anger. Landrieu blasted Bush the next day for staging a photo op with resources that were removed once he departed. "Yesterday we witnessed a hastily prepared stage set for a Presidential photo opportunity; and the desperately needed resources we saw were this morning reduced to a single, lonely piece of equipment. The good and decent people of southeast Louisiana and the Gulf Coast—black and white, rich and poor, young and old—deserve far better from their national government."[41]

Neither did Bush visit the trauma center that had been established at the Louis Armstrong International Airport. There images of untold suffering might further hamper his public relations blitzkrieg as a compassionate commander in chief in control of the situation. Ironically, Bush's effort to appear as the kindly facilitator of federal relief was temporarily thwarted when three tons of food that was to be delivered in the afternoon by helicopter to evacuees in St. Bernard Parish and Algiers Point had to be delayed on the Crescent City Connection bridge until Friday night because of the need to assure presidential security.[42] Just as Bush prepared to leave, he attempted to assure New Orleans, and the world, that he understood what had happened and what he must do to respond. "I'm going to fly out of here in a minute, but I want you to know that I'm not going to forget what I've seen. I understand the devastation requires more than one day's attention. It's going to require the attention of this country for a long period of time."[43]

Attention is a keyword in the political lexicon that Bush had forgotten, at least when it came to New Orleans and the rest of the Gulf Coast during the crisis of Katrina. To be sure, there are all sorts of attention that are at play in politics. After his first visit to the Gulf Coast, Bush finally seemed to recognize that he had to pay a different kind of attention to the business at hand, the kind of attention he had routinely paid to Iraq and the war on terror. As with most leaders, it was apparent that Bush had to juggle three intersecting forms of political attention. First, *common* attention is concentration on political matters that are important to our society in every epoch, including citizenship, security, liberty, and the common good. Second, *current* attention is concentration on political matters that shape contemporary society, for instance, racial justice, class and gender equality, and gay and lesbian rights. Third, *critical* attention is concentration on political matters that demand immediate resolution because they threaten the stability of society, for example, terror, poverty, and natural disasters.

Common attention to political matters assures that the values of democracy will get breathing space, though not necessarily for all citizens in equal fashion. Therefore, current attention to political matters suggests that the values of democracy must be refined and extended to include folk who have been deliberately dispossessed, shortchanged, or ignored in creating a just society. Effective leaders must wisely and humanely devote political attention to matters that are pushed to the periphery of society but that beg for greater play. The poverty, economic inequality, and racial injustice that were revealed in Katrina cry out for critical attention. At times, critical attention to current political matters becomes unjust because other compelling issues are slighted. The resistance to terror is critical—whether from beyond our borders or from within our society. But the defeat of social inequality is equally critical to the nation's health. Bush's obsession with fighting terror has weakened civil liberties. It has also led him to ignore current, and critical, issues like poverty and racial inequality that erode our society and chip away at our humanity and the common good.[44]

Bush's myopic attention to terror has also kept him from paying critical attention to natural disasters and environmental plagues in our current arena that are just as vexing to the social compact. Keeping his promise of giving "more than one day's attention" would require more than empty rhetoric. It would entail a significant shift in national priorities where the poor and black and relatively disenfranchised would gain greater prominence in our political deliberations. Katrina's furious aftermath forced Bush to concede that he couldn't fix what was wrong with a snap of his presidential finger or a wave of his administration's public relations wand. If he was serious, his approach would have to be about competence more than charisma, about substance more than slogans. But it became obvious by the evening of Friday, September 2, that the Bush administration would take the expedient way out of the crisis by paying more attention to public relations than political courage. When it came to Katrina they had more spin than spine.

GOVERNOR BLANCO TOOK ADVANTAGE of Bush's presence in New Orleans and engaged in a flurry of activities. She penned an open letter to Bush, reiterating her previous request for

40,000 troops and food, water, and supplies, and asking for a redeployment of a brigade of troops from Louisiana stationed in Iraq that had completed its mission because "they are urgently needed here at home."[45] (At a press briefing the day before Blanco's letter, White House spokesman Scott McClellan argued that it was unnecessary to bring troops back to Louisiana because there were sufficient numbers of the National Guard already in place to address the aftermath of Katrina.)[46] Blanco wrote that only Bush's "personal involvement" would "ensure the immediate delivery of federal assets needed to save lives that are in jeopardy hour by hour."[47] What she didn't realize is that the president and his men were plotting a hastily orchestrated campaign to seize from her the authority to evacuate New Orleans and to blame her for the government's wretched response.

In the meantime, Blanco issued two executive orders. The first order declared a state of public health emergency and suspended Louisiana medical licensing requirements for out-of-state physicians and medical personnel who were providing emergency treatment. The second order authorized the state Office of Homeland Security and Emergency Preparedness to commandeer all available school buses "to be used as necessary for the mass transportation of Hurricane Katrina evacuees, accompanying law enforcement personnel, and necessary supplies to and from areas of concern to areas of safety."[48] The latter executive order replaced the previous one she had issued on Wednesday, August 31, which was not as comprehensive, and didn't suspend, as the latest order did, the requirement that bus drivers have commercial driver's licenses—a change made in response to reports that many licensed bus drivers were unwilling to drive into poorer, tougher areas of New Orleans.[49]

Speaking from the tarmac at Armstrong airport, Bush reminisced briefly about his youthful days of carousing in the

Crescent City. He remembered New Orleans as "the town where I used to come from Houston, Texas, to enjoy myself—occasionally too much" to peals of laughter.[50] He thanked relief workers and told them that he believed that "New Orleans will rise again" and that "the people of Mississippi will recover."[51] Before he departed, Bush invited Landrieu, Blanco, and Nagin on board Air Force One for an impromptu meeting with various congressmen and senators.[52] The tension on the president's plane didn't revolve around Bush and Nagin, as might be expected, in light of Nagin's unvarnished WWL radio interview the night before.

Nagin later said on *60 Minutes* of his Air Force One encounter with Bush—who offered the New Orleans mayor his first shower in five days—that he hadn't expressed in person the anger he unleashed on his infamous radio interview. "But he was well aware of it," Nagin said. "And I pulled him on aside with the governor. I said, 'Look. That was uncharacteristic for me. But consider being in my shoes. What would you have done? And if I said anything disrespectable, disrespectful to the office of the president or the governor, I apologize. But tell me, what we gonna do now.'"[53] According to Nagin, Bush conceded the government's failure. "The president basically said, 'Mr. Mayor, I know we could've done a better job, and . . . we're gonna fix it." The mayor reports that Bush asked him to be completely honest. "He said to me, he said, 'Look. I think I've been hearing a lotta stuff that . . . may not be true. I wanna hear from you. Tell me the truth, and I will help you.' And I looked in his eyes, and he meant it. And when he meant it, I told him the truth."[54]

Nagin's truth telling on Air Force One came to a head, according to journalist Evan Thomas, when "Mayor Nagin blew up during a fraught discussion of 'who's in charge?' Nagin slammed his hand down on the table and told Bush, 'We just need to cut through this and do what it takes to have a more-controlled command structure. If that means federalizing it, let's do it."[55] Nagin undercut Governor Blanco's authority in advocating federalizing the National Guard, a debate that had been raging in D.C. over the previous three days. The National Guard is usually under the control of the governor, who can request that the federal government take over. Nagin urged the president to place in charge of the evacuation Lieutenant General Russel Honore—whom the mayor described in his WWL radio interview as "this John Wayne dude . . . that came off the doggone chopper, and he started cussing and people started moving," perhaps explaining the motivation behind Nagin's public profanity.[56] "Well, what do you think of that, Governor?" Bush asked as he turned to Blanco. "I'd rather talk to you about that privately," she responded. Nagin quickly retorted, "Well, why don't you do that now?"[57] The meeting disbanded. As one aide to Bush put it, this scenario was part of the confrontation on Air Force One that was "as blunt as you can get without the Secret Service getting involved."[58]

It was understandable that Nagin would cry out in desperation for the president to help his besieged city. But the conservative aversion to government as the true solution to the problems of the people lessened the likelihood that Bush would prove any more effective in getting the government to help New Orleans in a far more substantial manner than it had. Blanco's skepticism about the idea of federal takeover proved ultimately to be the wiser tactical and philosophical position on the matter.

In the meantime, Bush and Blanco huddled and talked before he departed. Around midnight, the power struggle was ratcheted up when the Bush administration sent Blanco a legal memorandum that proposed that the governor request that the federal government take charge of the evacuation of New Orleans.[59] It seems that Bush had sided with Nagin—who had in the previous election crossed Democratic Party lines to support Blanco's

Republican opponent for governor, now U.S. Representative Bobby Jindal, who had also been involved in the Air Force One meeting. The Bush administration sought control of the police and National Guard forces that reported to Blanco. After talking throughout the night with administration officials, Blanco and other Louisiana officials rejected the offer for fear that it would amount to a federal declaration of martial law.[60]

Bush administration officials claimed behind the scenes that the Insurrection Act granted the president the authority to put down civil disturbances by federalizing the National Guard and seizing the reins of the evacuation operations from Blanco.[61] But according to stipulations of the Insurrection Act, Blanco would have had to surrender authority before Bush could send active-duty combat forces to the state.[62] The last time the act was invoked was in 1992 during the civil unrest in Los Angeles following the Rodney King verdicts, but California governor Pete Wilson requested federal intervention. Not since the civil rights era has a president invoked the act against a governor's will.[63] The potential public relations fallout of a tug-of-war between federal and state chief executives quelled Bush administration plans as well. As one presidential aide rhetorically posited, "Can you imagine how it would have been perceived if a president of the United States of one party had preemptively taken from the female governor of another party the command and control of her forces, unless the security made it completely clear that she was unable to effectively execute her command authority and that lawlessness was the inevitable result?"[64]

Besides, state officials smelled a political skunk in the administration's request. As one of them anonymously said, "Quite frankly, if they'd been able to pull off taking it from the locals, they then could have blamed everything on the locals."[65] It is now clear that by Friday evening, that's exactly what the administration planned to do. Brown and Chertoff's disastrous media appearances the day before, coupled with their glaring misman-agement of the disaster, forced the White House to do damage control.[66] If they could do little to help the hurricane's victims, Karl Rove, Bush's ironfisted senior political adviser, and Don Bartlett, his communications director, could at least attempt to rescue the administration from drowning in its indifference and incompetence. Despite claiming in countless media outlets that they would wait to assign blame as they were being sharply crit-icized, Bush administration officials were now on the offensive. They deliberately and strategically shifted the blame to state and local officials.[67] They also attempted to deflect criticism of the administration by focusing not on problems in the past week but on what the federal government was doing right.

The first salvo of their offensive was Bush's regular Saturday morning radio spot. On this day, however, Bush did a rare thing and delivered it live from the White House's Rose Garden with Pentagon chief Donald Rumsfeld, DHS head Chertoff, and Joint Chiefs of Staff chairman Richard Myers by his side.[68] Bush said he was sending 7,200 active-duty troops to the area within 72 hours—the first significant commitment of ground troops since Katrina struck—joining the 4,000 troops already in place. The Pentagon announced that 10,000 more troops would be sent to Louisiana and Mississippi, raising the number of troops in the area to 40,000.[69] Bush subtly blamed state and local officials when he said that "despite their best efforts, the magnitude of responding to a crisis over a disaster area that is larger than the size of Great Britain has created tremendous problems that have strained state and local capabilities. The result is that many of our citizens simply are not getting the help they need, especially in New Orleans. And that is unacceptable."[70] By linking state and local actions to his earlier pronouncement that federal efforts were "not acceptable," Bush slyly transferred blame to Blanco and Nagin—guilt by word association.

Over the weekend, Rove and Bartlett's public relations crusade flooded the Gulf Coast with some of the Bush administration's most prominent faces, including those of Myers, Rumsfeld, and Secretary of State Condoleezza Rice, as they toured blighted communities.[71] Their visits coincided with troop and supply arrivals and were heavily covered throughout the media. Bush's disaster ambassadors took to the storm-damaged territory, in part, because of his spectacular failure in having given the wrecked geography a cool once-over before hightailing it home. His avoidance of the haunts most damaged by the hurricane, and his minimal contact with the region's homeless residents, created the impression of compassionless conservatism and made some Republicans wince in embarrassment.[72]

On Sunday, Chertoff blamed Democratic officials in New Orleans and Louisiana for the poor governmental response to Katrina when he appeared on *Meet the Press*. "The way emergency operations act under the law is the responsibility and the power, the authority, to order an evacuation rests with state and local officials. The federal government comes in and supports those officials."[73] FEMA chief Brown, a frequent victim of Nagin's ire, fired back on Saturday when he said "the mayor can order an evacuation and try to evacuate the city, but if the mayor does not have the resources to get the poor, elderly, the disabled, those who cannot, out, or if he does not even have police capacity to enforce the mandatory evacuation, to make people leave, then you end up with the kind of situation we have right now in New Orleans."[74]

Things are often different in theory than in practice; situations on the ground are often trickier than they are on paper, as Nagin discovered. Bush has made us learn that lesson again the hard way. It became clear when he announced an end to the war in Iraq—*before* the majority of soldiers in the region died, and before he had to borrow resources from home, including the National Guard, to supplement the military's ranks abroad. In so doing, he has left states like Alabama, Mississippi, and Louisiana stretched thin, and even more vulnerable to disaster. It was about to become painfully clear just how vulnerable the Gulf Coast was to both natural and political disaster.

The things that happened are unbelievable. And they're saying it was FEMA's fault, it was the governor's fault, it was the mayor's fault. FEMA was an hour away from New Orleans. Why didn't they rescue the people? Why didn't they save the people? Why'd the people have to go through what they went through? Why did those people suffer?

—*Darlene Mathieu, Katrina survivor*

CHAPTER 7

GUNS AND BUTTER
(or FEMA-nizing Disaster)

On Saturday morning, September 3, the Superdome had as many as 5,000 folk waiting to be evacuated, as substantial numbers had already been rescued. The remaining cluster of people had not been sequestered in the dome for days but had come to the Superdome in search of a ride out of town. Later Saturday, a dozen National Guard troops applauded as eighty-one-year-old Isaac Kelly, sporting a Houston Rockets cap, boarded a school bus, the last person to be evacuated from the Superdome.[1] The nation wouldn't as quickly return praise to the government for its horrendous mishandling of the storm's aftermath. For one, it appeared to insensitively shrug off the plight of poor blacks. Then, too, the government's inaction suggested that if more of the National Guard could have come earlier, the flood of suffering may have stopped sooner. Bush proved he couldn't balance domestic demands and foreign forays.

While the Superdome was emptying, the convention center had swollen to 25,000 people, most of whom had been there for the duration of the storm.[2] The National Guard had served nearly 70,000 meals at the convention center with enough supplies to serve 130,000 more. Altogether, 42,000 people had been evacuated from New Orleans by Saturday, with an equal number awaiting their turn to leave. Search-and-rescue teams continued to scour flooded areas, where some folk remained trapped in their homes, in attics, on rooftops, or in makeshift shelters.[3] Texas had taken in about 250,000 evacuees alone, while Baton Rouge doubled its population. A fleet of air-conditioned buses were suspended from serving the Superdome to begin evacuating the people stranded at the convention center. Outside, a man lay dead, his body covered with a blanket, a stream of blood running from his body onto the pavement, a casualty of Katrina's violent aftermath. In the end, six people died at the Superdome while four perished at the convention center, although the causes of their deaths are still not clear.[4] As a dozen people hunted food and water down the street from the convention center, they were rebuffed by a soldier with a drawn gun.[5]

Blanco's encounter with Bush may have left her feeling as if she were staring down the barrel of a gun, but on Saturday, after turning Bush back and dodging a federal bullet, she made two moves to secure her independence from Washington. First, she created a philanthropic fund for the victims of Katrina. Next, she hired James Lee Witt to advise her on relief efforts. Witt was Clinton's former FEMA chief, who had been critical of Bush for demoting the FEMA head from a cabinet level position to an undersecretary for DHS.[6] Had Brown been a cabinet member, his stature may have won him the president's ear and confidence. Chertoff claimed that he had "full confidence" in Brown's abilities even as he planned to fly overnight to New Orleans to take charge of the federal and military relief efforts.[7]

Before departing, Chertoff, Housing Secretary Alphonso Jackson, and White House domestic policy advisor Claude Allen met with black leaders to discuss the impact of race and class on the federal government's role in delivering, or in effect delaying, relief for several days.[8] According to White House press secretary Scott McClellan, the group's main focus was the process of evacuation, the desire to save and sustain lives, temporary housing, and finding ways to work with community and faith-based groups to address the long-term needs of the displaced.[9] The two-hour meeting was attended by former Congressional Black Caucus chair Elijah Cummings, NAACP president Bruce Gordon, and National Urban League head, and former New Orleans mayor, Marc Morial. The current Congressional Black Caucus chair, North Carolina U.S. representative Mel Watt, joined the meeting by phone.

Cummings, who had chided Bush and his administration the day before, said, according to his spokeswoman Devika Koppikar, that the gathering was meant in part to correct the perception that Bush was indifferent to black suffering. "I think a lot of people in the African American community—and others, by the way—share Bush's view that the results of his efforts have been unacceptable," Cummings commented after the White House meeting. "I think they wanted to make sure that the leaders of the Congressional Black Caucus, the Urban League and the NAACP knew that they were very sensitive to trying to make sure that things went right from here on out. And I think they wanted to try to dispel any kind of notions that the administration did not care about African American people—or anyone else."[10]

Cummings's last comment referred, of course, to Kanye West's comments on Friday night.[11] To be sure, West wasn't the only person frustrated by the cruelly slow pace at which help was sent to the largely black and poor evacuees who had been stranded or left to die on the Gulf Coast. Predictably, his sentiments revealed a divided nation: most whites disagreed, while the overwhelming majority of blacks felt the same as the articulate rapper.[12]

Although West's comments about Bush garnered the most media attention, he was equally critical of the diversion of resources and troops to Iraq and the "shoot to kill" orders given to the National Guard to restore order. "We already realize a lot of the people that could help are at war now fighting another way," West nervously said as he strayed further from his scripted remarks. "And they've given them permission to go down and shoot us."[13] West's views about the diversion of National Guard troops to Iraq reflect a belief shared by many critics of the administration. Bush's war chest, fit for a Brobdingnag, hoards needed and ever scarcer resources for domestic programs, including spending to strengthen levees and restore coastal wetlands.

Even military personnel have admitted that the bleeding of funds to fight in Iraq and patrol in Afghanistan have left domestic National Guard units strapped and thinned. Lieutenant General H. Steven Blum, the Guard's top commander, told a congressional committee held a month after Katrina that the National Guard lacks two-thirds of the equipment necessary to respond to domestic disasters and terrorist attacks. Blum said that the Guard needed an additional $7 billion to acquire radios, trucks, construction machinery, and medical gear required to adequately respond to catastrophe.[14] Blum testified that the situation with the Guard had been exacerbated by the deployment of units to Iraq and Afghanistan. They took with them the newest equipment and left it there for replacement soldiers. That meant that the home front was left with outdated and dwindling supplies of gear, only one-third of what was needed.

The link between Iraq and the faltering domestic agenda was clearly stated in an editorial in the *Pittsburgh Post-Gazette:*

> The 138,000 National Guard and other U.S. troops that are in Iraq, trying to assure security in Fallujah or even along the road from Baghdad to the airport, should have been in New Orleans, Mississippi and Alabama instead, providing relief, assuring the safety of rescue workers and deterring looters. . . . Why is the United States spending billions a week in Iraq when it is having to borrow $62.3 billion so far to help Americans recover and rebuild from a major domestic tragedy?[15]

The strain of diverted resources told on the Guard's efforts during the storm. The 222 soldiers who were sequestered at the convention center—partitioned away from the masses, and afraid to open their quarters to them for fear that the Guard's food and water supplies would provoke anger in hungry and thirsty evacuees—were trained in levee repair and not police work. They dared not confront thousands of storm victims who grew more desperate by the moment. The failed lines of communication—General Blum told one congressman who had served as a Marine in Korea and Vietnam, "I'm dealing with radios, sir, that you probably saw the last time you were in battle fatigues"—made it impossible for the Guard to speak with active-duty troops as they patrolled New Orleans.[16] Although Blum didn't think that the deployment of troops to Iraq slowed the hurricane response, Lieutenant Colonel Pete Schneider, a spokesman for the Louisiana Guard, disagreed. "We would have used them if we'd had them," Schneider said. "We've always known in the event of a catastrophic storm in New Orleans that we'd use our response up pretty fast."[17]

If Kanye West's comments about race and troop diversion seemed askew to some, his remark about the National Guard being "given permission to go down and shoot us" seemed far-fetched and paranoid. And yet, it was true. When a contingent of three hundred National Guard troops landed in New Orleans on September 2, Governor Blanco announced she had given them authorization to shoot and kill "hoodlums." The looting of New Orleans, though largely overplayed in the media, and often narrowly, and unfairly, viewed as the rioting of thugs and not largely the survival activity of folk abandoned by their government, raised once again the specter, splashed across national television, of blacks out of control.

Blanco's comments revived the ugly memory of a time when police, and occasionally military forces, were unjustly used by the state against blacks. Blanco angrily asserted her threat to the largely black masses. "These troops are fresh back from Iraq, well trained, experienced, battle-tested and under my orders to restore order in the streets. They have M-16s and they are locked and loaded. These troops know how to shoot and kill and they are more than willing to do so if necessary and I expect they will."[18] On Saturday, Brown warned of "idiots with a gun on a rooftop" and the remaining "hotspots" of crime in New Orleans. "Some of these kids think this is a game," Brown said at a press conference in Baton Rouge. "They have a gun and they think it is a game they are playing."[19]

Fortunately, when the man in charge of the troops—Lieutenant General Russel Honore, the three-star general Nagin wanted to invest with federal authority to evacuate New Orleans, a prospect Blanco resisted—witnessed his soldiers patrolling the streets with their guns up, he ordered them to lower their weapons. "This is not Baghdad," he snapped. "These are American citizens."[20] If only that message could have made the Bush administration move faster, more effectively, and with greater urgency, there might not be lingering suspicion about the role race and class played in the response to Katrina. As things stand, the federal government fumbled the ball, and its jersey read FEMA.

At a Saturday, September 3, press conference, DHS's Chertoff extended the administration's assault on local officials when he claimed that the federal government's hands were tied "because our constitutional system really places the primary authority in each state with the governor."[21] But Blanco and New Orleans City Council president Oliver Thomas fired back at Chertoff. Blanco argued that Louisiana "did not have enough resources here to do it all. . . . The magnitude is overwhelming."[22] Thomas admitted that New Orleans had been surprised and overwhelmed by the swell of evacuees stranded in the city. But he lashed out at the federal government for its inexcusable failures. "Everybody shares the blame here," Thomas acknowledged. "But when you talk about the mightiest government in the world, that's a ludicrous and lame excuse. You're FEMA, and you're the big dog. And you weren't prepared either."[23]

Perhaps New Orleans deputy police commander W.S. Riley offered the most skillful lashing of the federal government from a local official when he let loose on the National Guard. "My biggest disappointment is with the federal government and the National Guard," Riley said. "The Guard arrived 48 hours after the hurricane with 40 trucks. They drove their trucks in and went to sleep. For 72 hours this police department and the fire department and a handful of citizens were alone rescuing people. We have people who died while the National Guard sat and played cards. I understand why we are not winning the war in Iraq if this is what we have."

On Sunday, September 4, DHS tried to combat the perception of its incompetence by releasing figures about troop placements, National Guard activities, the mobilization of medical personnel, the evacuation of citizens, and the distribution of supplies, to prove the success of their "around the clock" federal "effort to save lives, sustain life, and support recovery and law enforcement operations in areas affected by Hurricane Katrina."[24] Not to be outdone by DHS, FEMA released its own statistics on Saturday to bolster its claims of competency in handling the catastrophe.[25] Their move is a sign of growing tension within the administration over the heavy criticism leveled at Brown. Homeland Security emails released after the crisis prove that Brown considered his designation as principal federal officer a demotion, and that when the White House created its task force to oversee Katrina, Brown's deputy chief of staff wrote, "Let them play their little rainder [sic] games as long as they are not turning around and tasking us with their stupid questions."[26]

The evacuees' dispersal eerily echoed earlier patterns of migration among black people in the nation's history. Before the early 1900s, nearly 90 percent of the black population lived in the South. As the mechanization of industry displaced black farmers and agrarian workers, the lure of better opportunities up north, and a release from de jure segregation—plus natural disasters like the 1927 Great Flood of Mississippi—drove black people to Detroit, Chicago, Cleveland, and further west out to California. The perils and possibilities of exile and migration are painfully familiar moments in the collective memory of black America.

Despite its self-congratulation on its efforts, it is only when one draws back and sees what FEMA *didn't* do—and views the help it turned down, before and after Katrina struck—that one gains a sense of the federal government's foul-ups. After FEMA grossly underestimated the storm's impact, it severely mismanaged its resources and responded in a dreadfully inadequate fashion. The agency sent only seven of its twenty-eight Urban Search and Rescue (US&R) teams to the region before Katrina struck, while not one of its workers was sent to New Orleans until after the storm vanished on Monday, August 29.[27] On Friday, August 26, as Katrina streaked across the Gulf of Mexico, FEMA officials in D.C. discussed the need for buses to evacuate folk, but failed to follow through. "We could all see it coming, like a guided missile," said Leo V. Bosner, a twenty-six-year FEMA employee. "We, as staff members at the agency, felt helpless. We knew that major steps needed to be taken fast, but, for whatever reasons, they were not taken."[28]

On Sunday, the Louisiana National Guard requested seven hundred buses from FEMA (they eventually only received one hundred on Wednesday). By Tuesday, August 30, as the waters rose, and rumors of violence spread, many of the women who drive buses in New Orleans were afraid to drive. Governor Blanco looked to FEMA, which only offered a fleet of buses, according to a spokeswoman, after a state request on Wednesday. But state officials had been requesting the buses all week, though it is unclear whether their method of request is another example of a procedural snafu. When Greyhound Lines finally received FEMA approval on Wednesday, they started sending buses to New Orleans. The slow pace of the buses' arrivals, and the increased desperation at the city's makeshift shelters inside the Superdome and convention center, made Blanco "blistering mad" and sent her into a fit inside Louisiana's emergency center in Baton Rouge. She was at her wit's end. "Does anybody in this building know anything about buses?" she cried out as she burst through the door.[29] It was this scene, sparked by FEMA's delayed and lackluster response, that drove Blanco to issue her executive orders commandeering the city's buses.

In truth, the story of the buses is even more convoluted and sad. On August 31, Peter Pantuso, head of the American Bus Association, tried unsuccessfully throughout the day to find someone at FEMA to tell him how many buses were needed for evacuation, where they should go, and who was in charge of the effort.[30] Pantuso said that "we never talked directly to FEMA or got a call back from them." The American Bus Association counts among its members some of the country's largest motor coach companies, including Greyhound and Coach USA. What Pantuso eventually discovered is that FEMA had outsourced the job of transporting the evacuees to Landstar Express America, a trucking logistics firm with a federal contract worth up to $100 million annually. Landstar Express in turn hired a limousine company, Carey Limousine, which hired a travel management company, Transportation Management Services.[31] According to Sally Snead, a senior VP at Carey, Landstar, after reading about the company's ability to move large groups of people on their Internet site, checked the availability of buses on Sunday, August 28, and early on Monday. However, the firm didn't ask the limousine company to order buses until early August 30, nearly eighteen hours after the storm hit. Snead then called Transportation Management Services, whose specialty is arranging buses for big events, to help fill an initial order of three hundred buses.

The day Katrina hit, Victor Parra, head of the United Motorcoach Association, called FEMA to offer help. FEMA didn't call back until the next day, directing Parra to the agency's Web page, "Doing Business with FEMA," which had no information about the storm relief effort.[32] The American Bus Association's Pantuso cut his vacation short on August 31, believing that his members would be called on in the relief effort. When he couldn't reach FEMA directly, Pantuso appealed to his Capitol Hill contacts and found out about Carey's role in the relief efforts. He then contacted Snead, who had wanted to call Pantuso earlier but had no number. At 5:00 P.M. on Wednesday, Pantuso and Parra had enough details to prevail upon their members to assist in the evacuation. By the weekend, more than 1,000 buses were available to transport stranded citizens of New Orleans to shelters across the country. FEMA's inefficiency certainly cost precious time, and, indirectly, may have cost hundreds of lives.

It was harmful enough that FEMA discouraged other first responders from aiding the besieged folk of the Gulf Coast without first being requested. That rule, of course, overlooks how the storm shattered the communications infrastructure with line breaks, destruction of base stations, and power failures, which affected most land-line and cell phones. This further hampered on-the-ground, up-to-the-second responses and activities that might save lives. For instance, fire officials in New Orleans had one channel for eight hundred people to communicate on. The National Guard couldn't communicate between units, while ground commanders lacked the ability to track the location of the units under their authority.[33] But the trail of rejections left by FEMA's refusal of assistance is a forceful indictment of the federal government's gross negligence of citizen safety.

The USS *Bataan*, an 844-foot ship that carries Marines in amphibious assaults, was in the Gulf before the storm, before any other military unit, awaiting authority for a full mobilization that never came.[34] The USS *Bataan* has helicopters, physicians, hospital beds, food, and water—and can make up to 100,000 gallons of its own water each day. The *Bataan* rode the storm out and followed it to the shore, preparing to help in emergency operations. Its helicopters were among the first to rescue stranded New Orleans citizens. But the *Bataan* was never asked to use its other considerable resources to help, including its six hundred patient beds, which remained empty throughout the storm's aftermath. None of its twelve hundred sailors were asked to go ashore to aid in the relief effort.

The ship's commander, Captain Nora Tyson, was frustrated. "Could we do more?" Tyson asked rhetorically. "Sure. I've got sailors who could be on the beach plucking through garbage or distributing water and food and stuff. But I can't force myself on people." Tyson said that the *Bataan* was ready to contribute. "If someone says you need to take on people, we're ready. If they say hospitals on the beach can't handle it . . . if they need to send the overflow out here, we're ready. We've got lots of room." FEMA's failure to mobilize the full resources of the *Bataan* was a tragic oversight. FEMA and the Bush administration were undoubtedly embarrassed when Lieutenant Commander Sean Kelly, Pentagon spokesman for the Northern Command (under whose jurisdiction the *Bataan* fell), gave an interview to BBC television explaining the failure of the federal government to engage the *Bataan* in relief efforts.

Northcom started planning before the storm even hit. We were ready for the storm when it hit Florida . . . and then we were planning once it was pointed towards the Gulf Coast. So . . . we activated what we call "defense coordinating officers" to work with the states to say, "OK, what do you think you will need?" And we set up staging these bases that could be started. We had the USS *Bataan* sailing almost behind the hurricane so that after the hurricane made landfall, its search and rescue helicopters would be available almost immediately. So, we had things ready. The only caveat is: we have to wait until the president authorizes us to do so. The laws of the United States say that the military can't just act in this fashion; we have to wait for the president to give us permission.[35]

FEMA's failure to take advantage of resources and to accept help didn't end with the *Bataan*. Three U.S. Customs Blackhawk helicopter crews stationed at Crestview Airport in Florida were upset because they weren't asked to provide full-time assistance in relief efforts.[36] A DHS official confirmed that the Blackhawks were brought in from as far away as San Diego to assist with rescue and recovery missions in the aftermath of Katrina. Mark Conrad, a former regional Internal Affairs supervisor for U.S. Customs, expressed anger and frustration over FEMA's failure to make use of the helicopter crews' talents. "They have three Blackhawk helicopters and crew just sitting there doing nothing, just so they can look good for CNN," Conrad said. "The crew is livid. They made one trip earlier and flew over Biloxi, (Mississippi) where there are dead bodies everywhere. Those are highly trained crews and Blackhawk helicopters can carry a lot of food and water. They could be doing something."[37]

What did FEMA have the helicopters do instead of flying rescue and recovery missions? Press duty. Instead of helping people in need, the Blackhawks were ordered to transport journalists to the region to film the misery they saw. When maintenance problems foiled those plans, the helicopter crews were ordered to fly to Biloxi to deliver supplies, but were immediately recalled. The crews had flown only one mission in two days. This was an incredible waste of their time and talent, and a loss of resources and rescue efforts for the stranded residents in the region.

FEMA's wasted efforts extended from the air to the sea. Nearly five hundred Florida airboat pilots who volunteered to rescue storm victims and to transport relief workers and supplies to New Orleans were kept from entering the city. Robert Dummett, state coordinator of the Florida Airboat Association, said that his group "cannot get deployed to save our behinds."[38] Or, for that matter, the behinds of those who most needed saving in the Gulf Coast region. FEMA wouldn't authorize their entry into New Orleans; without it, the pilots could be arrested, or they would have to labor without security and support services. Despite the pilots' complaining to several congressmen, who contacted FEMA on their behalf, FEMA refused their help because they claimed New Orleans wasn't safe. Although they were willing to help, the airboat pilots were barred from relief efforts. "To me, 500 airboats seems a perfect solution to the chaos and difficulty of getting people out of their flooded homes," U.S. Rep. Mark Foley said. "I'd love them to be able to go in and help, and that's what I've conveyed to FEMA."[39] But FEMA wouldn't budge.

Remarkably, neither would they budge with an organization well suited to handle such conditions: the Red Cross. "The Homeland Security Department has requested and continues to request that the American Red Cross not come back into New Orleans," Red Cross spokeswoman Renita Hosler said on September 2. "Right now access is controlled by the National Guard and local authorities. We have been at the table every single day [asking for access]. We cannot get into New Orleans against their orders."[40] The reason FEMA and DHS gave for blocking the entry of the Red Cross and other relief agencies into New Orleans is that it was too dangerous and that it might encourage people to believe it was safe to remain. By the same token, if the relief agencies had been allowed in, they might have facilitated the rescue and recovery of stranded citizens, providing them enough sustenance until they could be safely evacuated. The Red Cross was willing to go to the New Orleans Convention Center to deliver food and water. They have done so in far more dangerous circumstances than in New Orleans. FEMA and DHS simply seemed to shoot themselves in the foot at every turn.

FEMA even turned down the assistance of Chicago mayor Richard Daley. Before Katrina swooped down on the Gulf Coast, Chicago's Office of Emergency Management and Communications contacted emergency response agencies in Illinois and D.C. The city was generous in its offer: 44 Chicago Fire Department rescue and medical personnel and gear, over 100 Chicago police officers, 140 Streets and Sanitation workers, 146 Public Health workers, 8 Human Services workers, 29 trucks, 2 boats, and a mobile clinic. After the storm hit, FEMA only requested a single tank truck. Daley was frustrated and miffed. "I was shocked," Chicago's mayor said. "We were ready to provide considerably more help than they have requested. We are just waiting for the call."[41] The call never came.

FEMA rebuffed sheriffs' deputies and emergency personnel from Loudoun, Virginia, who were en route to Louisiana on September 1. They were forced to turn back when the federal government failed to produce the required paperwork.[42] After Sheriff Steve Simpson and his staff unsuccessfully tried reaching FEMA for twelve hours, the volunteers—twenty deputies and six emergency medical technicians—had to return home. They had been prepared to stay in Louisiana for fourteen days while living on their own supplies. FEMA also barred an Arizona mortician from entering the city because he was not certified by FEMA. Tom Dudelston sought to volunteer to help stranded residents in the Gulf Coast during his vacation, but unlike Arizona, which allows trained persons to assist during a catastrophe without FEMA certification, the federal government offered no such possibility. He was disappointed when he reported that "I am not going anywhere, I spoke with DMORT [Disaster Mortuary Operation Rescue Teams], a group of funeral directors and embalmers, and I cannot go."[43]

FEMA's foibles were far reaching. They blocked a five-hundred-boat citizen flotilla from delivering aid. They turned away three Wal-Mart trailer trucks loaded with water. The agency kept the Coast Guard from delivering one thousand gallons of diesel fuel. They cut Jefferson Parish's emergency communication lines, which the sheriff restored before posting armed guards to protect them from FEMA. They also turned back a German military plane transporting five tons of military rations for storm victims. FEMA claimed it lacked the required authorization (although a U.S. Embassy official cited technical and logistical problems in the federal government's recovery operations after the storm hit as the blame). FEMA tried to keep a Wal-Mart store from opening, an order that was eventually overridden by Jefferson Parish sheriff Harry Lee. The sheriff "commandeered" the Sam's and Wal-Mart stores in his parish and ordered that they be opened, against the wishes of FEMA, whose personnel Lee threatened to arrest if they interfered.

FEMA failed to properly use hundreds of firefighters who had volunteered their help. Instead of assisting in rescue and recovery efforts, they played cards, took classes on the history of FEMA, and lay around for days in an Atlanta airport awaiting instructions for duty. When the bodies began to pile up in New Orleans, FEMA refused journalists' requests to accompany rescue and recovery teams in their boats as they searched for victims, saying, "We have requested that no photographs of the deceased be made by the media." The agency eventually relented and permitted the media into New Orleans.

FEMA used a battalion of one thousand firefighters culled from Utah and around the country as community-relations officers to distribute flyers and a toll-free number, prompting some of the firefighters to tear off their shirts and stuff them in their backpacks, refusing to be demeaned and to promote the federal agency that misused their talents.[44] A FEMA spokeswoman indignantly reprimanded the firefighters for wanting to save lives instead of serving as FEMA propagandists. "I would go back and ask the firefighter to revisit his commitment to FEMA, to firefighting and to the citizens of this country," Mary Hudak said, equating service to the country with submission to FEMA's distorted vision and questionable practices.[45]

Perhaps the most egregious example of FEMA's dangerous failure came when Dr. Mark N. Perlmutter, a Pennsylvania orthopedic surgeon who volunteered his services in Louisiana, was ordered by a federal official to stop giving chest compressions to a dying woman because he wasn't registered with FEMA.[46] "I begged him to let me continue," Perlmutter said. "People were dying, and I was the only doctor on the tarmac [at the Louis Armstrong New Orleans International Airport] where scores of nonresponsive patients lay on stretchers. Two patients died in front of me. I showed him [the U.S. Coast Guard official in charge] my medical credentials. I had tried to get through to FEMA for twelve hours the day before and finally gave up. I asked him to let me stay until I was replaced by another doctor, but he refused. He said he was afraid of being sued. I informed him about the Good Samaritan laws and asked him if he was willing to let people die so the government wouldn't be sued, but he would not back down. I had to leave."[47]

In its formal response to Perlmutter's story, FEMA displayed an inflexibility and callousness that was unseemly. "We have a cadre of physicians of our own," FEMA spokeswoman Kim Pease said. "They are the National Disaster Medical Team. . . . The voluntary doctor was not a credentialed FEMA physician and, thus, was subject to law enforcement rules in a disaster area."[48]

On Sunday, September 4, Jefferson Parish president Aaron Broussard made an appearance on *Meet the Press*—made famous by his claim that a colleague's mother drowned while awaiting promised help, the details of which were later disputed.[49] But what couldn't be disputed was Broussard's compelling eloquence in delivering a biting indictment of FEMA.

We have been abandoned by our own country. Hurricane Katrina will go down in history as one of the worst storms ever to hit an American coast, but the aftermath of Hurricane Katrina will go down as one of the worst abandonments of Americans on American soil ever in U.S. history. I am personally asking our bipartisan congressional delegation here in Louisiana to immediately begin congressional hearings to find out just what happened here. Why did it happen? Who needs to be fired? And believe me, they need to be fired right away, because we still have weeks to go in this tragedy. We have months to go. We have years to go. And whoever is at the top of this totem pole, that totem pole needs to be chain-sawed off and we've got to start with some new leadership. It's not just Katrina that caused all these deaths in New Orleans here. Bureaucracy has committed murder here in the greater New Orleans area, and bureaucracy has to stand trial before Congress now. It's so obvious. FEMA needs more congressional funding. It needs more presidential support. It needs to be a Cabinet-level director. It needs to be an independent agency that will be able to fulfill its mission to work in partnership with state and local governments around America. FEMA needs to be empowered to do the things it was created to do. It needs to come somewhere, like New Orleans, with all of its force immediately, without red tape, without bureaucracy, act immediately with common sense and leadership, and save lives. Forget about the property. We can rebuild the property. It's got to be able to come in and save lives. We need strong leadership at the top of America right now in order to accomplish this and to reconstruct FEMA.[50]

It is little wonder, then, that on the same Sunday the *Times-Picayune*—after rejecting the federal government's claim that New Orleans was inaccessible to explain its delayed response, especially since many journalists, and entertainers like Harry Connick, Jr., found their way to the Crescent City just fine—stated in an open letter to Bush: "Every official at the Federal Emergency Management Agency should be fired, Director Michael Brown especially."[51] The *Times-Picayune* letter said that Brown's claim on Thursday, September 1, that FEMA had "provided food to the people at the Convention Center so that they've gotten at least one, if not two meals, every single day" was a "bald-faced" lie.[52] While Bush would move to shore up FEMA's fortunes, his gestures were largely cosmetic. Worse yet, he would deepen the wounds of the afflicted in the name of helping them, leaving them vulnerable to corporate vultures and, temporarily at least, work laws that robbed them of just wages. If the *Times-Picayune* expected Bush to prove that he had the best interests of New Orleans in mind before believing him, their wait, at least in the short run, would be in vain. FEMA's actions only exacerbated their plight.

Well, April [2005] was one of the first meetings where they had a presentation from a white group of men with money, who said they were the folk that were hired to give New Orleans a "new look." And they came into the meeting, and gave us a presentation about how New Orleans would change economically. And pretty much how they were going to "revitalize" downtown, where all of the tourists mainly come. And in the presentation, they were pointing out key areas [to be destroyed and rebuilt]. And one of the areas they were targeting was the Iberville Housing Project, which has been there forever.

—*Lennard Noble, Katrina survivor*

CHAPTER 8

CAPITALIZING ON DISASTER

UNDAUNTED BY THE HEAVY CRITICISM that came his way, and determined to make a better showing than on his Friday drop-in, Bush returned to Louisiana on Labor Day, Monday, September 5, visiting evacuees in Baton Rouge at the Bethany World Prayer Center and at Pearl River Community College in Poplarville.[1] Army engineers greeted Bush with good news: they had repaired two breached levees in New Orleans—the 17th Street Canal and the London Avenue Canal, which they plugged with hundreds of three-thousand-pound sandbags filled with cement and fragments of shattered roadways.[2] The engineers also began to carefully pump water out of the city and back into Lake Pontchartrain.

Still, Bush's visit wasn't without controversy. There was a dispute between staff members for the president and Governor Blanco about whether she was notified of Bush's visit. A White House staff member said she reached out to Blanco's office on Sunday and made contact Monday morning. Blanco's press secretary said they found out about Bush's trip late Sunday night on CNN, and that only after she called the White House did they extend an invitation to her.[3] The snub underscored the simmering tension between the president and governor over who should have authority in evacuating and reconstructing New Orleans. (Perhaps chilly is more like it, since Blanco gave Bush a terse introduction at an emergency operations center that signified their icy relations: "I know I don't need to make any other introduction other than 'Mr. President.'")[4]

Neither was Bush's visit to the Baton Rouge makeshift shelter, composed largely of black people, without strain. Accompanied by Bush friend T.D. Jakes—who was described in the *New York Times* as a "conservative African-American television evangelist with a megachurch in Dallas who has been courted by the White House as a partner in reaching out to the black vote"—the president thanked the preacher "for rallying the armies of compassion to help" Baton Rouge mayor "Kip" Holden, who joined the pair at the Bethany World Prayer Center shelter.[5] While some of the evacuees greeted Bush warmly, most kept their distance. Their sentiments were captured in the words of Mildred Brown, who had been at the shelter with her husband, mother-in-law, and cousin since Tuesday, August 30. "I'm not star-struck; I need answers. I'm not interested in hand-shaking. I'm not interested in photo ops. This is going to take a lot of money."[6]

The president's Louisiana visit wasn't the only Bush appearance at a shelter that made news on Labor Day.[7] Former First Lady Barbara Bush accompanied her husband, former president George H.W. Bush, former president Bill Clinton, and senators Hilary Clinton and Barack Obama on a tour of relief shelters in Houston, including the Astrodome, where thousands of evacuees were housed. In a moment of unsolicited candor, Mrs. Bush let on that she believed the poor black evacuees were surely in a better place than they were before, a prospect that both pleased and frightened her. "Almost everyone I've talked to says, 'We're moving to Houston,'" Bush said of the evacuees in an interview on American Public Media's *Marketplace* program. "What I'm hearing which is sort of scary is they all want to stay in Texas. Everyone is so overwhelmed by the hospitality. And so many of the people in the arena here, you know, were underprivileged anyway, so this—this (she chuckles slightly) is working very well for them."[8] Such rhetoric only raised the profile of the Bushes as clueless patricians.

Ironically, on Labor Day—a holiday intended to celebrate the American worker—it was big business that cashed in on what Naomi Klein has termed "disaster capitalism."[9] For Klein, disaster capitalism is a predatory force that "uses the desperation and fear created by catastrophe to engage in radical social and economic engineering," driven by the reconstruction industry, which "works so quickly and efficiently that the privatizations and land grabs are usually locked in before the local population knows what hit them."[10] On Labor Day, it was widely announced that Kellogg, Brown & Root Services, Inc. (KBR), an Arlington, Virginia–based subsidiary of Halliburton Co.—which Vice President Cheney headed between 1995 and 2000—had begun tapping a $500-million Navy no-bid contract to perform emergency repairs at Gulf Coast naval and marine facilities damaged by the storm.[11] KBR was contracted to receive $12 million for work at the Naval Air Station at Pascagoula, Mississippi; the Naval Station at Gulfport, Mississippi; and Stennis Space Center in Mississippi. It will also receive $4.6 million for its work at two smaller New Orleans Navy facilities and others in the South.[12]

Earlier in 2005, KBR—which hired former FEMA director Joseph Allbaugh as a lobbyist—had taken its share of $350 million awarded to four companies to repair naval facilities in northwest Florida damaged by Hurricane Ivan in 2004.[13] KBR has been extremely controversial because it garnered a five-year no-bid contract to restore oil fields in Iraq in 2003 right before the war began. When a senior Army official publicly criticized the contract, he was unceremoniously demoted.[14] Cheney's and Allbaugh's ties to the company smack of gross cronyism and cry out for systematic scrutiny of such contracts. In light of a sizable booty reaped from Katrina reconstruction efforts, it seems that Halliburton's contribution of more than $1 million to hurricane relief was but a drop in its energy bucket. "Halliburton has the Energy to help," said company chairman, president, and CEO Dave Lesar. "We remain prayerful for all survivors of this devastating storm and stand beside our colleagues and friends as they rebuild their lives."[15] Prayerful and *preyerful*.

But KBR was only the beginning of no-bid contracted reconstruction that carved a market in Katrina's misery and closed out members of the racial group most profoundly affected by the storm. The cronyism extended to the Shaw Group, which got a huge no-bid contract and also has been represented by Allbaugh.[16] A month after Katrina struck, more than fifteen contracts had been awarded for more than $100 million, including five contracts that were worth $500 million or more. The contracts were mostly for clearing trees, homes, and cars scattered across the Gulf Coast; buying trailers and mobile homes; and providing transportation, including trucks, ships, buses, and planes. More than 80 percent of the $1.5 billion in contracts awarded by FEMA were no-bid or limited-competition agreements.

The appearance of impropriety, cronyism, and abuse was so strong in the case of KBR and Shaw—combined with other instances of contracts clinched with a handshake and no paper to substantiate the deal—that it provoked the criticism of DHS inspector general Richard L. Skinner. "When you do something like this, you do increase the vulnerability for fraud, plain waste, abuse and mismanagement. We are very apprehensive about what we are seeing."[17] Also under investigation for the costs claimed for debris removal was the $568 million awarded to AshBritt, a company based in Pompano Beach, Florida, and a client of the lobbying firm to which Haley Barbour was connected before he became Mississippi's governor. Bechtel Corporation was awarded $100 million despite raising concerns with its oversight of a Boston "Big Dig" construction project. And KBR has been criticized by federal auditors for billing $100-per-bag laundry service and for overcharging in its Iraqi reconstruction.[18]

The demand for quick corporate and business response to reconstruction efforts heightens the possibility of fraud, abuse, and overcharging. It also favors those already in the pipeline and reinforces the practices of cronyism and racial exclusion and exploitation. Predictably, little of the contract money has flowed to black or other minority businesses. Only 1.5 percent of the $1.6 billion awarded in contracts by FEMA has gone to minority companies. Under regular contracting rules, the number is 5 percent. The Government Accountability Office launched an investigation as DHS arranged events to assist small businesses in gaining access to the $62.3 billion Congress had at the time appropriated for hurricane recovery.[19] It was only after broad public scrutiny that the Bush administration boosted the number of contracts awarded to small and minority-owned businesses after the federal government rebid the initial $100 million contracts given to four major construction firms—Shaw Group, Inc., Bechtel Corporation, CH2M Hill Inc., and Fluor Corporation—all of which enjoyed prior relations with the government.[20]

Still, this type of exclusion reflects preexisting patterns of discrimination that have prevented the flourishing of black businesses involved in reconstruction. It also reflects the lax rules that relieve companies of the obligation to abide by equal opportunity and affirmative action principles during a crisis or natural disaster.[21] As Lavern R. Kelly, the president of KNA Service, Inc., an Orlando, Florida–based firm that consults with minority businesses seeking government contracts, observed, "My concern is contracting and procurement is going on in the [affected] area and the 8(a) SBA requirements are being waived. [The federal government] is doing a lot of piggybacking off of non-minority 'prime' contracts and sole sourcing procurement with these firms, and not doing the same with qualified 8(a) firms who have existing contracts."[22]

When Bush issued an executive order on September 8 suspending the Davis-Bacon Act of 1931, thus allowing reconstruction companies to pay workers less than the prevailing local wages, he bolstered disaster capitalism, which had three effects. First, it increased the already substantial profits of corporations. Second, it made local wage workers even more financially unstable than they were before the storm. Third, it reinforced the harmful consequences of a racially segmented work force. "It sends a bad message," noted Harry Alford, president of the National Black Chamber of Commerce. "What they're basically saying to the minority in New Orleans is, 'We'll make it harder for you to find a job. And if you do, we'll make sure you get paid less.'"[23]

Even though the Bush administration reinstated the act on November 8, after significant pressure from Democrats and Republicans, a clear signal was nonetheless sent. Disaster capitalism's unintended racial consequences will have the greatest impact on those poor black workers seeking to recover from devastation. It may even force into permanent exile vulnerable evacuees who seek a promised land far different than the makeshift paradise imagined by Barbara Bush.

If Barbara Bush thought she had tapped into the weltanschau-ung of the desperately exiled wishing to shirk their domestic roots, there were thousands of others whose mind-set she may not have been able to divine. So determined were these citizens to remain in New Orleans, filth and flood and all, that the mayor had to force them to evacuate. On September 6, Nagin ordered an immediate evacuation of New Orleans as the local police and the National Guard went door-to-door to collect nearly 10,000 holdouts in boats and helicopters. The Army Corps of Engineers continued to pump water out of the city, which was still 60 per-cent submerged. The city's slow draining uncovered parts of buildings for the first time since the flooding, inspiring a bit of hope in Nagin for the future of New Orleans.

As senators Hilary Clinton and Barbara Mikulski called for FEMA chief Michael Brown to resign—the pair also introduced legislation that would restore FEMA to a cabinet-level agency in-dependent of Homeland Security—Bush vowed to investigate what went wrong with the response to the storm in order to pre-vent similar foul-ups with the next natural disaster or act of ter-ror.[24] Bush also announced that Vice President Dick Cheney would make his first visit to the Gulf on Thursday, September 7, a full week and a half after Katrina struck. While the White House sought congressional approval for a $51.8-billion emer-gency supplemental bill to fund recovery efforts in the Gulf Coast—a bill that eleven Republican lawmakers refused to sup-port—Speaker of the House Dennis Hastert and Senate Majority Leader Bill Frist announced a bipartisan joint committee to in-vestigate the hurricane relief effort.[25]

Democrats balked; they hadn't been invited to a meeting be-tween Bush and Hastert and Frist to discuss the committee, and believed that it was simply a political ruse to absolve the admin-istration and lay blame for the poor response to Katrina at the feet of the local and state government. When the committee eventually convened, however, Democratic Louisiana U.S. representative William Jefferson made sure to be front and center to register his bitter complaint about the foiled response to the disaster in his beloved state.

As political pressure mounted to fire FEMA's head, the White House abruptly removed Brown on September 9 from overseeing storm relief efforts. They replaced him with Vice Admiral Thad W. Allen, a Coast Guard officer who had been appointed earlier in the week to serve as Brown's special deputy for hurricane relief. The move came only a few hours after the media intensified its scrutiny of Brown's inflated résumé.[26]

Brown's removal wasn't driven by his incompetent management of the post-storm relief efforts alone. Rather, Brown was FEMA's, and the administration's, scapegoat. He was the public face of the agency's stark inefficiency and rampant dysfunction in channeling resources to hundreds of thousands of survivors exiled in shelters across the land. Computer systems crashed, distribution mechanisms faltered, and disaster recovery centers were overwhelmed, increasing the frustration and chaos around the evacuees. In effect, FEMA denied poor folk even minimal help from a government that had left them stranded for days. Chertoff appeared in Baton Rouge at a news conference with Brown awkwardly at his side to announce what the DHS chief said was his decision, one that grew out of the quest for a new direction in relief efforts. Chertoff praised Brown for doing "everything he possibly could to coordinate the federal response to this unprecedented challenge."[27]

But it was clear that Bush, a leader who demands and returns zealous loyalty, and who rarely calls his staff to account in public, sought a change of leadership. With that, he also sought a change in the perception that his administration had cruelly and ineptly left its most vulnerable citizens to drown in a gigantic sorrow not of their making. For his part, Brown put the best spin possible on his plight when he said that he would "go home and walk my dog and hug my wife, and maybe get a good Mexican meal and a stiff margarita and a full night's sleep. And then I'm going to go right back to FEMA and continue to do all I can to help these victims."[28]

The anger of the American people at the federal government's poor performance slapped Cheney in the face when he toured the Gulf Coast. As he was being interviewed on live television, Cheney got a bit of his own toxic medicine when a local physician who had lost his house screamed, "Go fuck yourself, Mr. Cheney," echoing a comment the vice president made to Senator Patrick Leahy in a heated exchange in the Senate chamber in 2004.[29] (In his role as Senate president, Cheney offered his "Fuck yourself" to Leahy on the day the Senate passed the Defense of Decency Act by a 99 to 1 margin.)

On September 12, Michael Brown resigned as head of FEMA. Stepping aside was his best management decision of the entire crisis. When Bush's press secretary Scott McClellan was asked whether the president asked Brown to step down, he maintained that "This was Mike Brown's decision, and [the president] respects that."[30] The sword of Damocles wasn't far away. Bush appointed R. David Paulison, a thirty-year veteran of fire and rescue work, as FEMA's acting director.

Brown's resignation brought a close to one of the most volatile chapters in the history of federal emergency management. But he managed to get in his digs at officials in Louisiana and at the White House. At a congressional hearing boycotted by most Democrats, Brown unsurprisingly laid blame for the disastrous response on local and state officials. He even testified that he had warned the White House of the coming disaster several days before the storm struck, although that contradicts Brown's claim that he hadn't known that Katrina would be so fierce and deadly. But Brown's resignation has not resolved a major cause of the botched recovery efforts: the Bush administration's animosity for a government geared to helping the most needy and vulnerable. Neither has it cleared up the chronic cronyism and strains of incompetence that blanket FEMA, other federal agencies, and the administration. Nor has it caused the administration to grapple with the need to pay moral and political attention to pressing domestic social issues.

Race and class are two of the most salient social issues that the administration has failed to come to grips with. Katrina blew their cover—and if we're honest, it blew our cover, too. We will remain imperiled if we postpone grappling with the lethal effects of race and class in our society. As horrifying as the actual events were, almost more disturbing was what Katrina revealed about the way the nation still thinks and feels about black people—whether in the media or in the culture more broadly. Ironically, this may also be the most opportune time in a while for the black elite to confront its own bigotry toward the poor and do something to help their plight.

My only challenge is with the news media. Because they're making blacks look [bad with] the few thugs and knuckleheads they've shown at the Astrodome and the Superdome. And that's not a correct portrayal of the majority of the black people that are here from New Orleans. We don't mind working; we're looking for jobs. Unfortunately, though, the media only likes to show the negative side of the African American community. We're a lot stronger and more intelligent than what's being shown. And I think through this [disaster] people are going to start seeing that.

—*Dwayne Woodfox, Katrina survivor*

We ran out of food and water, just like everybody else. So we ventured down and we went into one of the stores. People don't understand. When you're desperate, you've got to be resourceful. We tried to get some food. So we looted.

—*Nadine Jarmon, Ph.D., Executive Director of the*
New Orleans Housing Authority, Katrina survivor

CHAPTER 9

FRAMES OF REFERENCE
Class, Caste, Culture, and Cameras

IF RACE GRABBED THE BIGGEST HEADLINES in the aftermath of Katrina because of poverty and politics, its force was also felt in other dimensions of the cultural and personal response to the hurricane. The media became a big part of the story. Reporters' anger at the government's tragic delay leaped off allegedly neutral pages and TV screens even as the stories also reinforced stereotypes of black behavior in exaggerated reports of looting and social anarchy. The black elite stepped up to express support for the poor and outrage at their treatment, putting aside, perhaps even denying, elements of its own recent assaults on poor blacks. And despite its embattled status as the purveyor of perversity, patriarchy, and pornography, quarters of hip-hop responded admirably, reminding us that they have been one of the few dependable sources of commentary on the black poor all along. The disaster also sparked renewed interest in the "race or class" debate as to what element of the dyad accounted more reliably for the fate of the black poor.

But one of the untold stories of Katrina is how the hurricane impacted racial and ethnic minorities other than blacks. For instance, nearly 40,000 Mexican citizens who lived (mostly in trailers) and worked in New Orleans were displaced.[1] Altogether, nearly 145,000 Mexicans in the entire Gulf Coast region were scattered by Katrina. Latinos make up 3 percent of Louisiana's population, 124,222 people of the state's 4,515,770 residents. Many Latinos who live in the South are foreign born and are undocumented laborers on farms or in hotels, restaurants, and other service industry jobs.

The fear that government officials and police would target undocumented immigrants discouraged many Latinos from seeking hurricane relief, despite messages from Mexican president Vicente Fox that the American government had assured him that it wouldn't take such action. In fact, for the first time in more than 150 years, Mexico sent aid to the United States in the form of an army unit of nearly 200 soldiers and 45 vehicles that joined a Mexican Navy crew helping hurricane survivors.[2] It also sent food, medicine, nurses, and doctors to Louisiana, as well as a ship transporting ambulances and trucks. The League of United Latin American Citizens (LULAC) sent translators and established a relief fund, while its Arizona branch sent four container trucks with sleeping bags, water, and food.

Latinos in other areas were affected by the hurricane as well. In Bossier County, Louisiana, many Central Americans were employed in the service industry. And Baldwin County, Alabama, was home to many farm workers who lived in migrant camps. Many of them, and Jamaican immigrants as well, had either lost their documentation or had sought refuge in hotels, and not designated shelter areas, for fear of having their citizenship status scrutinized. That fear outweighed the fact that undocumented immigrants, at least in theory, do have rights to disaster relief.

Thousands of Native Americans on the Gulf Coast were hard hit by the storm as well. According to the National Congress of American Indians (NCAI), several Native American tribes were in harm's away across the damaged region, although early on there was little contact with affected members.[3] In the immediate aftermath of Katrina, there was little information about the death tolls among the six federally recognized Native American tribes in Alabama, Louisiana, and Mississippi, including the Parch Band Creek Indian Tribe in Alabama; the Coushatta Indian Tribe, Jena Band of Choctaw, and Tunica-Biloxi Tribe in Louisiana; and the Chitimacha Tribe and the Choctaw Indians in Mississippi. For one tribe near Chalmette, Louisiana, the local high school served as a tribal morgue, holding the bodies of Native American workers, including shrimpers and other fishermen, who were drowned in the flooding near New Orleans. The Mississippi Band of Choctaw Indians experienced power outages on their reservation and sought shelter at tribal hotels. The NCAI partnered with the National Indian Gaming Association (NIGA) to raise relief funds for Native Americans in the Gulf States.[4]

There were also nearly 50,000 Vietnamese fishermen who labored on the Louisiana coast—while others worked in the service and manufacturing industries—along with a large contingent of Filipino American shrimpers, part of the oldest Filipino community in North America.[5] A community of Vietnamese shrimpers also lived and worked near Mississippi; many of them were displaced, while others died in the horrible pounding of Katrina.[6] There were nearly 30,000 Vietnamese

evacuees dispersed to Houston, although many of them were denied entry into the Astrodome, finding shelter instead at Houston's Hong Kong City Mall.[7]

The oversight of Latino, Native American, and Vietnamese
and Filipino suffering in the catastrophe not only reinforces for
the latter three groups their relative invisibility in American culture, and for Latinos their relative marginalization in the region.
It shows as well that our analysis of minorities must constantly
be revised to accommodate a broader view of how race and ethnicity function in the culture. As important as it is, the black-
white racial paradigm simply does not exhaust the complex
realities and complicated interactions among various minority
groups and the broader society.

The black-white racial paradigm was also pressured by an en-
during question among social analysts that was revived in the
face of Katrina: is it race or class that determines the fate of poor
blacks? Critics came down on either side during the crisis, but
in this case, that might equate to six in one hand, half a dozen in
the other. It is true that class is often overlooked to explain social reality. Ironically, it is often a subject broached by the acid
conservatives who want to avoid confronting race, and who become raging parodies of Marxists in the bargain. They are only
concerned about class to deflect race; they have little interest in
unpacking the dynamics of class or engaging its deforming influence in the social scene. In this instance, race becomes a
marker for class, a proxy, blurring and bending the boundaries
that segregate them.[8]

Class certainly loomed large in Katrina's aftermath. Blacks of
means escaped the tragedy; blacks without them suffered and
died. In reality, it is how race and class interact that made the
situation for the poor so horrible on the Gulf Coast. The rigid
caste system that punishes poor blacks and other minorities also

targets poor whites. Even among the oppressed, however, there are stark differences. Concentrated poverty doesn't victimize poor whites in the same way it does poor blacks. For instance, the racial divide in car ownership discussed earlier partially reflects income differences between the races. However, as if to prove that not all inequalities are equal, even poor whites are far more likely to have access to cars than are poor blacks.[9] In New Orleans, 53 percent of poor blacks were without cars while just 17 percent of poor whites lacked access to cars.[10] The racial disparity in class effects shows up in education as well. Even poor white children are far less likely to live in, or to attend school in, neighborhoods where poverty is highly concentrated.

Moreover, one must also account for how the privileges of whiteness that transcend class open up opportunities for poor whites that are off limits to the black poor, whether it is a job offer at a restaurant wary of blacks or a schoolroom slot in a largely white, stable community. This is not to deny the vicious caste tensions that separate poor and working class whites from their middle-class and upper-class peers. Such tensions result in a dramatically different quality of life for the well-off and the have-nots. I simply aim to underscore the pull of racial familiarity that is often an unspoken variable, and sometimes the crucial difference, in the lives of the white and non-white poor. It is bad enough to be white and poor; it is worse still to be black, or brown, and female, and young, and poor. Simply said, race makes class hurt more.

In African American life, class and caste differences show up most dramatically in the chasms between the black fortunate and the black poor. As I watched Hurricane Katrina sweep waves of mostly poor and black folk into global view, I thought of the controversy stirred by Bill Cosby's assault on the black poor—that they are detrimentally promiscuous, disinclined to education, unappreciative of good speech, determined to saddle their kids with weird names, and bent on blaming the white man for all their ills. Cosby's views were widely celebrated in the press, and in many quarters of black America, especially among the black elite—the *Afristocracy*.[11] Those few who were publicly critical of Cosby were said to be making excuses for the black poor while denying their need to be responsible for their own destinies. Others agreed with Cosby that the poor hampered their own progress because they were either too lazy or too ignorant to do better. In any case, Cosby, and a slew of critics, believed that the black poor suffered because they desired or deserved to be poor.

In the aftermath of Katrina, some of the same black critics who had previously sided with Cosby suddenly decried conservative visions of the black poor that, interestingly enough, accord quite well with the comedian's views. For instance, *Atlanta Journal-Constitution* editorial page editor Cynthia Tucker penned a column, "Katrina Exposes Our Callous Treatment of the Poor," nearly a week after the storm struck.[12] She began dramatically—"Here in America, the land of opportunity, we gave up on the poor more than two decades ago." She writes that under Ronald Reagan "we learned that the poor were simply too lazy to improve their prospects and their misery was their own fault." Tucker argues that we "not only gave up trying to help the poor, but we also bought the argument that trying to assist them, especially through government programs, would just make matters worse."

The right-wingers, she says, convinced us that the poor are illiterate, sick, and unemployed because of welfare, and because they choose to be. "So we turned our backs on the impoverished and tuned them out, leaving them stranded in the worst neighborhoods, worst schools and the worst geography." Tucker writes that the images of the poor in the wake of Katrina shouldn't surprise us, since it is the outgrowth of a culture that has left the poor to their own devices. Tucker concludes her column with a rousing portrayal of the insular attitudes that deny the privileges of the well to do, blame the poor for their ills, and sweep the plight of the poor under our collective social carpet.

In fact, it's easy for all of us who live in relative prosperity to forget that most of us are here because we had the good sense to be born to the right parents. While a few impoverished young adults can still scratch and claw their way into the mainstream, it is getting harder and harder to do so as the industrial jobs that created the great middle class are disappearing. (Why do you think so many working-class sons and daughters volunteer for the armed forces?) Income inequality is increasing in this country; the latest census shows that the number of people living in poverty is rising. Still, a few predictable voices on the far-right fringe are already thinking up ways to blame Hurricane Katrina's victims for their plight. Some are playing up the lawlessness of a few thugs; others are casting responsibility for the crisis solely on local authorities. Haven't we listened to those callous self-promoters long enough? Hurricane Katrina overwhelmed levees and exploded the conventional wisdom about a shared American prosperity, exposing a group of people so poor they didn't have $50 for a bus ticket out of town. If we want to learn something from this disaster, the lesson ought to be: America's poor deserve better than this.[13]

But less than a year before Tucker's heroic defense of the vulnerable, she had heartily endorsed Cosby's equally callous condemnation of the black poor. In a column entitled "Bill Cosby's Pointed Remarks May Spark Much-Needed Debate," Tucker lauded the comedian–cum–social critic for his willingness to address the black poor's "self-inflicted wounds" in his "point-edly politically incorrect" diatribe against the black poor.[14] After briefly acknowledging that American society "still bears some responsibility for the failure of so many black Americans to join the economic and cultural mainstream," Tucker asked if black Americans shouldn't "acknowledge that, at the dawn of the 21st century, personal responsibility has at least as much to do with success in modern America as race, especially since the Supreme Court decision in *Brown v. Board* rolled back much of systemic racism?"[15]

A few months later, in a column entitled "Bill Cosby's Plain-Spokenness Comes Not a Moment Too Soon," Tucker affirmed the need for the Afristocracy to bear down on their less-fortunate kin by favorably citing the earlier example of black elites doing just that. "Throughout the first half of the 20th century, accomplished blacks routinely policed the behavior of their less-polished brethren, urging thrift, moderation, tidiness."[16] Such policing of black behavior gave way to a black leadership class during the civil rights movement that was loath to admit black failure for fear that it "would damage the movement," while black power advocates "denounced any black critic of black failure as a race traitor." Tucker concludes her column comparing American blacks to their kin throughout the diaspora who come to this country and succeed against the odds. She draws the lesson from their success that race simply isn't that big a barrier to black achievement.

But black parents ought to note this, as well: The success of black immigrants strongly suggests that race is no great barrier to achievement. While many black activists contend that there is still a grave disadvantage in being the descendant of slaves, it is hard to see what that could be. (Note, too, that black West Indians are also the descendants of slaves.) Yes, our ancestors suffered. But the 21st-century racist aims his hate at the color of our skin—not at where we came from or who our grandparents were.[17]

Nowhere does Tucker mention, as she did in her column after Katrina, the conservative philosophy and policies that hamper the progress and achievement of the black poor. No mention of deindustrialization, fortunate birth to middle-class parents, or the income inequality she previously addressed as reasons for poverty. Absent is the sense that blaming the poor for their problems is but the reflection of our callous refusal to acknowledge society's role in black poverty. Completely missing is the insight that Katrina brought to Tucker: that is, that we have collective responsibility for banishing the poor to the margins of the economy through horrible communities, schools, and living conditions. After Katrina, Tucker saw social and political responsibility; whereas after Cosby, she had seen only personal responsibility and self-determining fate. It is not that Tucker is unaware of the need to balance the call for personal and social responsibility—she pays lip service to the latter in her Cosby columns. But she tips the scales heavily in favor of the poor creating the conditions of their success or failure. Thus she relegates her citation of the social forces that constrain them to a footnote. When it concerns Cosby's carping, she is no longer outraged with society having turned its back on the poor—as if a black back turner is not as destructive and influential in his denunciations as a white conservative. Instead, Tucker joins Cosby in calling for Afristocrats to police the behavior of the poor. Tucker's endorsement of such elitism is telling, a symptom of the condescension and paternalism that the Afristocracy has historically displayed toward the poor.

It seems that Tucker only opposes assaults on the poor when

they originate from white society. She can only detect the heinous disregard for the social conditions that plague the poor when they emerge outside the race. But when the flag of attack waves broadly in black culture, especially under the leadership of an embittered Afristocrat such as Bill Cosby—an attack that is often joined by figures like talk show host Larry Elder or writer Shelby Steele—Tucker can only join the cavalry and ride roughshod over the nuanced and complex positions she otherwise upholds. As Tucker well knows, Cosby's words count even more because he is a celebrated comic whose race-neutral politics have endeared him to a white audience that he has never tested, or turned against, in the way he has the black poor.

Of course, Cosby doesn't stand alone. Katrina's waters washed up hard against the class bigotry of all those black figures such as economists Thomas Sowell and Walter Williams who chimed in on Bill Cosby's attack on the poor. There are many Afristocrats who actively fought against the poor, or who simply forgot them. There are even some who, like President George Bush, don't care about poor blacks. Such views prevailed even among some black elites in the Delta. The black upper classes in eastern New Orleans, for example, have educated their children at predominantly black magnet schools such as McDonogh No. 35 Senior High School, Warren Easton Fundamental, and Eleanor McMain Magnet Secondary School, while the masses of poor blacks suffer in substandard schools. When we black folk rail against the moral failings of the poor while overlooking the inequality and deprivation they confront, whether in New Orleans or in Washington, D.C., we only inflame the suffering of the vulnerable without relieving their plight.

There is, too, a curious color dynamic that sadly persists in our culture. In fact, New Orleans invented the brown paper bag party—usually at a gathering in a home—where anyone darker than the bag attached to the door was denied entrance. The brown bag criterion survives as a metaphor for how the black cultural elite quite literally establishes caste along color lines *within* black life. On my many trips to New Orleans, whether to lecture at one of its universities or colleges, to preach from one of its pulpits, or to speak at an empowerment seminar during the annual Essence Music Festival, I have observed color politics at work among black folk. The cruel color code has to be defeated by our love for one another.

Of course, it is a marvelous sight to see so many black folk rally around the poor after Katrina. The press noted how Katrina was a "generation-defining catastrophe" that galvanized black generosity and solidarity throughout the nation.[18] Black churches around the country raised millions of dollars for relief efforts. Several artists held or participated in fund-raisers. There was the S.O.S. (Saving OurSelves) Relief Telethon broadcast on BET and cosponsored by the National Urban League, the American Red Cross, the Hip-Hop Summit Action Network, and Essence Communications, which raised $10 million. The Jazz at Lincoln Center's "Higher Ground" relief benefit was spearheaded by New Orleans native and the center's artistic director Wynton Marsalis. There were several fund-raisers hosted by hip-hop artists, including Mississippi native David Banner's Heal the Hood Hurricane Relief Concert. There were also extensive fund-raising efforts made by New Orleans natives Master P and Juvenile, Chicago's Twista, and Brooklyn writer and activist Kevin Powell—joined by Common, Kanye West, Mos Def, and Talib Kweli. Many black professional athletes also visited the Gulf Coast and contributed money and time to relief efforts.[19]

We should be reminded, however, that the black poor are flooded daily by material misery; they are routinely buffeted by harsh racial winds. The obvious absence of the black blessed at times of ongoing difficulty—to defend and protect the poor in principled fashion—underscores the woefully episodic character of black social regard. Lots of well-to-do black folk are doing a lot to help, but too many of us have left the black poor stranded on islands of social isolation and class alienation. Episodes of goodwill and compassion are no replacement for structural change. As Martin Luther King, Jr., said at Riverside Church exactly a year before he was murdered:

> On the one hand we are called to play the good Samaritan on life's roadside; but that will be only an initial act. One day we must come to see that the whole Jericho road must be transformed so that men and women will not be constantly beaten and robbed as they make their journey on life's highway. True compassion is more than flinging a coin to a beggar; it is not haphazard and superficial. It comes to see that an edifice which produces beggars needs restructuring.[20]

Charity is no substitute for justice. If we never challenge a social order that allows some to accumulate wealth—even if they decide to help the less fortunate—while others are short-changed, then even acts of kindness end up supporting unjust arrangements. We must never ignore the injustices that make charity necessary, or the inequalities that make it possible.

What made Kanye West's defense of the black poor so admirable is that it suggested the willingness of a rich black celebrity to sacrifice his reputation, perhaps even his livelihood, and surely his comfort, to speak out on behalf of his less-fortunate brothers and sisters. The week after he was featured on the cover of *Time* magazine as the "smartest man in pop music," West made his stand against Bush and conservative social neglect on television.[21] West's comments brought a predictable firestorm of controversy and criticism. Television ingenue Kelly

Carlson, star of the series "Nip/Tuck," was offended. "I don't think a lot of people this day and age dislike black people," the young white starlet said. "I mean I think we've kind of moved on from that. So to go on television and say that, I think it's tacky, I think it's very low rent."[22]

Obviously Carlson is unaware of all the comments made by whites in the aftermath of Katrina as to why "lazy, ignorant blacks" didn't remove themselves from New Orleans when they heard the storm was coming. She must be oblivious to several incidents that occurred after Katrina struck that support West's comments and that render hers naive at best, and willfully ignorant at worst. As Tulane University professor Lawrence N. Powell contends, racial animosity for black folk flared when they were barred from the predominantly white neighborhood of Gretna outside of New Orleans, and when a congressman celebrated nature's destruction of public housing.

I don't how to get this point across without being blunt, but white supremacists have dropped the pretense of code-speak and are saying flat-out, "don't let them back in," using the n-word for emphasis. These raw words echoed at the police blockade on the Mississippi River bridge connecting New Orleans with the West Bank of suburban Jefferson parish, where policemen from Gretna, a notoriously racist town, fired shots over the heads of Convention Center evacuees as they walked toward the on-ramp pursuant to instructions that buses were waiting on the other side to carry them to safety. . . . A friend who rode out the storm in Uptown New Orleans . . . tells of witnessing gas station owners urging the military to keep blacks out. Several Uptown swells and white-shoe lawyers who huddled in the Hyatt Hotel across from the crowded misery inside the sodden and unsanitary Superdome were almost jubilant about the ethnic cleansing wrought by Katrina, so friends in the media report. Republican Congressman Richard Baker, representing a prosperous area of Baton Rouge, said this of the storm's aftermath: "We finally cleaned up public housing in New Orleans. We couldn't do it, but God did."[23]

New Orleans rapper Master P questioned whether West's comments were genuine or inspired by commercial interests. "I hope the comments that Kanye West made is sincere and this is not a promotional thing to sell records," Master P commented. "I know he's got a new album out right now." Master P's personal involvement may have clouded his understanding of the critical relationship between politics and the relief for the poor he so desperately desired. "We gotta save people. We need George Bush, we need the Mayor [of New Orleans], we need the [Louisiana] Governor. I've lost people, I know how real it is. This ain't about a promotional thing with me. I've got loved ones out there missing."[24] But unlike Carlson, West understood, indeed felt, the profound disregard for black life that the president's policies reinforced. And unlike Master P, West understood that one of the reasons more help hadn't gotten to the black poor more quickly is because of a delayed governmental response that had racial roots.

West proved that his comments were anchored in reason and passionate commitment, and not a one-off rant that was more cathartic than critical, when he defended himself a week later. "People are like, 'Yo, aren't you scared that something's going to happen to you?'" West said. "I was like, 'I can think of a lot worse things that could happen to me, like how about not eating for five days? Or how about not knowing where my f*** family is? Everybody's always concerned about theyself."[25] West was critical of the nation's denial of poverty, but he warned that it would come back to haunt us. "I just feel like America's always been pushing the [impoverished] under the counter, trying to act like it's not really there. And what happens if you're cleaning the kitchen and you're always dusting something under the counter? If you spill something, it's going come up and be in your . . . face."[26]

Not only did West redeem the sometimes sorry state of a hip-hop world careening on the gaudy trinkets of its own success—booze, broads, and bling—but his gesture signaled a political courage on the part of the black blessed that is today all too rare. Many hip-hop artists were encouraged by West's words, affirming that he echoed the sentiments of less-known artists. Still others took them as the occasion to challenge themselves and their peers to bridge the gap between their art and their practice. "We've been screaming this for five years," David Banner proclaimed about the critique of the Bush administration put forth by many rap artists. "You listen to your David Banners, Dead Prez, listen to rap music period. This is what rappers have been screaming all the time. The problem is America concentrates more on our cuss words. They don't hear the pain in the music all the time. You just finally had somebody who has the power Kanye has, who said it at the right time."[27]

Fellow Southern rapper T.I. challenged the tall-talking em-cees, who brag about living a lavish lifestyle, to furnish proof of their treasure in their philanthropy. "I called everybody's bluff who be talking all that ballin' sh**," T.I. said. "Popping all them bottles in the club . . . talking about how much girls and jewelry and cars they got. Let's see how much money they've got for a good cause. Basically, I told everybody to put their money where their mouths are, and if you ain't got no money to give to the cause, I don't want to hear that sh** no more."[28] Chicago rapper Twista challenged black people to embrace the poor, who are wrongfully neglected by the government. "They've been bogus, so what is everybody so shocked about?" Twista said of the political establishment. "I feel the response was real slow, but I look at my own harder than I look at them. I feel like us as black folks were supposed to stop what we was doing, put all that sh** down and get these [disaster victims] straight."[29]

New Orleans rapper Juvenile, best known in the mainstream for the trend-setting single "Back That Thang Up," lost his home and cars in the flood, but was critical of the poverty and corruption that plagued his beloved hometown before Katrina. "All we lost was our home," he said. "A lot of people lost their lives. But we lost beyond a house or a door. We lost an environment. So we lost everybody. Everybody lost. We lost that spirit . . . There ain't nothing like New Orleans. We got spirit. We the smallest city, the highest in poverty. We was the lowest in the education system. We was just about to go on strike with the teachers. The school board system was corrupt. Our police system is corrupt. Our judicial system is corrupt."[30] Juvenile criticized the federal government but also suggested that, given the extreme poverty of many residents, the storm clouds of Katrina may have contained a silver lining. "It didn't take a hurricane for me to do nothing for New Orleans," he said, "'cause like Chris Rock said, we was f***** up before the hurricane hit. Y'all should've *been* sending us . . . FEMA. We've been f***** up. For a lot of us that sh** was a blessing."[31]

Perhaps the most articulate, well-spoken supporter of Kanye West's perspective is an NBA athlete whose political bona fides were established long before Katrina. "I definitely agree with Kanye West," said the Washington Wizards' Etan Thomas, who raised cash and gathered supplies for the hurricane survivors. "Had this been a rich, lily-white suburban area that got hit, you think they would have had to wait five days to get food or water? When the hurricane hit in Florida, Bush made sure those people got help the next day. But now, when you are dealing with a majority poorer class of black people, it takes five days? Then you still don't send help but instead send the National Guard to 'maintain order'? Are you kidding me?"[32] The author of *More Than an Athlete*, a collection of verse that assails racism, the death penalty, and materialism, Thomas has made a conscious choice to embrace the heroic legacies of outspoken athletes who made their marks in their professions as a springboard to raising social consciousness. "I admire athletes of the past, like Bill Russell, Muhammad Ali, Jim Brown, John Carlos and Tommie Smith, Kareem [Abdul-Jabbar]—athletes who used their position as a platform to speak out on social issues and stand up for a cause. Basketball is not my life. A quote I live by is: 'I speak my mind because biting my tongue would make my pride bleed.'"[33]

Kanye West's words, and those of the figures who supported him, suggest that not nearly enough of us are invested in consistently raising our voices for the voiceless. Narrow career interests and risk aversion define our number. Too many of us are "safe Negroes" who don't realize that we can never really be safe until all black people are safe. Kanye West saw his identity tied to the identity of the poor, and realized that the people who were drowning were "my people." That simple act of identification is the primal scream of recognition of kin through the bonds of shared history and conscience.

If Bush and black elites have forgotten the poor, black artists from the Delta have remembered their peers with eloquence. It began with the incredibly fertile traditions of the blues, and with the jazz that found its originating moments in the thick intersection of complex black identities in New Orleans. Poor blacks felt their humanity affirmed in the soaring sounds of a music whose ambition was to reshape the world it encountered—and to let everyone listen in on the worlds it had created. The black poor of New Orleans—and the tough neighborhoods from which they emerged and the even tougher urban forces they had to negotiate to survive—gained coverage in the hip-hop narratives, and entrepreneurial energies, of Master P, Juvenile, Lil Wayne, Baby, Mannie Fresh, Mia X, and Lil Mo. When Master P, for instance, tired of critics blaming poor blacks for the underground drug economy, he retorted in rhyme, pointing a finger at bigger forces: "I don't own no plane / I don't own no boat / I don't ship no dope from coast to coast." In another rap, Master P writes to the president: "Dear Mr. President I live in the hood / Where people live bad but say its all good." Later in the song Master P addresses the disparate treatment of poor blacks and white people, saying black folk "die in the ghetto / Put they face on a shirt / White folks get killed and it's a city wide search."

It is perhaps ironic that wretchedly poor New Orleans is the birthplace of bling, the ostentatious, flashy brilliance of eye-popping jewelry and the lavish lifestyles on which it rests. And yet those same projects and slums about which these stars rap— and the invisible-at-any-other-time dwellers they shout out, and the attendant social miseries and pathologies that they meticulously detail—are hardly ever engaged or thought about, except as fodder for the local media's fascination with blacks spilling other blacks' blood, or to foster even more paranoia in largely white suburbs.

But there are also hip-hop artists who mined the rich cultural resources in the Delta even before its heritage was stormed by Katrina. While many hip-hoppers from the Delta spin woeful tales of absent fathers, some have tapped the roots of paternal influence to feed their artistic imagination. In 2005, hip-hop legend

Nas joined his noted musician father Olu Dara for an imaginative duet on the song "Bridging the Gap" that plunged deeply into the region's distinctive musical history. From its opening blues vamp, drenched in a Bo Diddley–meets–Muddy Waters rhythmic swagger, it is clear that Nas and Olu Dara have wed two powerful art forms in exploring the area's vibrant musical tradition. By now it's a cliché for hip-hoppers to join the rap-rock brigade. But there are precious few rappers who've bothered to tap the fertile sonic vein that produced rock—and hip-hop as well. After all, with their double entendres, colorful language, relentless boasting, homespun machismo, and tragicomic sensibility, the blues are a forceful parent to rap. Olu Dara and Nas brilliantly play off of the kinship of their music and manhood on their breathtaking collaboration. "Bridging the Gap" is a soulful tribute to the roots shared by father and son, by the rural and the urban, and by two supremely gifted artists.

"This is a song that, without us even trying . . . [shows that] his music and my music in reality are the same," Nas says to me about his spirited teaming up with Dara. "No matter if it started years ago in the Delta, or if it was out in Queensbridge, it all comes back around." In the song's opening lines, Dara tersely spits his lyrics as the weeping harmonica and the shuffling cadence of African-flavored drums snake around his beautifully thrashing vocals. Like his son has done for New York, Dara declares his Mississippi roots and his wild youth. The elder statesman then tells of conceiving a son as he cleverly adapts Muddy Waters's bravado to his musical tree in a prophetic couplet: "I named the boy Nasir, all the boys called him Nas / I told him as a youngster, he'll be the greatest man alive." Nas picks up the conceptual thread and, taking a cue from his father, pares production back to the basics and spins a poignant tale of his artistic mastery and familial roots, proclaiming that he and Dara are "bridging the gap / from the blues to jazz to rap / the history of music on this track."

But "Bridging the Gap" also celebrates the strong moral and physical presence of the father, an uplifting counterpoint to the plague of fatherlessness in hip-hop. "I grew up around my father and grandfather, then here I come, and here's Nas," Dara testifies. "That's four generations that I've witnessed, and been a part of. To me that was a natural thing, because I grew up in Natchez. . . . It was very unusual *not* to have a father around." It was only after he migrated to New York and had two sons that Dara discovered the oddness of being congratulated for a paternal bond he took for granted. "I remember when Nas and his brother were born, and I would be with them all the time. And people would stop me on the street [and say], 'It's so nice to see a father with his son.' I was taken aback by that. . . . I looked around and I thought, 'I'm an anomaly,' which is a sad thing."

If they are indeed an anomaly, Nas and Dara intend with their bracing song to encourage others by their example of mutual respect and love. "I really look at this record as an example of how things can turn out positive later on," Nas says reflectively. "My father's made it, he survived, and a lot of his peers are dead and gone. Some of my peers are dead and gone, but I still made it to where I am today. Through all the trials and tribulations of life, here we are, we can smile at each other, we can stand strong together, and say life is good and the love is there. It's a great, great example for all American families to look at. And for those kids, and those rappers, who didn't have their fathers around, now it's their turn to be responsible when they have their kids. They've got to try that much harder to stick around."

"Bridging the Gap" is also remarkable for its heartening vision of masculinity nurtured by learning, tradition, and affection rather than brutality or violence. "I learned from [my father] the difference between a tough guy putting on a front—because he didn't know anything and he had to protect himself and he felt unloved—and a real man," Nas emphasizes in animated fashion. "A real man can let you see his vulnerability, and use it as bait, because he opens himself up to you, and [when] he opens you up to his vulnerability, he's testing himself. . . . Because at the end of the day, our confidence about our strength is where our power is. So we can open up that vulnerability that all these other so-called men are trying to protect and [use to] feel safe. I feel safe in my skin. I feel safe walking in my shoes. I feel safe about who I am. And I trust that I'm always going to be on top of my game."

The song reaffirms Nas's standing as one of hip-hop's most fiercely gifted lyricists. Listening to it in the aftermath of Katrina, "Bridging the Gap" also confirms Nas's courage to go where few rappers have gone as successfully before: into the vibrant heart of the Delta, into the edifying love between father and son, and into the murky waters of American manhood. This time around, he's looked back to move us forward. As he insightfully observers, "the blues came from gospel, gospel from blues / the slaves were harmonizing them 'ahs' and 'oohs' / old school new school no school rules / all these years I been voicin' my blues." In that pithy rhyme, Nas captures the finely mingled lineage of black music. He also articulates black music's willingness to tell the truth about darkness and to offer hope in defiance of life's utter bleakness. At their best, that's what Nas, Olu Dara, the blues, and hip-hop are all about. That message of hope offers moral recovery for the black folk in the Delta who can cling to their musical roots and nurture the future through their artistic vision.

I also heard echoes of the Delta at the 2005 annual gathering of the Congressional Black Caucus. At a program on education sponsored by Congressman Major Owens, I listened to the powerful lyrics of The Militant Advocates, a rap group associated with the social activist Bob Moses—who risked life and limb and went bravely to Mississippi at the height of the civil rights movement to teach the people and to register them to vote.[34] The Militant Advocates—composed of Baltimore high school students Wayne Washington, Chris Goodman, Xzavier Cheaton, and Bryant Muldrew—poignantly portrayed the political and natural circumstances that victimized folk in the storm in New Orleans. Their mature perspective on "Tribute to the Hurricane" was heartening and offered hope that hip-hop still inspires youth to critical reflection on social misery. Two of the verses amply illustrate their gift.

> (CHORUS: all together)
> What if, your hopes, your dreams, your goals, your love,
>   your life
> Went straight down the drain
> And it wasn't because of a gun or a knife, or some drugs, but
> Bad weather had the Hurricane pouring down rain
> And y'all know that we know how y'all feel, so be a man and
>   stand tall
> And shed those tears, cause that stuff that's going down in
>   New Orleans
> Let's turn a nightmare straight to a dream.
>
> (1ST VERSE: Wayne a.k.a. snook)
> I have these tears in my eyes & they ain't coming out
> Like the ocean of my body just become a doubt
> & my mouth wide open & I cannot shout
> About the stuff that got people squeezing out
> My eyes is on the screen of fox 45

And I'm scared it's talking about the people's lives
About the husband, the kid, the seniors, & wives
About the struggle, the stress, & the life that they strive
So I'm rapping to the peeps that got it going on
Be men, stand tall, & give out a arm
We a family so don't be scared to share
So let's extend the hand & destroy the nightmare.

(VERSE 4: Chris a.k.a. CMG)
Natural disasters
Catastrophes
They produce evacuees
Where's the help the A.I.D.
It just seems so strange to me
The time it took to look at the state and federal checkbook
Didn't you see the eyes that cried for help?
Broadcast on the news all over the TV
People's lives straight down the tube
They lost it all even if they had nothing to lose
But let's look at the facts and clues
Let's seek the truth
Baltimore is very similar to the N.O.
As far as kin folks and how we blast pistols
And many issues
Are nearly identical
So our after effects would be identical
Education is minimal
Very few can fill out A.I.D. forms
No one's afraid for 'em
So the National Guard put the aim on 'em
And let rounds spray then they lay and decay
In a way that's ok for the men in charge.

If the Militant Advocates helped to frame for their generation the racial consequences of a natural and economic disaster, the media was critical in framing perceptions of people and events surrounding the catastrophe. This was painfully evident with a set of photos, and their accompanying captions (parts of which I will italicize for emphasis), that were widely circulated on the Internet the day after the storm struck. In the first photo, a young black man clasps items in each arm as he forges through the flood waters. The caption to the AP (Associated Press) photo of him reads: "A young man walks through chest deep flood water after *looting a grocery store* in New Orleans on Tuesday, Aug. 20, 2005. Flood waters continue to rise in New Orleans after Hurricane Katrina did extensive damage when it made landfall on Monday."[35] In the second photo, also from AP, a young white man and woman tote food items in their hands as they carry backpacks and slush through the flood waters. The caption accompanying their photograph reads: "Two residents wade through chest-deep water after *finding bread and soda from a local grocery store* after Hurricane Katrina came through the area in New Orleans, Louisiana."[36]

In this case, the captions say it all: the young black man *loots* his groceries, the white youth *find* theirs. With no stores open, the white youth clearly couldn't have found their groceries, and would have had to obtain them the same way the young black man did. It didn't appear in either photo that someone's charity was responsible for any of the people pictured receiving food, which probably means that the young black man and the white youth stormed a store to get groceries, a quite understandable move under the circumstances. While the white youth's move is rendered "quite understandable" by the language—what else were they to do, after all, and the language lessens the obvious means of their acquiring groceries—the black youth's move is rendered as legally and morally questionable. If he has "looted" then he has broken the legal and moral codes of society.

He is further alienated from his civic standing by simply being described as "a young man" while his white peers are cited as citizens—"two residents." The value judgment communicated by the photo and its caption is largely implicit, though strongly implied by the language. The captions help lend value, and a slant, to essentially neutral photographs, pictures that, on their own, suggest solidarity of circumstance between the black and white youth. But the identical character of their experience is shattered by the language, which casts their actions in contrasting lights: the white youth have been favored by serendipity and thus "naturally" exploit their luck in "finding" food, a gesture that relieves them of culpability; the black youth, by comparison, has interrupted the natural order of things to seize what didn't belong to him and thus remains responsible for his behavior.

To be sure, none of this is expressly articulated; the existing framework of racial reference suggests its meaning. Such a framework, one that weaves white innocence and black guilt into the fabric of cultural myths and racial narratives, is deeply embedded in society and affects every major American institution, including the media. How black folk are "framed"—how we are discussed, pictured, imagined, conjured to fit a negative idea of blackness, or called on to fill a slot reserved for the outlaw, thug, or savage—shapes how we are frowned on or favored in mainstream society. Words help to interpret images; language and pictures in combination reinforce ideas and stories about black identity. The words that accompany these photos, like the reams of words that accompany the images of black folk in society throughout history, help to underscore hidden bias and sleeping bigotry, often in the most innocent, gentle, and subtle form imaginable. Hence, plausible deniability is critical to such maneuvers, allowing invested parties to reply when called to account: "I didn't mean it that way"; "You're too sensitive"; "You're exaggerating"; or "You're reading too much into things." Thus, the burden to explain or justify behavior is shifted from offender to victim.

The media's role in framing blacks as outlaws and savages achieved a rare blatancy when it endlessly looped on television the same few frames of stranded blacks "looting" food and other items, largely for survival. The repetition of the scenes of black "looting" contains its own indictment: there wasn't enough film of vandalizing behavior to feature several instances. By repeating the same few scenes the media helped to spread the notion that black folk were in a state of social anarchy and were tearing violently at the fabric of civility and order. The framework didn't allow for blacks to receive the benefit of the doubt extended to the white couple that "found" food. Neither was the compelling imagery often accompanied by commentary to suggest that people who had been abandoned by their government had a right to help themselves—a theme that surely ought to have pleased the bootstrapping Republicans at the helm of the federal government. Instead, many critics bitterly lamented the actions of people who did what they had to do to survive.

To be sure, besides taking food and items to survive—as did local officials and authorities, including aides to the mayor and the police, who were given the sort of pass that the masses would never receive—black folk took clothes and appliances, and a few took guns. These blacks were drowned in a second flood of media and social criticism that vilified them for their inexcusable behavior. Even those critics who were sympathetic to the urgent conditions of the abandoned blacks felt pressured to embrace the frame of reference of black criminality before otherwise defending poor blacks. Such critics had to acknowledge that yes, these were awful and heinous acts, but still, distinctions must be made between acts of survival and acts of greed, wanton cynicism, or reckless morality. In order to defend them, their supporters had to prove that they were willing to establish a hierarchy of the "good Negro" and the "bad Negro." They often failed to realize that such moral ordering is futile in a society where the inclination to misbehavior is viewed as true of black folk in general. Although separating "worthy" from "unworthy" blacks is supposed to strengthen the cause of the "good Negro," such distinctions ultimately make all blacks more vulnerable because they grant legitimacy to a distorted racial framework. Thus, the looting for looting's sake, versus the looting for survival's sake, may appear to be a legitimate ordering of black morality, but it is just as likely to obscure how black identity is seen through a muddy lens. The very act of black folk taking food, even when conditions are oppressive, generates the sort of suspicion that white folk will not as a rule be subject to—as in the case of "looting" versus "finding" food.

Thus, when a moral distinction is made between taking food and taking other items, it denies the stigma already attached to blacks who simply sought to survive. I am not arguing that because of the ethical distortion found in drawing faulty distinctions among black folk, one cannot thereby condemn immoral behavior. I am simply suggesting that what constitutes "immoral" black behavior conveniently shifts in reference to black folk to suit the social or racial purposes of a given moment, or crisis, in the culture. Katrina was one of those moments of crisis. By exaggerating the crisis, the media proved it was caught in a crisis of exaggeration.

Moreover, the hand wringing over poor black folk "looting" exposes the ugly reality that may explain the apparent glee with which some black folk "looted": that property matters more than poor and black people in many quarters of the culture. Some people took clothing items because they needed to change from their soiled clothing where they had to urinate or defecate on themselves. Some people took televisions to barter for food. Some saw luxury items as capital to purchase momentary relief from their misery, whether through exchanging those for food or for money that might, however illusorily, get them and their families free of their situation. Perhaps they could pay somebody with a car to drive them to safety on higher ground. And some of them must have learned their seemingly illogical behavior—that is, for those critics who suggest the black poor couldn't do anything practical or purposeful with the items they filched—from a culture of consumption from which they had been barred. The lesson of that culture seemed to be: have it because you want it.

Of course some were greedy, but that greed wasn't any different—in fact, was its naked face in miniature—than the greed that passed as normal and desirable when it showed up in the upper, richer, whiter classes. To begrudge poor people a gleeful moment of rebellion against property—by taking it, by possessing it, by hoarding it, and by having a taste of things they had been denied all their lives, nice things that they saw the people for whom they slaved routinely enjoy and treasure even more than they did the poor black folk who stoked their leisure, is an act of arrogant and self-righteous indifference to the plight of the black poor, most of whom, mind you, would never in a million years take anything that didn't belong to them. But desperate people do in desperation what capitalist and political and cultural looters do daily—steal and give little thought to its moral consequence. In a comparative ethical framework, the black poor come out looking a lot more justified than do the disingenuous critics who lambaste them.

That is why New Orleans rapper Juvenile expressed compassion for the black poor and called into question the sanctification of property that would be washed away anyhow. "I don't call it looting," the rapper said. "They stole everything from out of my house, and I'm not mad at the person that stole out of my house. Because the hurricane was gonna hit and the house was gonna get hit with 25 feet of storm surging. It was gonna be damaging. I couldn't do nothing with it anyway. . . . And I think the looting in New Orleans, I don't call it looting, I call it survival."[37] Juvenile explains the logic of folk stealing televisions in order to better their chances of survival. "I might could get this TV and sell it to somebody and get some money. They talking about the TVs and VCRs, 'Why would you take that?' There's still people that got money that could buy where money was still useful. We don't know. The average person don't know. They wasn't down there in the waters. They had people who just wanted some herb to calm they damn nerves."[38]

As journalist Jordan Flaherty argues, the real criminal activity in Katrina can't be laid at the feet of the black poor, but at those who benefited from unjust economic and racial arrangements long before the storm struck. Moreover, the media framed black survivors as lawless thugs while ignoring the social conditions that made their lives hell.

While the rich escaped New Orleans, those with nowhere to go and no way to get there were left behind. Adding salt to the wound, the local and national media have spent the last week demonizing those left behind. As someone that loves New Orleans and the people in it, this is the part of this tragedy that hurts me the most, and it hurts me deeply. No sane person should classify someone who takes food from indefinitely closed stores in a desperate, starving city as a "looter," but that's just what the media did over and over again. Sheriffs and politicians talked of having troops protect stores instead of perform rescue operations. Images of New Orleans' hurricane-ravaged population were transformed into black, out-of-control, criminals. As if taking a stereo from a store that will clearly be insured against loss is a greater crime than the governmental neglect and incompetence that did billions of dollars of damage and destroyed a city. This media focus is a tactic, just as the eighties focus on "welfare queens" and "super-predators" obscured the simultaneous and much larger crimes of the Savings and Loan scams and mass layoffs, the hyper-exploited people of New Orleans are being used as a scapegoat to cover up much larger crimes.[39]

The media also framed the black poor when it helped to spread rumors about violent and animalistic black behavior in the shelters to which they fled. Television reports and newspaper accounts brimmed with the unutterable horror of what black folk were doing to each other and their helpers in the Superdome and the convention center: the rape of women and babies, sniper attacks on military helicopters, folk killed for food and water, armed gang members assaulting the vulnerable, dozens of bodies being shoved into a freezer.[40] As the *Times-Picayune* reported, the "picture that emerged was one of the impoverished masses of flood victims resorting to utter depravity, randomly attacking each other, as well as the police trying to protect them and the rescue workers trying to save them."[41] Nearly every one of the allegations proved to be baseless rumor. Of course, the mayor and police commissioner of New Orleans helped spread the rumors as well in famous interviews on *Oprah*. Police commissioner Eddie Compass broke down crying while describing "the little babies getting raped," and Mayor Nagin spoke of the mayhem of people "in that frickin' Superdome for five days watching dead bodies, watching hooligans killing people, raping people."[42]

But hyperbole pervaded the media as well. A day before evacuations began at the Superdome, *Fox News* television issued an "alert" warning of "robberies, rapes, carjackings, riots and murder. Violent gangs are roaming the streets at night, hidden by the cover of darkness." The *Los Angeles Times* featured a lead news story that dramatically reported National Guard troops taking "positions on rooftops, scanning for snipers and armed mobs as seething crowds of refugees milled below, desperate to flee. Gunfire crackled in the distance." Although the *New York Times* was more cautious in its reporting, noting that reports couldn't be verified, it still repeated stories and reports about widespread violence and unrest. And neither was the exaggeration quarantined to the states. The *Ottawa Sun*, a Canadian tabloid, reported unverified news of "a man seeking help gunned down by a National Guard Soldier" and "a young man run down and then shot by a New Orleans police officer." And the *Evening Standard*, a London newspaper, compared the carnage and chaos to the Mel Gibson futuristic film *Mad Max* and to the novel *Lord of the Flies*.[43]

Most of the information reported by the media proved to be urban legends and cultural myths that swirled in the toxic stew unleashed by Katrina. "It just morphed into this mythical place where the most unthinkable deeds were being done," said National Guard spokesman Major Ed Bush. As government help failed to arrive, a conceptual vacuum opened up that was filled with a powerful mix of lies and legends. There were reports that an infant's body was found in a trash can, that there were sharks unschooled from Lake Pontchartrain swimming through the city's business district, and that hundreds of bodies had been stashed in the basement of the Superdome.[44] A physician from FEMA arrived at the Superdome after international reports of the killings, rapes, murders, and gang violence, expecting a huge cache of bodies. "I've got a report of 200 bodies," National Guard Colonel Thomas Beron recalls the doctor saying to him. "The real total was six."[45] Four people had died of natural causes, one overdosed on drugs, and the other committed suicide by jumping to his death.

Eddie Jordan, the Orleans Parish District Attorney, was outraged by the media's glaring inaccuracies in framing the shelter survivors as animals. "I had the impression that at least 40 or 50 murders had occurred at the two sites," Jordan said. "It's unfortunate we saw these kinds of stories saying crime had taken place on a massive scale when that wasn't the case. And they [national media outlets] have done nothing to follow up on any of these cases, they just accepted what people [on the street] told them. . . . It's not consistent with the highest standards of journalism."[46]

Of course, given the nature of rape—a crime that is dramatically underreported under normal conditions—it is likely that such crimes indeed did occur, but, it seems, with nothing near the frequency as reported. Neither has there been any verification of widespread reports of murder—in fact, only one person in the convention center appears to have been a victim of homicide, by stabbing, but even that case is murky. It is likely that there were indeed some thugs present, but is seems clear that they were Antediluvian Thugs—thugs before the flood. But they didn't have much of an impact on the crowds at the Superdome and the convention center. Later, before he was asked to resign by Mayor Nagin, Compass admitted that he was wrong, adding, "The information I had at the time, I thought it was credible." Nagin, too, acknowledged that he didn't have, and probably never would have, an accurate picture of the alleged anarchy that prevailed. "I'm having a hard time getting a good body count."[47]

The *Times-Picayune* captured the remarkable dignity of the crowds and the grossly exaggerated nature of the reports of social disarray that occurred among the evacuees when it concluded that

> Few of the widely reported atrocities have been backed with evidence. The piles of bodies never materialized, and soldiers, police officers and rescue personnel on the front lines say that although anarchy reigned at times and people suffered unimaginable indignities, most of the worst crimes reported at the time never happened. Military, law enforcement and medical workers agree that the flood of evacuees—about 30,000 at the Dome and an estimated 10,000 to 20,000 at the Convention Center—overwhelmed their security personnel. The 400 to 500 soldiers in the Dome could have been easily overrun by increasingly agitated crowds, but that never happened, said Col. James Knotts, a midlevel commander there. Security was nonexistent at the Convention Center, which was never designated as a shelter. Authorities provided no food, water or medical care until troops secured the building the Friday after the storm. While the Convention Center saw plenty of mischief, including massive looting and isolated gunfire, and many inside cowered in fear, the hordes of evacuees for the most part did not resort to violence, as legend has it.[48]

What fed the rumors? It seems that poor communications fostered by the breakdowns of telephones made it nearly impossible for reporters to get accurate information. But the major reason seems to be—as *Times-Picayune* editor Jim Amoss admitted—a matter of race and class. "If the dome and Convention Center had harbored large numbers of middle class white people," Amoss said, "it would not have been a fertile ground for this kind of rumor-mongering."[49] It is safe to say that the media's framework was ready to receive and recycle rumors of vicious black behavior because such rumors seemed to confirm a widely held view about poor blacks. The more outrageous the reports, the juicier the alleged details, the more poetic and breathless the news reports became. Journalists outdid each other in the competitive urge to describe and remythologize the sheer horror of the huddled black masses. No adjective or metaphor seemed alien to reporters seeking to adequately conjure the chaos of blackness being unleashed on the world in all of its despotic wizardry and evil inventiveness. The cruelty, and crudity, of the poor black evacuees seemed to be a necessary analogue to the environmental misery they endured.

Besides, the media's framing of the black poor seemed to exonerate those who hadn't gotten there quickly enough to help them. The message seemed to be: "If this is how they act, if this is who they are, then their inhumanity is a justification for not rushing to their rescue." The government seemed to be let off the hook. Other folk may have argued that such negative actions among poor blacks could have been arrested had the government arrived on time. Still others thought that the government should have gotten there earlier to arrest the folk themselves. Law and order was a recurring motif of the criticism lobbed at the black evacuees: there was simply no excuse—not even one of the worst natural disasters in the nation's history—for them to misbehave in such fashion. It seems that the status quo and the powers that be needed precisely the sociological framework of the poor that the media presented.

How ironic, then, that the media should have gathered such kudos for locating again that part of their skeletal structure that threads down their backs. It is really doubly ironic. First, because it was at the expense of black suffering—which television reporters and cameras undoubtedly brought home to America in full color—that journalists got credit for regaining their voice. The edifying skepticism displayed by nearly the entire crew of frontline reporters, and on occasion those stationed at a safer distance at their home studios, was a lively and refreshing departure from the predictable banter that sadly passes for refined suspicion. It may have not been very refined, but the outright combativeness that frequently flared for a few days in the media was positively bracing. But the fact that it took such an utter tragedy for the media to stop pretending it was neutral—and to find a way between disingenuous claims of objectivity and crushing bias dressed up as fairness—is ultimately sad. That means that unless another crisis comes along—and already, despite protests to the contrary, America, and the media, have largely moved on past the tragic revelations of Katrina—the media will slink back into spineless endorsements of black pathology, especially for the poor, in one form or another.

The celebration of the media during Katrina is perhaps ultimately ironic since it is the media that has largely been responsible for communicating the culture's spleenful bigotry toward the black poor. To be championed as the defenders of the very population the media has harmed so much, whether intending to or not, should provide more than one occasion of intense discomfort and squirming for journalists. Unless the media reframe their very reference to blackness and poverty, which is not likely to occur without intense pressure, they will have not only failed to earn the encomiums they've received, but worse, they will have set back the quest to truly expose the problems the black poor face by pretending to have done so. As framers of black life, the media can either illumine for the world our complexity or shutter the dizzying dynamism of our identities behind stale stereotypes and callous clichés.

The media framed the evacuees at first as refugees, a term that caused denunciations by black leaders because it seemed to deny that black folk were citizens of the nation. A few critics responded by suggesting that, technically, the black poor could be considered refugees because they were fleeing a catastrophe and seeking refuge away from their homes. But what such clarifications missed is the spiritual truth of black identity that rested more in connotation than denotation, more in signification than grammar. Black folk felt that they had already, for so long, been treated as foreigners in their own land. We desperately sought to claim the rights and privileges that our bitterly fought-for membership in the society should provide.

I saw flashes of this when I visited one of the shelters in Houston for the black displaced, dislocated, and dispersed. When I stepped into the Reliant Center, where thousands of mostly black and poor folk from New Orleans, Mississippi, and Alabama had been chased by Hurricane Katrina's ugly force, I felt the hurt and desperation of a people whose middle name throughout history has been exile. A sea of green nylon cots was all that separated displaced bodies from pavement floors. Some of the folk needed medicine and healing talk. Their ailments of flesh and mind were indifferent to their current plight, as indifferent, it seems, as the government that miserably failed them in their hour of need. Grown men openly wept; resourceful women were emotionally depleted; younger folk had whatever innocence remained from childhoods already battered by poverty cruelly washed away. They were desperate for a glimpse of hope beyond the hell and high water into which they had been plunged. Instead, the richest nation in the world shuttled them to harsh makeshift quarters. But many of the evacuees called upon their faith to see them through. And some of them undoubtedly wondered where God was in all of this. Perhaps they even believed that this was God's will. Could it be that God caused Katrina?

I prayed, "God, enough is enough. I need to hear from [my 85-year-old father] today." About an hour or two later, I got a call from CNN. The news reporter said, "I have your father here." And she said, "I just need to talk to you about it. When he came out of the apartment, he was dressed in a suit. Shoes polished. He came walking down Interstate 10 and everybody wondered, 'Where'd he come from'"? No dirt, clean from head to toe, top hat like he was living in the '20s. She said she never saw anybody like that, with this type of personality, during all of her assignments in rough areas around the world. She said he put so much hope in her. I realized he had the peace of God inside him.

—*Leonard Butler, Katrina survivor*

When Jesus said "You've done it to the least of these," it wasn't real to me. But it's real because of Katrina. But it wasn't real when I pulled up at the red light and saw the least of my brothers stand there with the sign [begging for money]. I did not act like that was *me* out there. I said, "Well, the reason why he's there is, he doesn't want to work." But right now I'm in the same situation.

—*Antoine Barriere, New Orleans pastor, Katrina survivor*

CHAPTER 10

SUPERNATURAL DISASTERS?
Theodicy and Prophetic Faith

IF EARTHQUAKES HAVE AFTERSHOCKS, then hurricanes have reverberations that shake the moral foundations of the geographies they destroy. In the wake of Katrina, a number of figures spoke about the meaning of the storm. Some argued that it was God's will, while others explored the question of human and natural responsibility for the catastrophe. It is clear that we must come to grips with the suffering Katrina unleashed. The faithful must also provide a thoughtful response to those who purport to discern God's vengeance, and to those who just as eagerly seek to avoid the unsettling question of God's role in suffering. Finally, only a revival of black prophetic religion will aid the largely black survivors to stand on solid ground after swimming in the toxic waters of Katrina.

Not long after Katrina made landfall, voices from every corner of the religious map weighed in on how God had used the

hurricane to punish the nation. A prominent ultra-Orthodox Is-
raeli rabbi, Ovadia Yosef, announced—his defenders say jok-
ingly—that Katrina was God's punishment for President Bush's
support of the August 2005 withdrawal of Jewish settlers from
the Gaza Strip. "It was God's retribution," Rabbi Yosef said.[1] Al-
Qaida in Iraq said that "God attacked America and the prayers of
the oppressed were answered."[2] Minister Louis Farrakhan argued that Hurricane Katrina was God's way of punishing America for its warmongering and racism. "Maybe God ain't pleased,"
Farrakhan said. "Maybe this caste system that pits us against
each other has to be destroyed and something new and better
put in its place."[3]

But in the theological arena where interpreters fought over
God's design for the disaster, conservative Christians battered
the victims of Katrina all over again. Many ministers argued that
New Orleans faced divine retribution because it was a haven for
sin. "They openly practice voodoo and devil worship in New
Orleans," black Baptist pastor Dwight McKissic said. "You can't
shake your fist in God's face 364 days a year and then ask,
'Where was God when Katrina struck?'"[4] God's wrath may have
howled in Katrina's winds because New Orleans thumbed its
nose at the Almighty. "We've known for decades and longer that
New Orleans has been a place where immorality is flaunted and
Christian values are laughed at," said conservative minister
David Crowe, the executive director of the Christian group
Restore America. "It is the epitome of a place where they mock
God."[5]

Conservative black minister Wellington Boone on national television assailed "the culture of those people stranded in New
Orleans" for their fate, claiming that the "looting of property,
the trashing of property, etc. speaks to the basic character of the
people" and that "these people who have gone through slavery,

segregation and the Voting Rights Act are doing this to themselves."[6] Other conservative Christian ministers argued that because of its abortion clinics, its annual gay pride parade known as Southern Decadence, and the slavish dependence of blacks on welfare, God punished New Orleans and washed away their sins in a flood of retribution brought on by Katrina—which, several of them pointed out, means "to purify."[7]

The belief that the poor black population of New Orleans brought their suffering on themselves reflects the views of conservative television and radio talk show hosts. Bill O'Reilly, on his Fox News Channel program *The O'Reilly Factor*, issued a stern warning to the poor. "So every American kid should be required to watch videotape of the poor in New Orleans and see how they suffered [after Hurricane Katrina], because they couldn't get out of town," O'Reilly opined. "And then, every teacher should tell the students, 'If you refuse to learn, if you refuse to work hard, if you become addicted, if you live a gangsta-life, you will be poor and powerless just like many of those in New Orleans."[8] O'Reilly, of course, was seeking to deflect criticism of the Bush administration in light of its atrocious performance in the aftermath of Katrina, and to prove the foolishness of overreliance on government. But as one journalist argued, the "larger implications of his words also are obvious. These often poor, often black hurricane victims brought all the misery and death on themselves, because they weren't motivated enough to succeed in America."[9] Rush Limbaugh argued that a "welfare state mentality" prevented the black poor of New Orleans from escaping their fate. "The nonblack population was just as devastated, but apparently they were able to get out," Limbaugh said in blasting the hurricane's victims. "Race, in this circumstance, is a poisonous weapon, and it's why the liberals are now gravitating to it."[10]

The belief in a God who punishes errant believers and enemies alike is a relic of ancient, if narrow, interpretations of Judaism, Islam, and Christianity. The notion that God will bring judgment on the wicked has often been viewed favorably by religious communities that suffered oppression at the hands of superior political powers. A rich prophetic tradition rose, in part, on the denunciation of the abuse of power by political forces that sought to unseat divine authority in the social order. Just as often, of course, the most stinging critiques were reserved for those within a religious community's arc of moral judgment. The prophetic gaze was cast most reliably on the failures of fellow believers to live up to the ideals expressed in the scriptures of one's faith. To be sure, crude authenticity tests, and tribal theological visions, often flourished in the name of keeping the faith right and pure, just as they do today. But such tests and visions mock the best prophetic spirit of history's great faiths.

Contemporary versions of tribal theologies persist in pronouncements that are more pathetic than prophetic. Too often, crude cultural bias infects the bitter statements of religious zealots who use God to sanction their beliefs. This is especially visible in Christian communities that are teetotalers on drink, yet drunk on arrogant analyses of divine punishment rooted in their confidence in knowing what gets God's goat—or, worse still, in knowing who God's sacrificial scapegoat is. In the case of Katrina, such views drip with hubris and hate. To suggest that God chose to use the storm to speak is presumptuous, and anachronistic, enough; but to posit its rage as person- and issue-specific—to rid New Orleans of gays, practitioners of voodoo and abortion, and poor blacks—is contemptuous of the precious human life God cherishes, not to mention homophobic and racist.

Further, such perspectives are immediately deflated on the sharp edges of their theological contradiction. To assume that New Orleans was a greater divine target for wiping out poor blacks than bigger cities with bigger black populations is to accuse God of poor sight or planning. And if God wanted to destroy abortion clinics, there are more in other states—say in California or New York—than in Louisiana. Does New Orleans contain more gay folk than Los Angeles? Of course, one supposes by this logic that where wind fails, quaking earth quenches queer desire all the same. But thousands of straight people die in earthquakes, just as they do in hurricanes. Did no conservative Christians die in the flood? Either God's aim is off, or the advocates of divine wrath believe that these innocents are *theolateral* damage. But does God punish the innocent to get a message to the guilty? What about the babies who died, who practiced neither abortion nor voodoo, and who hadn't claimed their sexual orientation or engaged in racial politics? Such a gesture is dirty pool, even for divinity.

That's why God usually warns the righteous to scram before disaster descends—remember Noah? Before curses come, ships are constructed to collect the righteous creatures to be saved from the flood. Did all the righteous make it out of New Orleans, or, to shift Biblical stories, were there some wives of Lot who looked back and got frozen in the fury? Even so, that assumes that they had a way of escape laid out and simply reneged on the route to rescue. For the most part, the poor in New Orleans lacked cars and a useful emergency exit plan provided by the government. The rule of divine anger usually operates like this: If God gets ready to strike, God usually offers up ample chariots, or a whale—it was good enough for Jonah—or plenty of Fords or Chevys, to let folk scamper out of town. At the very least,

God leaves enough stable earth in place long enough to permit the potentially pummeled to beat a path to safety. In missing this, the conservatives often turn out to be both bigoted believers and terrible theologians.

The conservatives' theology also fails them when they become so obsessed about the folk outside their fold that they miss the cutting edge of God's displeasure within their gates. For many of the most determinedly right-wing theologues, divine displeasure usually means that they're not being hateful enough to others—they're not lambasting gay marriage enough, or they're not pointing out the manifest pitfalls of siding with poor blacks, even if these critics happen to be black themselves. What usually fails to register with conservative Christians is that God might be tired of the tirades that are the bread and butter of right-wing faith. What about God's judgment on them, a pox on their theological houses?

Such an idea, central to the prophets' calls for Israel to clean up her own house lest she risk the anger of the Almighty, is almost always missing in such circles. God forbid that such believers might actually apply to themselves the litmus tests they give to others. When trouble or tragedy befalls conservative Christians, do they conclude that God is calling them to depart from their "wicked ways"? Do they believe that their downfall is linked to their religious or moral views? Is it possible that God is punishing them for their racist, sexist, or homophobic beliefs? Such prophetic self-reflection is noticeably muted in the aftermath of suffering for the self-righteous. In the end, it may be more important to them to maintain their beliefs in a rigidly ordered universe of ethical meaning than to sacrifice their ideas on the altar of bigger, more humane truths about God and human community.

One of the bigger truths that many conservative Christians fail successfully to come to grips with is the idea implied in even their crude pronouncements: the link between sin and suffering. For many conservative Christians, the matter is settled, cut and dried, black and white: sinners suffer, the saved are spared.[11] But for many Christians, and believers of other faiths, the problem of suffering presents a peculiar problem: how one can maintain that God has all the power and goodness in the world and yet allows evil to flourish. In classic theological terms, that is the problem of theodicy, a problem that, after Katrina, cries out for an answer. It rushes forth in the question: where was God in this crisis? Like latter day Jobs, the faithful wrestle with why God allows bad things to happen to good people.[12] (For many conservative Christians, bad things mostly happen to bad people.)

One religious figure assures us that God allowed Katrina to do damage out of respect for the play of human choice. "Why did God allow Katrina to lash out?" asks Thomas Rosica, a Catholic priest. "God doesn't intervene to prevent such things, because God love us too much. If we had a God who simply swooped down to halt natural catastrophes, prevent human tragedy and sinfulness, then religion and faith would simply be reduced to some form of magic or fate, and we would be helpless pawns on some divine chess board."[13] In making the familiar argument that God refrains from imposing on us the divine will, and instead permits human action to count, for ill or good, Rosica illumined an odd twist in such a position: that it is God's love for us that allows us to suffer. At first blush, such a reading appears headed toward theological masochism. On second thought, perhaps it is proper to highlight the paradox nonetheless, if for no other reason than to show that God is caught in the same dilemma we are, but from the other side, and shares a frustration born of love and respect for human freedom of not being able to derail the machinery of time and circumstance to help us, since that very machinery has at other moments brought such pleasure and profit—from great works of art to splendid human uses of nature's forces.

Another religious figure curiously exempts the government from responsibility in worsening the effects of the hurricane, even as he claims that God's role in nature remains a mystery. He also contends that the behavior of the Katrina victims revealed the worst in human nature. "There are really three mysteries at work here," says Patrick LaBelle, O.P., director of the Catholic Community at Stanford University. "The first is, of course, the mystery of God's powerful hand at work in nature, and there is no clear answer for this perennial question."[14] LaBelle suggests that we invoke the phrase "acts of God" when "there is nobody to sue," and while "there is no possibility of a divine lawsuit, there is a tendency to lay blame. And it is easy to blame God for this tragedy." LaBelle argues that holding God accountable for tragedy "provides an escape from what we should really be doing"—helping the suffering.[15] Although his focus on service is admirable, LaBelle sidesteps the question of God's role in human suffering by resorting to the familiar nostrum "it's a mystery" to get God off the hook.

Interestingly, he lets the government off the hook as well. While acknowledging that the "first movement to help was slow," LaBelle claims that "when it came it was powerful," a statement contradicted even by the president, who called the results "unacceptable." LaBelle is even more defensive about the administration, arguing that their mistakes "will surely be turned into political weapons, but after all is said and done the essential goodness of people will surface, survive, and reign."[16]

Thus, in his discussion of where God was in the storm, LaBelle deflects criticism of God and the government, and, although not conflating them, he certainly draws them together in a single explanatory swoop. When LaBelle discusses the second mystery— "the almost incredible violence on the part of some few who have gone so far as to attack men and women trying to rescue people in need, along with the looting and other forms of criminal behavior"—he concludes that such behavior is an example "of what people call original sin . . . that imbalance, often without reason, that makes us, in a paraphrase of St. Paul's words, do what we do not want to do and avoid what we know we should do."[17]

It is remarkable that LaBelle finds evidence of original sin in the alleged misbehavior (most of which has been proved to be false) of the twice-victimized Katrina survivors—first by nature and then by the government's delayed and botched response— but not in the much more lethal lapses of the federal government. While LaBelle hesitates to blame God, he exhibits no reluctance in blaming the hurricane victims. (LaBelle's stance is all the more curious since he failed to find original sin in the priests found guilty of sexually abusing children and youth in the clergy abuse scandal that rocked the Catholic Church.)[18] Third, for LaBelle, "there is the mystery that breaks through every standard barrier and division in society, liberating the best in people, freeing so many to enter into virtual acts of heroism in trying to help others."[19] It's all true, but it's not all that's true about the situation. LaBelle thus avoids any discussion of the social injustices that trapped the black poor in the Gulf Coast, and which bring out the worst in human beings. LaBelle's theodicy is disappointing because it doesn't adequately address the divine role in suffering. Neither does it come to grips with the religious justification for the status quo that buttresses social suffering. LaBelle's theodicy only temporarily defers the question of divine responsibility for that suffering.

Critics Edward Rothstein and Peter Steinfels pursue a more rigorous and satisfying engagement with theodicy after Katrina. In a sleek essay, Rothstein offers an abbreviated genealogy of theodicy, the term coined by philosopher Gottfried Liebniz in the eighteenth century that derives from the Greek words θξοσ (*theós*, "god") and δικη (*díke*, "justice"), which translates literally as "the justice of God." Leibniz was arguing against the skeptic Pierre Bayle, who denied God's goodness and omnipotence because of the existence of human suffering. As Rothstein says, the point of Leibniz's concept is to prove that justice exists, and that we live in "the best of all possible worlds."[20] Rothstein points out how theodicies have sprung up in their wake to explain natural disasters like earthquakes, floods, and droughts. Some theodicies maintain that disasters are the wages of sin, some argue that they are signs of the apocalypse, while still others contend that they cleanse evil from the earth.[21] A theodicy preserves the moral order by explaining the disruption caused by disaster. A theodicy points to sources of meaning that transcend human cause and power.

The Lisbon earthquake of 1755, which wrought huge devastation and wiped out a third of the city's population, ended for many the appeal of theodicy. The Enlightenment also helped to defeat the idea that a theodicy might reasonably account for catastrophe. But if the Enlightenment was helped by the earthquake—Kant wrote about it, it sparked scientific investigation, and the governmental response to it was practical, not religious—it also conceptually segregated moral evil and natural disaster. An earthquake or flood could no longer be neatly subsumed under traditional religious theodicies.[22] God got booted offstage as the author of causality while human agency took center stage. Unlike McArthur's old soldiers, theodicies neither died nor faded away; instead, they were reborn in other guises. As history replaced theology, secular explanations for suffering shined, spotlighting thinkers like Hegel ("[who] saw history as an evolutionary series of transformations in which destruction was as inevitable as birth") and Marx ("[who] believed other kinds of economic and human laws accounted for destruction and evolution").[23] Natural disasters, meanwhile, were banished to the realm of science.

Rothstein argues that the advent of Katrina spurs the formation of other kinds of theodicy. This time around, human agency has been seen as a major culprit in the suffering, "as if failures in planning were almost evidence of cause, as if forces of nature were subject to human oversight," leading Rothstein to conclude that the "hurricane has been humanized."[24] Such thinking marks a critical shift in our thinking about the natural world because it inflates human knowledge by extending scientific and political power "into the realm of nature."[25] There are no explanations in that realm for the origins of catastrophe, but there is an exploration of the human failings that make us experience disaster. Rothstein probes the political roots of theodicy while measuring the religious equivalencies that attend its path of explaining disaster.

There is a theodicy at work here, in the ways in which the reaction to natural catastrophe so readily becomes political. Nature becomes something to be managed or mismanaged; it lies within the political order, not outside it. Theodicy, if successful, does not overturn belief but confirms it. So, for some commentators, the flood and its aftermath provided confirmation of their previous doubts about the Bush administration. Actually, in some respects, this theodicy has gone even beyond the political: just as a religious theodicy might have shown natural catastrophe to be the result of human misdeed, many of the early commentators about the flood did the same, creating a kind of scientific/moral theodicy in which human sin is still a dominant factor. . . . All of these explanations are subject to examination and debate of course, but in the heart of a secular age, they are also something else. They are theodicies. And in the face of nature's awesome and horrific powers, the prospect of political retribution is as prevalent as the promise of divine retribution once was.[26]

Rothstein has offered a nuanced and literate exploration of politically charged theodicy after Katrina—where religious modes of expression have been baptized by secular ideas that assign responsibility to, and anticipate retribution from, political forces. In a provocative essay, however, Peter Steinfels argues that it is only individuals who have played Job and asked God about their suffering. Traditional theodicy, however, has hardly troubled the "public conscience."[27] Steinfels thinks that questions of human agency and responsibility, which form for Rothstein a political theodicy, have obscured the question of God's absence or presence in Katrina. The reluctance of theodicy in secular culture is partially explained by the Enlightenment's displacement of God and the appeal to reason and science to sort out human responsibility for catastrophe. That means that the focus in Katrina has been on how New Orleans was fatefully built on marsh, the relative political indifference to approaching disaster in the region, the horrid response by the government in the storm's aftermath, the racial and economic inequities that riddled the rescue and relief efforts, and the toll of human error and the breakdown of man-made networks of communication, transportation, potable water, disposal of sewage, and food, gasoline, and medical supplies.[28]

For Steinfels, however, the attribution of responsibility to human beings still points a theological finger back to God. The focus on human agency suggests a strong American belief in freedom and responsibility. But failing to ask the question of evil beyond human hands betrays an avoidance of the profound self-examination that religious theodicies invite.

> For believers, humanity, with all its faults and contrivances, is no less God's creation than hurricanes and ocean surges and the law that water seeks its own level. So one might logically step back from asking how God could allow the brimming, turbulent Lake Pontchartrain to break the levees to asking how God could allow self-interested or shortsighted politicians to put off reinforcing the levees or allow enterprising engineers and developers to decrease the capacity of the environment to buffer storms. How could God allow the negligence, racism, indifference or hard-heartedness that long gnawed at the social fabric of New Orleans—or the blindness or incompetence of officials who should have understood the brewing human storm, as well the meteorological one? That such questions about divine providence have been so little pressed in this way testifies to a tremendous modern—and American—belief in human freedom and responsibility. On the Gulf Coast, humans fell short, not God; humans and human institutions should be called to account, not God. Certainly, such calls to accountability are morally preferable to simply blaming the heavens. But at what point does this practical-minded shying away from examining further the ultimate sources of evil and injury also testify to the culture's resistance to genuine self-scrutiny?[29]

If the failure to press Providence about its role in human suffering deflects critical self-inventory, an aversion to facing up to tragedy, along with an exorbitant belief in American know-how to solve nearly all problems, is equally vexing. These features of our contemporary world are even more reason to ask the tough questions of God that form classic theodicy. Steinfels admits that asking such questions might not bring us any closer to satisfactorily squaring evil's existence, and God's goodness and power, but he refuses to see it as a waste of time. He elegantly argues that "delving into such mysteries might at least lead to a more profound understanding of the human condition and the untidiness of reality generally."[30]

Rothstein's and Steinfels's views of theodicy are quite helpful in addressing the urgent problems posed by Katrina. Both Rothstein and Steinfels offer a seasoned and wise rebuttal to the often vicious pronouncements of the *punitive theodicies* advocated by conservative and fundamentalist religious believers. Punitive theodicies drape tribal biases in religious symbols and make God a cosmic enforcer. Rothstein's *attributive theodicy* suggests the political makeover of a concept that has far too long gotten caught in the thickets of abstract theorizing and that remains at a great distance from the pain and suffering it supposedly addressed. The theoretical and philosophical gist of theodicy has often discouraged tangible engagement with practical problems. Rothstein's attributive theodicy finds human fingerprints on suffering in a way that validates the moral dimensions of religious theodicies while holding true to the demand for human culpability that an appeal to God might cloak.

Steinfels's *redistributive theodicy* refocuses critical attention on the vital link between moral self-examination and wrestling with the weighty problem of Providence's role in our individual and public lives. By insisting on asking if the hand of God—or its absence—has shaped the social order, redistributive theodicy seeks to understand the relation between religious belief and personal and public ethical self-inventory. And by raising the problem of evil as an issue that is but one remove from the theological landscape when it probes human responsibility and agency, redistributive theodicy seeks to clarify the ultimate cause of human suffering and disaster.

All three theodicies crop up when the suffering of the black poor of New Orleans is at stake. Did God cause the wind to roar and the waters of New Orleans to rage? Did God cause the destruction and death and mayhem we see? Is it ever God's will for black people to suffer? Can good come from black suffering, as even Martin Luther King, Jr., argued? Does that mean that black suffering, then, is God's way to redeem black people or the nation? Is that a sadomasochistic theology that black people should give up? Or is such an explanation a way for blacks to steel themselves against the meaninglessness of events so as not to suffer psychic and literal death? Some critics have claimed that God saved Africans from their savagery and their heathenism through slavery. Is the same true for catastrophes like Katrina? Is this a punishment from God—as one black Katrina survivor was heard to ask, "What did we do wrong for God to do this to us?"

When the vicious winds and turbulent waters of Hurricane Katrina crashed into the Gulf States, black people's prayers flooded the earth. Of course, water is central to African American culture; it symbolizes freedom, separation and purity, and birth and death, all at the same time. It is important in the religious stories we tell to narrate our identity and destiny. The Red Sea opened up in the Bible to clear a path for escaping Hebrew slaves, but closed and drowned Pharaoh's pursuing army. The angry sea consumed, and disgorged, black bodies during the Middle Passage, a watery grave that provided freedom from the brutal chattel slavery ahead. But water is also the symbol of spiritual redemption, of burying sins and cleansing the soul of moral dirt.

"Wade in the Water" is a favorite spiritual, or slave song, one that promises the ebony children of God that "God's gonna trouble the waters."

Their faith has long provided black folk safe harbor in ugly storms and disasters, both natural and man-made. When Africans were torn from their mother soil and forced into bondage in the New World, millions of lives were lost on the angry seas. Still, even as their brothers and sisters perished, their faith allowed many Africans to preserve life and limb and to symbolically book passage on the "Ol' Ship of Zion." When blacks were plunged beneath the harsh waves of chattel slavery, they sought refuge in the community of faith they carved out of their brutal existence. When the civil rights movement was drenched with the foul spray of white supremacy and Jim Crow, it took cover in sanctuaries across the land.

Black faith and spirituality offer believers at least three resources in the face of Hurricane Katrina. First, black faith and spirituality provide moral and theological insight into "natural disaster." Many religious folk, some under the sway of punitive theodicy, have claimed that this calamitous storm was "God's will." Others ask what "we" did wrong to deserve such a cataclysmic rebuke from nature, and, hence, from God, if Steinfels's redistributive theodicy rings true. Black religious faith, especially Christianity, discourages such a narrow interpretation of nature and God. The suffering that human beings endure is never God's will. The evil that is wrought by human beings—and here Rothstein's attributive theodicy is vital—and the chaos that is unleashed by nature express neither God's vision nor vengeance, as punitive theodicies suggest. God's will is for human beings to flourish and for us to live in harmony with each other and nature.

To be sure, our shortcomings poison human community. The

vicious and sinful character of human beings constantly inter-
rupts God's ideal of love as the basis of our relations with one
another. And nature's unpredictable fury can with little notice
crush or destroy human life. God intends none of this. This does
not mean, however, that our faith cannot help us to extract
meaning from our misery, or to make sense of our suffering. Our
faith can give us the comfort that God walks with us, and will
not forsake us. That may seem like small solace in the face of our
finitude. But the knowledge that God refuses to let us go ultimately calms the soul in distress. That is the only guarantee we
have that the universe that has betrayed us at one turn through
wind and water will stand behind us through the divine Word.

Even if God does not wish for us to experience tragedy, our
suffering, when viewed through mature faith, can provide a
window into existence and a measure of relief. Suffering is an
unavoidable aspect of our human pilgrimage; the deepest faith
cannot prevent our walk through the valley of the shadow of
death. For the victims, and survivors, of Hurricane Katrina,
black faith refuses to offer pat answers or theological clichés. It
is a tragedy of untold proportion, a catastrophe that causes the
heart of God to break. And while the survivors are surely
blessed, we must resist the notion that they are better than those
who died. Black spiritual wisdom cautions against such presumptuous faith, which feeds on pride.[31] It helps us to resist the
temptation to ethical arrogance. Those who lost their lives were
victims of a force of nature that might have as easily drowned
those who escaped. This is one of the paradoxes of black faith
that we must not let collapse into black-and-white theological
certitude: yes, God's grace spared the survivors, but that doesn't
mean that they are superior. The survivors are, therefore,
charged with responsibility to live even more fully and purpose-
fully in the awareness of their mysterious fortune. And the full

force of an attributive theodicy commissions the rest of us to hold society responsible for the healthy and just reconstruction of poor black communities.

Second, black faith offers a stirring critique of the racial and class elements swept to the surface by Katrina. As Martin Luther King, Jr., was fond of paraphrasing the prophet Amos, we must work for a world where "justice rolls down like waters, and righteousness like a mighty stream."[32] The biblical mandate of Jesus to care for "the least of these"—and to visit prisoners, attend to widows, and preach hope to the poor—supports the black church's mission to address salient social issues. It is clear that the vast majority of victims in this catastrophe were black and poor. Although God's grace may account for why some poor folk lived—a perspective not easily adopted when either an attributive or redistributive theodicy prevails—it appears that class position and skin color kept others from facing the fury of the storm. Those who were able to escape before the wind and water did their worst were richer, and often whiter, than those who were left behind to sink or swim.

It is little wonder that the desperate and destitute took easily to "conspiracy theories" about the possible dynamiting of some of the levees in New Orleans to protect the whites and drown the blacks. After all, such an event happened in the Great Flood of 1927. And since the forces that fueled such a heinous act still thrive, including white supremacy and a deep dislike for poor blacks, it stands to reason that many blacks might believe it could happen again. In this instance, conspiracy theories are secular, grassroots theodicies—most likely of the attributive mode—that seek to explain the evil that poor blacks endure at the hands of a culpable and callous white society.

Black religious faith offers prophetic criticism of persistent racial and economic inequality. This inequality, of course, renders millions of our fellow citizens more vulnerable to natural disaster. That is why the sorrow song from slavery, "Go Down Moses," still resonates in black sacred circles. It instructs the leader to "tell ol' Pharaoh to let my people go"—to release them from the brutal conditions that cause their suffering. From Henry Highland Garnett to Martin Luther King, Jr., from Frederick Douglass to Jesse Jackson, and from Sojourner Truth to Bishop Vashti McKenzie, black prophetic leaders have argued that the gospel must transform society and bring the Kingdom of God closer to our time and community. Even as right-wing evangelical faith sanctifies the state, worships the market, and genuflects before conservative government, black prophetic faith must uphold the blood-stained banner of a God who identified with human suffering and oppression, and who came to earth to die as one of the poor and outcast. Otherwise, our declaration of a "preferential option for the poor" will echo as an empty theological slogan.

Black prophetic faith must also help guide the national discussion about race in the aftermath of the traumatic dispersion and migration of Katrina's poor black survivors across the country. Black migrations have sometimes been spurred by natural disaster and racial violence. Like generations of black Southerners before them—who left the region because of white supremacy and natural disasters like the Great Mississippi Flood of 1927—many black folk from the Gulf Coast may end up seeking habitat and livelihood far from their native shores. Thousands upon thousands of mostly poor black folk cannot afford to wait while New Orleans is rebuilt. Given trends of gentrification that favor business elites and corporate interests, the poor won't be able to afford their homes or communities once they are rebuilt.

Prominent white businessmen in New Orleans—the same ones who hired private security firms during the storm to protect

their property—met in the immediate wake of Katrina to plan
for the city a future that was whiter and richer than before.
James Reiss, a white businessman who is one of Mayor Nagin's
biggest backers, and who serves in the mayor's administration as
chairman of the Regional Transit Authority, was explicit in the
plans he and nearly forty other white businessmen are hatching.
"Those who want to see this city rebuilt want to see it done in a
completely different way: demographically, geographically and
politically," Reiss said. "I'm not just speaking for myself here.
The way we've been living is not going to happen again, or we're
out."[33] As the old saw goes, urban renewal amounts to Negro removal. Black folk have been a pilgrim people, a wayfaring group,
a folk who are rarely ever really at home, unsettled, always up-
rooted, forever migrating from place to place, exiles in their own
country, their movements spurred as much by tragedy as opportunity.

Although many of the evacuees were initially welcomed with
open arms, the racial hostilities that usually accompany the in-
flux of black people into white enclaves must be anticipated.
And we must address the fear that the black poor carry with
them of being displaced from one home only to find themselves
in even more tenuous conditions as they attempt to build new
lives. Moreover, if New Orleans is rebuilt with an eye to the gentrification imagined by white business elites, one that pushes already economically marginal folk further to the social periphery,
then we have done little more than collude with nature's despot-
ically indifferent will to uproot and exploit the poor.

Third, Katrina challenges black churches to recapture their
prophetic anger and to transform that passion into social action.
During the 2004 election, many conservative blacks voted for
Bush because of his opposition to gay marriage. This political
red herring diverted critical attention from Bush's failure to ad-

dress the social and economic inequities that still hamper progress and equality for millions of poor blacks. This shift among black voters reinforced ugly homophobia. But it also absorbed precious cultural resources that might have relieved the suffering of the black poor instead of increasing the suffering of gay, lesbian, transgender, and bisexual brothers and sisters. The greater tragedy is that such efforts were sparked by conservative figures that have proved hostile to the interests of black folk.

Even when it appears that our interests are being embraced, we must be cautious. Under the guise of supporting faith, President Bush has shifted the burden of social services from the government to faith-based institutions. It is a gesture that the prophetic black church and religious leaders must resist. As James Carroll argues, that shift undermines governmental responsibility for the poor. It also may have contributed to the federal government's failure to respond to Katrina's victims in an effective and timely manner. Carroll also argues that placing religious groups in charge of social services permits the expression of antipublic viewpoints on the public dime. And he argues that citizens deserve relief during catastrophe. Governmental help is a form of self-help since the citizenry owns the government. The failure to recognize this point has facilitated a transition from the war on poverty to a punitive war on the poor.

I find myself wondering if the abysmal performance of government agencies in responding to this crisis isn't related to the unprecedented emphasis the government itself has been putting on "faith-based" groups as key providers of social services? . . . But politicians from Washington to the state capitols have exploited this tradition of religious generosity to justify the rollback of programs dating to the New Deal. . . . The church-state divide, undercutting norms of supervision and accountability, means religious groups, even while entrusted with public functions, can embody antipublic values. . . . The problem is redoubled when religiously sponsored good works supply needs in place of government responses. Something essential to democracy is at stake here. The rights of citizens to basic relief, especially in times of crisis, are rooted not in charity, but in justice. . . . Citizens in a democracy, after all, are the owners of government; therefore government help is a form of self-help. . . . The destruction of public social services has been nothing less than an attack on people in need, as if their need itself is deserving of punishment. The war on poverty has become a war on the poor. That it is waged in the name of God, in alliance with those who claim to honor God, is blasphemy.[34]

Black prophetic churches must also be sharply critical of the gospel of prosperity as the measure of authentic faith that has swept our sanctuaries. The black church has been flooded by theological justifications of material acquisition that threaten to drown our heritage of radical identification with "the least of these." It is tragic that so many in the black church have been seduced by facile formulas of upward mobility and social status. In the meantime, we have surrendered Micah's prophetic imperative to love mercy, do justice, and walk humbly with God. Katrina reminds us that black pastors and their flocks must refocus on their mission to the downtrodden, the heavy laden, the socially outcast, the bereaved, and those imprisoned by hopelessness and despair. Too many black churches have reneged on the translation of the gospel into concrete demands for social justice. Instead, we have tailored our theologies to fit the market and morality of a conservative culture that despises our history and tramples on our best traditions.

The black church must reclaim its legacy of prophetic anger at the forces that make the lives of the poor and vulnerable an unrelieved hell. Otherwise, we forfeit our right to be called sons and daughters of a God whose first love is always those who are last. Katrina didn't happen to make us learn these lessons. But if we act on the horror we have witnessed, then Katrina's hellish fury, and the injustices it washed into our faces, won't have the last word. And our poor brothers and sisters won't have died in vain.

In my opinion, I think we need to rethink Black America and unite, and have our own black banks and a black Red Cross. We have enough black millionaires, athletes and celebrities, and we can do this independently if we all stick together.

—*Sherry Browning, Katrina volunteer*

I was in my apartment in New York City, and on days two and three, I distinctly remember watching the news and seeing faces of desperation of all ages—young and old—just crying out for help. I just could not stand [the sight of the suffering]. I ended up through phone calls finding two other guys who were going down to New Orleans—one of them was a paramedic—who wanted to do the same thing. We rented a SUV and drove down, literally from Brooklyn, New York all the way, straight to Louisiana.

—*Lisa Aptaker, M.D., Katrina volunteer*

One of the concerns I have, that I hope we address as a people coming out of this, is the lack of leadership in the African American community. No one agency or institution in the African American community stepped up and gave leadership and charge to what amounted to the devastation and displacement of a predominantly African American population.

—*D. Z. Cofield, Houston pastor and Katrina volunteer*

EPILOGUE
Transforming the Jericho Road

THE PEOPLE OF AMERICA have done a remarkable job in responding to Hurricane Katrina, and to Hurricanes Rita and Wilma: the charitable giving to the victims of these three disasters has topped $2 billion, an amount approaching the $2.2 billion total donated to the victims of 9/11.[1] But charity is episodic and often driven by disaster. What is needed are structures of justice that perpetuate the goodwill intended in charity. Justice allows charity to live beyond crisis. Justice is what love sounds like when it speaks in public. As Martin Luther King, Jr., warned us, compassion for the victim along the Jericho road is never enough; we must transform the Jericho road. After Hurricane Katrina, the need for such transformation is clearer and more urgent than ever. We all have a role to play.

The government has a big role to play in addressing the issues swept to the fore by Katrina. The present administration will no doubt resist such a role because of its hostility to the idea that government ought to help the nation's citizens. Their atrocious performance during the disaster suggests that limited government offers poor protection to the most vulnerable among us. Still, we the people must insist that they make the effort.

FEMA must be fixed. It should be upgraded once again to a cabinet-level position to ensure greater attention from the president. Disaster relief must once again be made a national priority. The agency must combat internal forces that view it as what former head Joseph Allbaugh termed "an oversized entitlement program."[2] It must once again find its mission in relieving and mitigating disaster. FEMA must also shore up its leadership culture by purging the agency of crippling cronyism; it must bring in capable professionals to head the various divisions within the agency. Moreover, FEMA's nearly all-white leadership receives more discrimination complaints than any other federal agency.[3] This has proved to be quite a liability after recent hurricanes in getting the agency's leadership to understand the plight of the poor minorities it is charged to serve.

The local, state, and federal governments must outline effective plans to evacuate the poorest and most besieged communities. Anticipating the needs of the poor who lack cars should spur the government to use municipal transportation to speed evacuation. Consulting with leaders of blighted communities, and the poor themselves, is necessary to design effective measures that assure their safety during natural disasters.

The government must also find just and creative ways to rebuild New Orleans and the rest of the Gulf Coast decimated by the disaster. So far, the signs point to Republicans' exploiting tragedy as an opportunity for disaster capitalism. The Republicans gave fat contracts to huge corporations with previous ties to the federal government. As we know, President Bush temporarily suspended the Davis-Bacon Act. More broadly, the Republicans have proposed a number of measures to undercut just reconstruction for the poor. Some of their proposals include making the entire affected area a flat-tax free-enterprise zone, or an economic competitive zone; arguing for first-year business expensing in lieu of depreciation for all assets, including personal property and buildings, in the blighted region; offering a zero rate on the capital gains and dividends for residents and businesses located or investing in the affected region; waiving the death tax for all deaths in the affected area between August 20, 2005, and December 31, 2005; waiving environmental regulations that prevent rebuilding; eliminating regulatory barriers that prevent faith-based and charitable groups from participating in reconstruction efforts; offering a permanent reduction in the gas tax; and permitting an increase in offshore oil drilling.[4] Hardly any of this will benefit the poor.

The reconstruction process must include the voices and visions of the black folk who are, at 67.9 percent of the population, the *majority* in New Orleans. To be sure, business elites have already galvanized their resources to make New Orleans a whiter and wealthier place. This would mean that New Orleans would be devoid of the rich cultural gumbo of black and ethnic identities that lent the city its irresistible charm. Whitewashing New Orleans, however, is not just bad for its aesthetic and cultural values; it is horrible as well for its democratic and political sensibilities. By encouraging the poor folk in the region to help plan the city's reconstruction, the government could help prevent the vast demographic shift—hoped for by some to shore up conservative white interests, and feared by others for just that reason—that would amount to "ethnic cleansing." The Latino, Native American, and Asian populations that supply vital labor in service industries must also be included in rebuilding efforts.

As Naomi Klein argues, the poor people of New Orleans should benefit from rebuilding even as they are allowed to build on valuable solutions to some of the area's most pressing problems:

> New Orleans could be reconstructed by and for the very people most victimized by the flood. Schools and hospitals that were falling apart before could finally have adequate resources; the rebuilding could create thousands of local jobs and provide massive skills training in decent paying industries. Rather than handing over the reconstruction to the same corrupt elite that failed the city so spectacularly, the effort could be led by groups like Douglass Community Coalition. Before the hurricane this remarkable assembly of parents, teachers, students and artists was trying to reconstruct the city from the ravages of poverty by transforming Frederick Douglass Senior High School into a model of community learning. They have already done the painstaking work of building consensus around education reform. Now that the funds are flowing, shouldn't they have the tools to rebuild every ailing public school in the city?[5]

The federal government must preserve coastal wetlands and barrier islands to beat back the violent winds of hurricanes. Environmental policies that favor energy companies scarcely protect the nation's citizens in vulnerable geographies. The Bush administration's hostility to many scientific ideas, including the science related to stem cell research, missile defense, climate change, product safety, environmental regulation, evolution, and global warming, is well known. That doesn't lessen the need for science free of ideological blinders. Whether we like it or not, human behavior affects in demonstrable measure which way the winds blow. We are, after all, cosmic citizens, and unless we mind our ecological store, we will all pay the price for our criminal negligence.

The government should also set up a Katrina victims' fund like it did for the victims of 9/11. Tragically, the victims of 8/29 are widely seen as undeserving of the respect and cultural empathy that go to the victims of 9/11. The fund is needed because the more than $2 billion in charitable donations is offset by soaring costs that consume a lot of the funds raised.[6] It is doubtful that most of that money gets into the hands of the poor. There is also the widespread belief discussed earlier that the black poor basically got what they deserved because they were too stubborn or stupid to leave. A conservative government frowns on the black poor because of the belief that they should be responsible for their own lives. That belief didn't stop the funds flowing to the families of victims of 9/11, some of whom were white, wealthy, and could afford to speak for themselves in a fashion the poor simply can't match.

The director of the 9/11 fund, Kenneth Feinberg, was asked about the idea of a fund for 8/29 victims. He doubted that it would be set up, and even doubted that the Katrina victims deserved it. When the host of a television program asked Feinberg if it was because of "the underlying philosophy here . . . that 'I'm responsible for my own life and if something bad happens, too bad,'" he affirmed that view. "That's part of it, I think," Feinberg said. "It's the United States after all. Our heritage is limited government. The government is not a guarantor of life's misfortunes. I think the 9/11 fund was an aberration. I don't think you will find anywhere in American history, two million dollars on average, tax-free, to every eligible claimant."[7] Except when it involves people of means, people who had names, people whose bodies were identified with a picture in the papers—

more than can be said for the largely nameless, faceless victims of 8/29.[8] If the federal government is serious about righting societal wrongs in the wake of Katrina, it must start by ensuring the futures of those families devastated by the disaster.

Society has a role to play as well. We must foster a national conversation on race, poverty, and class. Sure, government should have a hand in this as well. But expecting folk who bungled a job helping poor people of color to lead such a discussion is like expecting the wolves to guard the sheep. That's not to let them off the hook. The government gets its chance to have a conversation on race, poverty, and class whenever it makes laws to enhance or erode the prospects of the poor. It should be obvious that lawmakers must establish measures on every level that protect the poor—at their schools, on their jobs, and in the social sphere they must negotiate.

But we in civic society bear a responsibility as well to force the government to take note of the poor, and to act on their behalf. Major foundations must forge alliances among thinkers who are already ahead of the curve on the matter of race, poverty, and class. We must get the information right, which is quite critical. We must also distribute it in a timely and effective fashion to public policy makers and politicians. But that is only the beginning. We have a huge job of educating ourselves in the general public about the true nature of poverty, about who is poor and why, and about what we can and should do about it. We have enough information at our fingertips about the complex lives of the poor. Now, we must in good conscience act on it.

There are surely ideological and intellectual differences among those who study the problem. This is by no means a politically neutral enterprise. Resources are at stake, and so are the lives of the poor we steady or stigmatize by our study. We must recognize the grammar of despair that chokes the life from the poor and makes their lives a kind of hell we only read about. But we must also learn the language of social possibility that inspires them to find even more fulfillment as agents of their own destinies. If, as James Carroll contends, governmental assistance is self-help because the people own the government, there is no shame or harm in encouraging the government to do its best to uplift and rescue its citizenry from the weariest social margins.

Our educational system must be involved as well. Our schools, from elementary classrooms to university halls, should help to deepen and broaden perspectives on race, class, and poverty, and thus provide a ready basis to understand and to act for, and with, the poor. Education is obviously critical to thinning the ranks of the poor by offering them a way out of poverty. But we must also pay attention to structural factors in the economy, and in the racial order, that prevent quality education for the poor. Unless we talk and learn about class, poverty, and color, and the distinctive fashion in which they collude to deprive people of healthy life chances, we are perpetuating a legacy of injustice.

The media, too, is critical in facilitating this conversation. I have already discussed how the media regained a bit of its necessary skepticism about the government while covering Katrina— and how it squandered its capital on unverified reports of black behavior that played to persistent stereotypes. It only underscored how powerful the media remains while emphasizing its need to turn the cameras on itself. As part of its ritual of self-examination, the media can forge a greater awareness of how race, poverty, and class intersect. By hosting town-hall meetings in local communities, the media might instigate ongoing attention to specific examples of how race, class, and poverty affect various communities. The media can shed light on what measures have succeeded or failed, and thus help clarify the solutions that might be duplicated around the nation.

The media can also explore previously unimagined links between class, poverty, race, and other issues in the mainstream— the war on terror, for instance, or AIDS in Africa, as the poor of color in our nation see themselves tied to the poor the world over. Such liberating and illuminating habits don't merely benefit people of color and the poor alone; they strengthen our yen to be truly democratic, with as much information and insight as we can muster. Our abhorrent ignorance of the poor can at least be partially reduced by seeing them in non-stereotypical settings and roles where their often-unappreciated grace and humanity resonate most powerfully.

There must also be grassroots efforts to encourage environmental justice. Although the focus on the ecology is long-standing, considerations of environmental racism are often shunted to the periphery. Many of the most urgent environmental issues involve poor people of color. Many of them live, for instance, in the fence-line communities that dot the Mississippi River. Their communities face dangerous racial injustices, economic inequalities, and vulnerabilities to environmental forces that should be steadily highlighted. Many poor people of color in Louisiana live in the "Louisiana Petrochemical Corridor," an eighty-five-mile stretch of the river from Baton Rouge to New Orleans where there are more than 125 refineries and chemical plants. It has also been dubbed "Cancer Alley" because of the high incidence of cancer and respiratory problems. The media, universities, charitable foundations, civic society, and the government should hold fast to these ugly truths. The media and the rest of us should help keep the issues of race, poverty, and class before the American public, long after the initial waves of sympathy have subsided—as they already have.

Black communities have a role to play as well. We must confront the often bitter bias against the poor that grows in our own black yards. Pockets of disdain for the less fortunate in our race mock our commitment to freedom from oppression. Yet, while the black middle class has expanded, and black elites have multiplied, we have failed to address the persistent poverty of a third of our communities. We have been victimized by a narrow emphasis on personal responsibility—a critical element in upward mobility and economic stability—while neglecting the social and racial forces that make the exercise of such responsibility far more difficult than it should be.

Black fraternities, sororities, civil rights groups, and voluntary organizations must pool resources and direct attention to the plight of the poor. Black media, including radio programs and television stations, magazines, and Websites, must continually hammer away at the forces of economic and racial injustice that were revealed in Katrina.

Moreover, we must criticize the materialism that has restricted the prophetic reach of the black church into our communities to rescue the vulnerable. We have latched on to theological visions of the church's mission that only reinforce the social and class inequalities between poor and well-to-do blacks. In part, the expanded black middle class is looking for permission, and justification, to free itself from responsibility and compassion for the less fortunate of our number. We must recover the fundamental commitment to the poor that allowed us to rise in the first place. That is the only guarantee that our poorer brothers and sisters will be able to rise as well. Social justice is the lifeblood of the black church; we must not sacrifice our liberating heritage for the pottage of prosperity.

Finally, we must engage in memory warfare. We must confess that Katrina not only revealed the callous disregard for poverty's colored face to the nation, but also exposed our failure to mother and father our race into its best future through our social nurture and political care. We must never let the nation forget what it has learned from Katrina, and we must never let those lessons fall flat on our ears. The only way Katrina can be kept from becoming a passing moment of self-reflection along the national path to even more carnage is if we continue to tell the truth about poverty, race, class, environment, government, the media, and our culture. Memory warfare pits us against the forces of cultural, racial, and class amnesia. And it protects us from *Aframnesia*, a paralyzing form of black forgetfulness of our beleaguered brothers and sisters. We must embrace the sometimes painful but ultimately healing remembrance that makes us human and wise. If we forget, then poor people of color become little more than fodder for the imperial imagination of a nation that has exploited them and thrown them away. God forbid we count ourselves in that number.

AFTERWORD
Great Migrations?

IN THE AFTERMATH of Hurricane Katrina, black folk in the Gulf Coast faced the cruel reality of yet another "storm induced diaspora."[1] Earlier storms, especially the Great Mississippi Flood of 1927, had flushed black Americans from their homes in search of relief from the desperate poverty and brutal racism that the disaster revealed. But this most recent tragedy harkened back even further: the deadly waters of slavery's middle passage flooded the black collective memory. One of the unifying themes of slavery and storms in the black imagination is the traumatic dispersal of black folk across rugged, even resistant, geographies. Black folk have built communities in the most hostile conditions imaginable. They have beat back both natural and man-made disasters to stake bold claims of citizenship and common humanity.

Of course, black folk have, over the centuries, endured various qualities and versions of dispersion, including the familiar migrations black folk have undertaken or been forced into.

Apart from slavery, perhaps the most memorable exodus of black folk is the Great Migration that stretched from the early twentieth century into the 1930s, as black folk shirked their rural southern roots to embrace northern urban life. To be sure, the Great Migration is a complex story of forces that pushed and pulled blacks from their native haunts—southern white backlash after Reconstruction; the decline of southern agrarian capitalism; and the lure of northern economic opportunity in a region whose landscape was not as violently marked by the visible signposts of white supremacy.

But migration is also never merely physical and spatial. It also involves political, psychic, social, and spiritual forces that affect the shape and duration of black diaspora. Neither is migration a static process. Rather, it is dynamic, fluid, and evolutionary, unfolding in both layers of dispersal and various points of entry into, and exit from, the diasporic identity. The restless black quest for home suggests the search for common roots with other citizens. It also points to an unquenchable desire for a unique black identity forged in the give and take of black comings and goings in the world.

If black migrations don't stay put, and measure both the kick in the pants and the tug of dreams that motivate black movement, they also aren't simple phenomena that can be explained by single theories of mobility. Among many others, there are at least three kinds of movement that Hurricane Katrina revealed: submerged, subversive, and subsidized migrations. How these play out will say a lot about how black folk will wake from this latest racial and economic nightmare.

Submerged migrations occur when there is a shift in concentrations of population within specific geographical regions. More particularly, such internal migrations count as submerged migrations when minority populations are economically dislocated, socially displaced, and spatially segregated. Thus, folk are shifted within, or immediately outside of, cities in the effort to protect wealthier communities (such as when Chicago project dwellings like Cabrini Green are dismantled and their populations displaced from the wealthy Gold Coast area) or to physically quarantine poor populations in working class exurbs to make room for the production of entrepreneurial projects (such as the building of sports stadiums), the construction of new highways, or the development of new properties.

Submerged migrations are also sparked, and exacerbated, by shifts in the political economy, and in urban geography and demography, that have a negative impact on poor black people. The shift from manufacturing to high-end service industries drives millions of workers to the bottom of the economy. In this pivotal transitional moment in the economy, high-tech, knowledge-based jobs proliferate while low-wage jobs in the service sector are occupied by the working poor. Furthermore, the gentrification of poor, mixed-waged neighborhoods by upwardly mobile professionals weakens the already fragile hold of working poor households on economic stability. The possibility of homeownership is almost nil in such communities among the lower classes, and access to rental homes is nearly impossible. Thus, the poor are forced into bleaker neighborhoods with little capital concentration, entrepreneurial energy, or upward mobility. This is the doorway into one of the most vicious aspects of submerged migration—concentrated poverty, which leads to poor homes, communities, jobs, and education, all of which produce more material deprivation and social suffering.

New Orleans has suffered the lethal consequences of the submerged migration of black populations for decades. Some middle class blacks, and many more working class and working poor blacks, have been concentrated in the city's ninth ward for several decades. As New Orleans city council member Cynthia Willard-Lewis says, the ninth ward is

> a community with many economic challenges—chronic and systemic poverty in a core group. However, there are also many families that are middle class and own multiple properties, have professional backgrounds, and have educated their children. And because of the roots, the fact that mama and grandmama and daughters all live in the same neighborhood, there's a real connectivity of home and family. There is a diversity of income, but the greater portion, because of the challenge of poverty and the elderly population, primarily has fixed incomes. The numbers are lower on the economic street, but higher on the home owner street.

The linchpin to submerged migration of the poor is chronic undereducation. As Willard-Lewis notes, poor education worsens the effects of concentrated poverty and extends its reach into every area of black life.

> There are many challenges with the public systems that provide resources and services to the poor—our public education, first and foremost. And the fact that all of those things that inhibit quality education were present, from oversized classrooms, lack of resources, stressed teachers, poor infrastructure, crumbling buildings, limited extracurricular activities—all of those things that work against children having the right to great educational opportunities, which then open doors to a future where they can earn significant wages—were in place in New Orleans. So you will probably have . . . high illiteracy rates and high dropout rates. In addition to that, the standardized test taking experiences forced many of the children out of the classroom because they knew they couldn't pass those tests. . . . So there were many barriers and re-

quirements that the children had to deal with when they went through the door of a crumbling old school, without books in an overcrowded classroom, that didn't equip them and didn't speak to their emotional, spiritual, academic, physical needs. And the ravages of Katrina have hit all the systems: our health care system, our public education system, our law enforcement system. They're all now working under great burdens of rebuilding. And my hope is that Katrina presents an opportunity to really address what the needs of the people are as they have articulated them.[2]

If submerged migrations drive poor people into poor neighborhoods through economic dislocation and social displacement, then *subversive migrations* disperse black folk across regional and national boundaries through both natural and social disasters. Subversive migrations occur when, for instance, storms or floods force black folk from their native regions into foreign territories—both within their nations and beyond—and when racist practices cause blacks to flee their homes. On the face of it, natural disaster is race-neutral, since its fury falls fiercely on all populations in a vulnerable region. But in New Orleans, the higher, safer ground has always been occupied by richer, whiter folk, while the lower, more dangerous ground has always been the province of poorer people. That poor black people have been exiled to vulnerable territory suggests the racial politics of both demographic and geographical shifts and trends. It also points to the fact that while nature's fury may be color-blind, the consequences of such fury surely aren't, since they track the social and racial hierarchies of those cultures.

Many of the migrations undertaken by black folk have been in response to the vicious acts of white terror, violence, and dominance. As Steven Hahn argues, migration's political character could be clearly and painfully apparent, as in Grimes County, Texas, where the violent seizure of power by the White Man's Union in 1900 sparked an "exodus" of hundreds (perhaps one-third) of the black inhabitants. More commonly, the politics were to be found in smaller-scale rejections of the hardships, humiliations, and coercions that black migrants believed whites were determined to inflict on them and in the established institutions and social networks that were their vehicles of change.[3]

Moreover, traumatic events like the 1927 Great Flood of Mississippi reveal the racial hurricanes and cultural floods that are the cruel aftermath of natural disaster. When black folk were forcibly exiled from their homes in the Great Flood, they were subject to the naked aggression of the state as it imposed sanctions on black life that intensified the affects of the natural disaster. Black folk were herded into work camps where they were forced to rebuild ravaged regions without compensation. They were also denied both their citizenship rights and the right to occupy land and structures they had helped to restore and reconstruct. Their treatment during the Great Flood reflected broader trends in the treatment of blacks at the hands of whites: their formally organized towns were often the target of racial terror, including, most famously, the bombing of an all-black community in 1921 in Tulsa, Oklahoma; their places of recreation were resented and closed; and their families, especially their more vocal members, were run off and forced to seek refuge in safer corners of the black diaspora.

Subversive migrations thrive not only on the coercion of poor black populations into vulnerable geographies, but also on the social chaos and racial disarray encouraged by the opportunistic exploitation of natural disaster for racist purposes. When, for instance, black folk were forced to work against their wills in the aftermath of the Great Flood, whites were able to utilize black labor to their racial, and societal, advantage. Moreover, subversive migrations compound the oppression that spatial and psychic dislocation breeds. As Jesse Jackson argues, such forces shouldn't be confused with the planned and desired mobility that characterize migration.

Dislocation, in the name of relocation, is not to be confused with migration. Blacks migrate of their own volition. Because it's more oppressive economically and militarily, blacks have been forced to rebuild at gunpoint. Here [in Katrina] people are put on planes for uncertain destinations and landing in Utah, or in California. This became an exile. I would distinguish between exile and migrations. To paraphrase the Bible, "They took us away, so we sat by the rivers of Babylon and there we wept." They took people away. They didn't migrate; they were taken away. Forcibly. In exile. And now, FEMA will not give the addresses to the State Board of Elections so they can get their voting material for the upcoming elections. They plan to keep them in exile so it'll affect the state's political demographics.

Jackson also spotted in the subversive migration of black folk in Katrina a haunting echo of slavery.

I saw people where their family was separated— men from women, children from the old and the sick from the well. And with no communication. They didn't know where others had gone, and they just began to panic in desperation. "Where's my wife? Where's my mother? Where's my child? Where's my daddy? What happened to our house?" They were, like, disoriented. It looked like the hull of a slave ship experience.[4]

In this latest act of subversive migration, black folk have been dispersed over 44 states in the nation, recalling the dreadful dispersal of their forbearers during slavery. While Katrina may lack the explicitly racist overtones of earlier natural disasters, the undeniable racial consequences of the subversive migration of hundreds of thousands of blacks underscores persistent patterns of racial hierarchy in the nation.

Finally, *subsidized migrations* occur when black masses are drawn forth by the promise of work or a style of life that zreflects an investment in black survival or a patronage of black skill and talent. It is widely known, of course, that poor black folk were drawn north away from their impoverished southern existence by the possibility of wage work that would adequately compensate blacks beyond the debt peonage of the sharecropper's plantation. Hence, northern industrialists subsidized black migration by offering fair pay for hard work, an offer that, in the context of black life, established a revolutionary predicate: that black workers were, in some ways, if not quite equal to white workers, then at least much further along the path to parity than in the south.

But it was not only the black poor who benefited from the push north. Recent historians have argued that the black elite were also lured north for greater professional opportunities and freedoms. As James Gregory contends, black professionals

were leaving at very high rates, especially graduates of the Negro colleges who, unless they went into the ministry or teaching, had little chance of finding appropriate work in the South. Their numbers were small, but attorneys, social workers, writers, musicians, and other professionals along with merchants, preachers, and teachers were an important part of the Great Migration. When Asa Philip Randolph followed his thirst for education to New York in 1911, when William Dawson left Tennessee to study law in Chicago in 1915, when George Baker decided to move his ministry to Brooklyn and call himself Father Divine, and when Bessie Smith and

Louis Armstrong took their music north in the 1920s, they too were part of the Southern Diaspora and part of why it became such a momentous force in the reorganization of American society.[5]

Although Gregory highlights the intersecting racial interests of poor and middle class blacks in a migration subsidized, in part, by northern economic and social forces, his argument also underscores the fact that, even among blacks, there were, and are, parallel migrations. In Katrina, both racial and class elements converged in the subsidized migration of black folk. More well-to-do blacks, and whites, enjoyed an experience of evacuation significantly different from that of the black masses. As it turns out, the parallel migrations of the well-to-do and the worse-off are sharply distinct.

First, the poor were, and remain, dependent upon government to subsidize their exodus, while wealthier citizens had, and still have, independent means to subsidize their evacuation and migration from New Orleans. Second, the more well-to-do are able to squeeze out greater advantage from their evacuations and migrations, either by finding work in locales away from New Orleans, in sustaining themselves through independent means, or in exploiting the tragedy through reconstruction and development contracts that subsidize their migration and their repatriation to the city in a far different manner than the poor. And third, the well-to-do have only been faced with temporary exiles, exoduses, and migrations; the poor face permanent displacements, dislocations, and forced migrations. Although their evacuations-turned-permanent migrations are allegedly subsidized through federal government aid, the meager-to-modest payments most are able to draw down mean that the black poor face far more difficult circumstances even when their living situation has greatly improved.

The migrations of black folk reveal as much about the nation's response to black pain and suffering as they do about the self-determining mobility of the masses of blacks. Whether they are submerged, subversive, or subsidized, black migrations reveal the moral, political, and racial backdrop of black movement. Each meaning of migration showed up in the tragedy of Katrina, but only a future that we shape by our principled and determined action will reveal which element of black migration prevails.

April 2007

NOTES

PREFACE

1. Lawrence N. Powell, "New Orleans: An American Pompeii?" September 2005, paper in author's possession.

CHAPTER 1

1. Jacques Amalric, "Crises in New Orleans Is History Repeating Itself," WatchingAmerica.com, September 8, 2005, http://www.watchingamerica. com/liberation000040.html.

2. "Who Are Katrina's Victims?" Center for American Progress, September 6, 2005, p. 1. www.americanprogress.org.

3. Ibid.

4. Alan Berube and Bruce Katz, "Katrina's Window: Confronting Concentrated Poverty Across America," Brookings Institution, October 2005, http:// www.brookings.edu/metro/pubs/20051012_concentratedpoverty.htm.

5. "Who Are Katrina's Victims?" pp. 1–2.

6. Ibid., p. 2.

7. Alan Berube and Steven Raphael, "Access to Cars in New Orleans," Brookings Institution, September 15, 2005, http://www.brookings.edu/ metro/20050915_katrinacarstables.pdf.

8. Ibid.

9. Ibid.

10. Ibid.

11. Ibid.

12. Ibid.

13. Ibid.

14. Berube and Katz, "Katrina's Window."

15. Ibid.

16. Ibid.

17. Ibid. I first used the term "black track" to describe a pattern of black out-migration that mimics patterns of earlier out-migration of white middle-class families to suburban communities. See Michael Eric Dyson, *Reflecting Black: African-American Cultural Criticism* (Minneapolis: University of Minnesota Press, 1993), p. 188.

18. As historian Lawrence N. Powell argues: "Because habitable land was so scarce, the population of New Orleans had to squeeze together, cheek-by-jowl—upper-class gents next door to or one street over from raw-boned stevedores, Irish next to German, black next to white, in a salt-and-pepper pattern that still baffles visitors to the city. New Orleans never had ethnically and racially pure enclaves until modern suburbanization began slotting the population into segregated subdivisions." Lawrence N. Powell, "New Orleans: An American Pompeii?" September 2005, p. 21. Paper in author's possession.

19. Anthony Fontenot, "How to Rebuild New Orleans" (compiled by Aaron Kinney and Page Rockwell), Salon.com, September 30, 2005, http://www.salon.com/news/feature/2005/09/30/rebuild_reaction.

20. "The Racial Wealth Gap Has Become a Huge Chasm that Severely Limits Black Access to Higher Education," *The Journal of Blacks in Higher Education*, 2005, pp. 23–25.

21. Jordan Flaherty, "Notes from Inside New Orleans," *New Orleans Independent Media Center*, September 2, 2005, http://neworleans.indymedia.org/news/2005/4043.php.

22. Ibid.

23. Ibid.

24. "Bush: 'We Will Do What It Takes'" (transcript of Bush speech from Jackson Square in the French Quarter of New Orleans), CNN.com, September 17, 2005, http://www.cnn.com/2005/POLITICS/09/15/bush.transcript/index.html.

25. "Who Are Katrina's Victims?" p. 2.

26. Manuel Roig-Franzia, "Once More, a Neighborhood Sees the Worst," *Washington Post*, September 8, 2005, p. A18.

27. "Lower Ninth Ward Neighborhood Snapshot," Greater New Orleans Community Data Center, October 10, 2002, http://www.gnocdc.org/orleans/8/22/snapshot.html.

28. Ibid.

29. Ibid.

30. Ibid.

31. Ibid.; Roig-Franzia, "Once More," p. A18.

32. Roig-Franzia, "Once More," p. A18; Ceci Connolly, "9th Ward: History, Yes, but a Future?; Race and Class Frame Debate on Rebuilding New Orleans District," *Washington Post*, October 3, 2005, p. A01.

33. Connolly, "9th Ward."

34. Ibid.; Roig-Franzia, "Once More."

35. Michael Ignatieff, "The Broken Contract," *The New York Times Magazine*, September 25, 2005, p. 15.

36. Ibid.

37. Ibid.

CHAPTER 2

1. For instance, in an interview with me in October 2005, Reverend Jesse Jackson supported Kanye West's views while expanding on them. "Well, Bush has not shown that he cares for civil rights or cares for the interest of black people. And there are several outstanding examples. Bush put a wreath at Dr. King's gravesite one day and the next day sent Olson [the solicitor general] to the Supreme Court to kill affirmative action. Like today Rosa Parks is lying in repose in the Rotunda. So he . . . nominates an extreme right-wing states' rights judge to the Supreme Court, who is against everything Ms. Parks stood for. Another example is the U.N. Commission on Racism in South Africa. He wouldn't send Colin Powell. He put a man [in] the attorney general's office, John Ashcroft, who was very hostile to civil rights. He has refused to meet with civil rights leadership for four years. So his administration has been quite hostile to the civil rights struggle, period. Women, labor, African Americans—[all have been] locked out."

2. *Access Hollywood*, September 5, 2005.

3. *Sunday Morning*, September 4, 2005.

4. Barack Obama, "Statement of Senator Barack Obama on Hurricane Relief Efforts," September 6, 2005, http://obama.senate.gov/statement/050906-statement_of_senator_barack_obama_on_hurricane_katrina_relief_efforts.

5. Ibid.

6. Philip Shenon, "Clinton Levels Sharp Criticism at the President's Relief Effort," *The New York Times,* September 19, 2005, p. A21.

7. W. Fitzhugh Brundage, *The Southern Past: A Clash of Race and Memory* (Cambridge, Mass.: The Belknap Press of Harvard University Press, 2005), pp. 99–100.

8. "A Concert for Hurricane Relief," NBC, September 2, 2005.

9. Ibid.

10. Ibid.

11. "First Lady: Charges that Racism Slowed Aid 'Disgusting,'" CNN.com, September 9, 2005, http://www.cnn.com/2005/POLITICS/09/08/katrina.laura bush.

12. "Interview with George H.W. Bush, Barbara Bush," *Larry King Live,* CNN, September 5, 2005.

13. Jacob Weisberg, "An Imperfect Storm: How Race Shaped Bush's Response to Katrina," *Slate*, September 7, 2005, http://www.slate.com/id/2125812/?nav=navoa.

14. Ibid.

15. Ibid.

16. Ibid.

17. Ibid.

18. Susan Page and Mario Puente, "Poll Shows Racial Divide on Storm Response," *USA TODAY*, September 13, 2005.

19. Alan Berube and Bruce Katz, "Katrina's Window: Confronting Concentrated Poverty Across America," Brookings Institution, October 2005, http://www.brookings.edu/metro/pubs/20051012_concentratedpoverty.htm.

20. Robert Pear, "Buying of News by Bush's Aides Is Ruled Illegal," *The New York Times*, October 1, 2005.

21. Bruce Weber, "CRITIC'S NOTEBOOK: Power, Pitfalls and 'The Great White Hope'; A Washington Company Revisits a Shining Moment from a Decidedly Different Era," *The New York Times,* September 14, 2000, p. E1.

22. Dave Goldiner, "Who Is to Blame? Terror War Crippled FEMA, Say Experts," *New York Daily News,* September 5, 2005. p. 7.

23. "Reaction to Katrina Split on Racial Lines," CNN.com, September 13, 2005, http://www.cnn.com/2005/12/katrina.race.poll/index.html.

CHAPTER 3

1. See the transcript of Bush's speech ("George Bush Delivers Remarks at the Republican National Convention") at http://www.cnn.com/ELECTION/2000/conventions/republican/transcripts/bush.html.

2. See "Welcome to the Hackocracy," *The New Republic*, October 17, 2005. Also see Ken Silverstein, "Shades of FEMA's Brown in Bush Pick," *The Los Angeles Times*, October 1, 2005, p. 1.

3. Naomi Klein, "The Rise of Disaster Capitalism," *The Nation*, May 2, 2005.

4. Roy S. Popkin, "The History and Politics of Disaster Management in the United States," in Andrew Kirby, editor, *Nothing to Fear: Risks and Hazards in American Society* (Tucson: University of Arizona Press, 1990), p. 101.

5. Ibid.; Rutherford H. Platt, et al., *Disasters and Democracy: The Politics of Extreme Natural Events* (Washington, D.C.: Island Press), 1999, p. 1; George D. Haddow and Jane A. Bullock, *Introduction to Emergency Management* (Boston: Butterworth-Heinemann, 2003), p. 2.

6. Platt et al., *Disasters and Democracy*, p. 1; Popkin, in *Nothing to Fear*, p. 101.

7. Platt, *Disasters and Democracy*, p. 1.

8. Platt, *Disasters and Democracy*, p. 1; Mary Comerio, *Disaster Hits Home: New Policy for Urban Housing Recovery* (Berkeley: University of California Press, 1998), p. 198.

9. Popkin, in *Nothing to Fear*, pp. 103–104; Comerio, *Disaster Hits Home*, p. 198. As Popkin writes on p. 104: "The agency came into being in 1881 after the United States Senate ratified the Geneva Conventions. But . . . Barton saw that, in addition to aid to war victims, disaster relief could be an equally

important activity for the organization. Paradoxically, she could not sell the idea to the international Red Cross movement at the time; her disaster proposals, known as the 'American amendment,' were soundly defeated at conferences in Geneva. The American Red Cross was only a few months old when she sent a representative to the scene of a major forest fire. . . . The very first Red Cross disaster supplies were sent to Port Huron for victims of that fire."

10. Popkin, in *Nothing to Fear*, p. 103.

11. Comerio, *Disaster Hits Home*, p. 198.

12. Platt, *Disasters and Democracy*, pp. 2–3.

13. Ibid., p. 4.

14. Gordon Thomas and Max Morgan Witt, *The San Francisco Earthquake* (New York: Stein and Day, 1971), p. 274, cited in Platt, *Disasters and Democracy*, p. 248.

15. Platt, *Disasters and Democracy*, p. 4; Richard Hofstadter, *The Age of Reform* (New York: Knopf, 1955).

16. "Progressivism," in *The Columbia Encyclopedia, Sixth Edition* (New York: Columbia University Press, 2004), p. 38819; Hofstadter, *The Age of Reform*.

17. Seymour Toll, *Zoned American* (New York: Grossman Publishers, 1969), p. 26, cited in Platt, *Disasters and Democracy*, p. 4.

18. Wynn Craig Wade, *Titanic: End of the Dream* (New York: Penguin, 1979), cited in Platt, *Disasters and Democracy*, p. 4.

19. Platt, *Disasters and Democracy*, pp. 4–6.

20. Ibid., p. 6.

21. Comerio, *Disaster Hits Home*, p. 198.

22. Ibid.

23. Haddow and Bullock, *Emergency Management*, p. 2.; Popkin, in *Nothing to Fear*, p. 107.

24. Ibid. Haddow and Bullock argue on p. 2 that, despite the act's great influence, it rested on a faulty philosophical premise of humans' ability to control nature, giving a sense of false security and leading to dangerous consequences. "This act has had a significant and long-lasting impact on emergency management in this country. This act reflected a philosophy that man could control nature, thereby eliminating the risk of floods. Although this program would promote economic and population growth patterns along the nation's rivers, history has proven that this attempt at emergency management was shortsighted and costly."

25. Ibid.; Comerio, *Disaster Hits Home*, p. 199; Popkin, in *Nothing to Fear*, pp. 106–108; Platt, *Disasters and Democracy*, pp. 6–7.

26. Comerio, *Disaster Hits Home*, p. 199; Platt, *Disasters and Democracy*, p. 12.

27. Haddow and Bullock, *Emergency Management*, p. 3.

28. This legislation is charted in Popkin, in *Nothing to Fear*, pp. 109–110.

29. Platt, *Disasters and Democracy*, p. 15.

30. Haddow and Bullock, *Emergency Management*, pp. 2–3; Platt, *Disasters and Democracy*, p. 15.

31. Haddow and Bullock, *Emergency Management*, p. 5.

32. As Haddow and Bullock point out, the fact that Carter had been a governor was critical to his development of FEMA as president to resolve the fragmentation of federal emergency management. "The states and the governors grew increasingly frustrated over this fragmentation. In the absence of one clear federal lead agency in emergency management, a group of State Civil Defense Directors led by Lacy Suiter of Tennessee and Erie Jones of Illinois launched an effort through the National Governor's Association (NGA) to consolidate federal emergency management activities in one agency." *Emergency Management*, p. 5.

33. Haddow and Bullock, *Emergency Management*, p. 7.

34. Ibid., pp. 7–8.

35. Ibid., p. 8.

36. Ibid., p. 9.

37. Ibid., p. 9.

38. As with Jimmy Carter, Clinton's governorship prepared him to highlight the work of FEMA. As Haddow and Bullock write, "As Governor of Arkansas, President Clinton had experience responding to several major flooding disasters and realized how important an effective response and quick recovery was to communities and to voters." *Emergency Management*, p. 9.

39. Haddow and Bullock, *Emergency Management*, p. 10.

40. Ibid., pp. 10–12.

41. Ibid., p. 11.

42. Ibid., p. 12.

43. Kevin Drum, "Chronology," *Washington Monthly* (Political Animal), September 1, 2005, http://www.washingtonmonthly.com/archives/individual/2005_09/007023.php.

44. Haddow and Bullock, *Emergency Management*, p. 13.

45. Drum, "Chronology."

46. Vernon Leob, "Cheney to Lead Anti-Terrorism Plan Team; New FEMA Office Will Coordinate Response Efforts of More Than 40 Agencies, Officials Say," *The Washington Post*, May 9, A29; Haddow and Bullock, *Emergency Management*, p. 12.

47. Haddow and Bullock, *Emergency Management*, p. 12.

48. Leob, "Cheney to Lead," p. A29.

49. Ibid.

50. The newly formed department was initially called the National Military Establishment, but when the National Security Act of 1947 that created the department was amended in 1949, it gained its present name.

51. Drum, "Chronology."

52. Scott Shane, "STORM AND CRISIS: Man in the News—Michael De-

Wayne Brown: Facing Blame in a Disaster," *New York Times*, September 7, 2005, p. A22.

53. Daren Fonda and Rita Healy, "How Reliable Is Brown's Resume?" *Time*, September 12, 2005.

54. Ibid.

55. Ibid.

56. Ibid.

57. Drum, "Chronology."

58. The phrase, from the *Washington Post*, is cited in "Bush Should Join Outrage over Botched Hurricane Relief," Editorial, *Tampa Tribune*, September 7, 2005.

59. Spencer S. Hsu, "Leaders Lacking Disaster Experience," *Washington Post*, September 9, 2005, p. A01.

60. Ibid.; Eric Lipton, Christopher Drew, Scott Shane, and David Rohde, "Breakdowns Marked Path from Hurricane to Anarchy," *The New York Times*, September 11, 2005, p. 1.

61. Ibid.

62. Seth Borenstein and Shannon McCaffrey, "Brown Is Merely a Symbol of the Problems at FEMA, Experts Say," *Knight Ridder Newspapers*, September 9, 2005, http://www.realcities.com/mld/krwashington/12605339.htm.

63. Hsu, "Leaders Lacking."

CHAPTER 4

1. National Hurricane Center, "Tropical Depression TWELVE" [5 PM EDT TUE AUG 23 2005], http://www.nhc.noaa.gov/archive/2005/dis/al122005.discus.001.shtml?; National Hurricane Center, "Tropical Storm KATRINA" [11 AM EDT WED AUG 24 2005], http://www.nhc.noaa.gov/archive/2005/dis/al122005.discus.004.shtml?.

2. National Hurricane Center, "Hurricane KATRINA" [5 PM EDT THU AUG 25 2005], http://www.nhc.noaa.gov/archive/2005/pub/al122005.public.009.shtml?; "2 Killed by Trees as Katrina Makes Land," *The Washington Times* (United Press International), August 25, 2005, http://washingtontimes.com/upi/20050825-043734-9093r.htm; Mike Davis, "The Predators of New Orleans," *Le Monde Diplomatique,* October 2005.

3. National Hurricane Center, "Hurricane KATRINA" [1130 AM EDT FRI AUG 26 2005], http://www.nhc.noaa.gov/archive/2005/pub/al122005.public.013.shtml?; National Hurricane Center, "Hurricane KATRINA" [5 PM EDT FRI AUG 26 2005], http://www.nhc.noaa.gov/archive/2005/pub/al122005.public.014.shtml?.

4. Press Release, August 26, 2005, "Governor Blanco Declares State of Emergency," http://gov.louisiana.gov/index.cfm?md=newsroom&tmp=detail&articleID=776; Governor Haley Barbour, August 27, 2005, Executive Order No. 939, http://www.governorbarbour.com/EO939.htm.

5. United States Department of Defense, News Transcript, "Special Defense Department Briefing with Commander of Joint Task Force Katrina," Thursday, September 1, 2005, http://www.dod.gov/transcripts/2005/tr2005 0901-3843.html; "Lt. Gen. Honore a 'John Wayne Dude,'" September 3, 2005, http://www.cnn.com/2005/US/09/02/honore.profile; Kevin Chappell, "The Aftermath of Hurricane Katrina: And the Man Who's Helping Put Things Back Together," *Ebony*, November 2005, pp. 284–287.

6. Larry Eichel et al., "Katrina: Failure at Every Turn," *Knight Ridder Newspapers*, September 11, 2005, http://www.philly.com/mld/philly/news/special_packages/hurricane_katrina/12611879.htm.

7. Fox News, "Official: Astrodome Can't Take More Refugees," FoxNews.Com, September 2, 2005, http://www.foxnews.com/story/0,2933,168112,00.html.

8. Press Release, August 27, 2005, "Governor Blanco Asks President to Declare an Emergency for the State of Louisiana due to Hurricane Katrina," http://gov.louisiana.gov/index.cfm?md=newsroom&tmp=detail&articleID=778.

9. White House press release, August 27, 2005, "Statement on Federal Emergency Assistance for Louisiana," http://www.whitehouse.gov/news/releases/2005/08/20050827–1.html; White House press release, August 28, 2005, "Statement on Federal Emergency Assistance for Mississippi," http://www.whitehouse.gov/news/releases/2005/08/20050828.html; White House press release, August 28, "Statement on Federal Emergency Assistance for Alabama," http://www.whitehouse.gov/news/releases/2005/08/20050828-3.html; White House press release, August 28, 2005, "Statement on Federal Disaster Assistance for Florida," http://www.whitehouse.gov/news/releases/2005/08/20050828–2.html; Eichel et al., "Katrina."

10. Eichel et al., "Katrina."

11. White House, August 27, "President's Radio Address," http://www.whitehouse.gov/news/releases/2005/08/20050827.html.

12. "Katrina Aims for Louisiana; Contraflow Begins at 4pm," 8/27/05, http://www.2theadvocate.com/stories/082705/new_kat2001.shtml.

13. Bruce Nolan, "Katrina Takes Aim," *The Times-Picayune*, August 28, 2005; Susan B. Glasser and Michael Grunwald, "The Steady Buildup to a City's Chaos," *The Washington Post*, September 11, 2005, p. A01.

14. Glasser and Grunwald, "The Steady Buildup."

15. Ibid.

16. Ibid.

17. Tamara Lush, "For Forecasting Chief, No Joy in Being Right," *St. Petersburg Times*, August 30, 2005.

18. Eichel et al., "Katrina."

19. State of Louisiana Emergency Operations Plan, Supplement 1A: Southeast Louisiana Hurricane Evacuation and Sheltering Plan, Revised, January 2000, p. II–2.

20. Ralph R. Reiland, "Comedy of Deadly Errors," *Pittsburgh Tribune-*

Review, September 19, 2005, http://www.pittsburghlive.com/x/tribune-review/opinion/columnists/reiland/s_374919.html.

21. Ibid.

22. Ibid.; National Hurricane Center, "Hurricane KATRINA" [1 AM CDT SUN AUG 28 2005], http://www.nhc.noaa.gov/archive/2005/pub/al122005.public.020.shtml?; National Hurricane Center, "Hurricane KATRINA" [8 AM EDT SUN AUG 28 2005], http://www.nhc.noaa.gov/archive/2005/dis/al122005.discus.022.shtml?; Gordon Russell, "Nagin Orders First-Ever Mandatory Evacuation of New Orleans," *Times-Picayune*, August 28, 2005, http://www.nola.com/newslogs/breakingtp/index.ssf?/mtlogs/nola_Times-Picayune/archives/2005_08_28.html#074564.

23. Russell, "Nagin Orders."

24. Some have said the number is 112,000.

25. Lush, "For Forecasting Chief"; The White House, Photo Essays, http://www.whitehouse.gov/news/releases/2005/08/images/20050828-1_p082805pm-0101-515h.html.

26. "26,000 Shelter at Superdome," *Times Picayune*, August 28, 2005, http://www.nola.com/newslogs/breakingtp/index.ssf?/mtlogs/nola_Times-Picayune/archives/2005_08_28.html#074657; Eichel et al., "Katrina."

27. Doug MacCash and James O. Byrne, "Catastrophic: Storm Surge Swamps 9th Ward, St. Bernard; Lakeview Levee Breach Threatens to Inundate City," *The Times-Picayune*, August 30, 2005, http://www.nola.com/hurricane/tp/katrina.ssf?/hurricane/katrina/stories/083005catastrophic.html; Eichel et al., "Katrina"; NASA's Earth Observatory, "New Orleans 17th Street Canal Levee Breach Satellite Image," September 1, 2005, http://yubanet.com/artman/publish/article_24515.shtml.

28. Eichel et al., "Katrina."

29. NASA, "Katrina Intensifies into a Powerful Hurricane, Strikes Northern Gulf Coast," 8.30.05, http://www.nasa.gov/vision/earth/lookingatearth/katrina_trmm_0828_0829.html.

30. Eichel et al., "Katrina."

31. Ibid.

32. Ibid.

33. Ibid.

34. Ibid.

35. Eric Lipton, Christopher Drew, Scott Shane, and David Rohde, "Breakdowns Marked Path from Hurricane to Anarchy," *The New York Times*, September 11, 2005, p. 1.

36. Ibid.

37. Ibid.

38. Landrieu threatened to punch Bush if he criticized local officials on ABC's *This Week* with George Stephanopoulos, September 4, 2005.

39. Memorandum, August 29, 2005, Michael D. Brown, FEMA, http://wid.ap.org/documents/dhs.katrina.pdf; Ted Bridis, *Associated Press*, "FEMA

Chief Sent Help Only After Storm Hit," September 7, 2005, http://abcnews.go.com/Politics/HurricaneKatrina/wireStory?id=1104514&CMP=OTC-RSS-Feeds0312.

40. Memorandum, August 29, 2005, Michael D. Brown, FEMA, http://wid.ap.org/documents/dhs.katrina.pdf.

41. The White House, "Press Gaggle with Scott McClellan and Dr. Mark McClellan," August 29, 2005, http://www.whitehouse.gov/news/releases/2005/08/20050829-1.html; The White House, "President Participates in Conversation on Medicare," August 29, 2005, http://www.whitehouse.gov/news/releases/2005/08/20050829-5.html.

42. Mary Foster, "Super Storm Rips Piece Off Superdome's Roof," *Associated Press*, August 29, 2005, http://www.sfgate.com/cgi-bin/article.cgi?f=/n/a/2005/08/29/national/a163816D53.DTL.

43. The White House, Photo Essays, August 29, 2005, http://www.whitehouse.gov/news/releases/2005/08/images/20050829-5_p082905pm-0125-515h.html.

44. FEMA News, "First Responders Urged Not to Respond to Hurricane Impact Areas Unless Dispatched by State, Local Authorities," August 29, 2005, http://www.fema.gov/news/newsrelease.fema?id=18470.

45. American Red Cross, Press Room, "American Red Cross Launches Largest Mobilization Effort in History for Hurricane Katrina," August 29, 2005, http://www.redcross.org/pressrelease/0,1077,0_314_4473,00.html. Even in the announcement of FEMA's support of the Red Cross and other charitable organizations, the agency, in the title of its press release, emphasized due process and procedural correctness even in the midst of its bungling of the Gulf States emergency. See FEMA News, "Cash Sought to Help Hurricane Victims, Volunteers Should Not Self-Dispatch," August 29, 2005, http://www.fema.gov/news/newsrelease.fema?id=18473.

46. E&P Staff, "Revealed: Rumsfeld at Padres Game as New Orleans Sank," *Editor & Publisher*, September 6, 2005.

47. Eichel et al., "Katrina."

48. Evan Thomas, "How Bush Blew It," *Newsweek*, September 19, 2005, http://www.msnbc.msn.com/id/9287434/.

49. Ibid.

50. The White House, "President Commemorates 60th Anniversary of V-J Day," August 30, 2005. http://www.whitehouse.gov/news/releases/2005/08/20050830-1.html.

51. Ibid.

52. Jennifer Loven (Associated Press), *The San Diego Union-Tribune*, August 30, 2005; The White House, "Press Gaggle by Scott McClellan," August 30, 2005, http://www.whitehouse.gov/news/releases/2005/08/20050830-4.html; Thomas, "How Bush Blew It." The task of getting the president to cut his historic, extended vacation short was no simple matter. As Evan Thomas reports, Bush's surly private demeanor often makes it difficult for his aides to

bring him bad news. "The bad news on this early morning, Tuesday, Aug. 30, some twenty-four hours after Hurricane Katrina had ripped through New Orleans, was that the president would have to cut short his five-week vacation by a couple of days and return to Washington. The president's chief of staff, Andrew Card; his deputy chief of staff, Joe Hagin; his counselor, Dan Bartlett; and his spokesman, Scott McClellan, held a conference call to discuss the question of the president's early return and the delicate task of telling him. Hagin, it was decided, as senior aide on the ground, would do the deed." Thomas, "How Bush Blew It."

53. *Meet the Press*, Transcript for September 4, 2005, http://www.msnbc. msn.com/id/9179790.

54. John Hill, "Level of Devastation in New Orleans Area Continues to Rise," *The Shreveport Times*, August 31, 2005.

55. Ibid.

56. *The Situation Room*, CNN, Transcript, "Hurricane Katrina Aftermath; Rescue Efforts and Assessing the Damage," http://transcripts.cnn.com/ TRANSCRIPTS/0508/30/sitroom.02.html.

57. David Remnick, "High Water: How Presidents and Citizens React to Disaster," *The New Yorker*, October 3, 2005, http://www.newyorker.com/fact/ content/articles/051003fa_fact.

58. "Federal Agencies Dispatch Help," Associated Press, *St. Petersburg Times*, August 30, 2005, http://www.sptimes.com/2005/08/30/Worldand nation/Federal_agencies_disp.shtml.

59. Richard Roeper, "Say That Again? 'Things Are Going Relatively Well,'" *Chicago Sun-Times*, September 12, 2005, p. 6.

60. Department of Homeland Security, Michael Chertoff Memorandum, "Designation of Principal Federal Official for Hurricane Katrina," http:// www.dhs.gov; Department of Homeland Security, *National Response Plan*, December 2004, http://www.dhs.gov/interweb/assetlibrary/NRP_FullText. pdf.

61. Department of Homeland Security, *National Response Plan*.

62. Jonathan S. Linday, Alison Young, and Shannon McCaffrey, "Chertoff Delayed Federal Response, Memo Shows," Knight Ridder Newspapers, Knight Ridder, Washington Bureau, September 13, 2005, http://www.realcities.com/ mld/krwashington/12637172.htm.

63. Department of Homeland Security, Michael Chertoff Memorandum.

64. Also see Eric Lipton and Eric Schmitt, "Navy Ships and Maritime Rescue Teams Sent to Region," *The New York Times*, August 31, 2005, p. 14.

65. The White House, "Press Gaggle with Scott McClellan," August 31, 2005, http://www.whitehouse.gov/news/releases/2005/08/20050831-2.html.

66. Ibid.

67. Fox News, "Bush Meets with Disaster Relief Task Force in D.C.," September 1, 2005, http://www.foxnews.com/story/0,2933,167908,00.html.

68. Ibid.; The White House, "President Outlines Hurricane Katrina Relief

Efforts," August 31, 2005, http://www.whitehouse.gov/news/releases/2005/08/20050831-3.html.

69. Scott Gold, "Katrina's Rising Toll; Trapped in an Arena of Suffering; 'We Are Like Animals,' a Mother Says Inside the Louisiana Superdome, Where Hope and Supplies Are Sparse," *Los Angeles Times*, September 1, 2005, p. 1; Will Haygood, "'It Was as if All of Us Were Already Pronounced Dead': Convention Center Left a Five-Day Legacy of Chaos and Violence," *The Washington Post*, September 15, 2005, p. A1.

70. State of Louisiana, Executive Department, Executive Order No. KBB 2005-31, *Emergency Evacuation by Buses*, August 31, 2005, http://69.2.43.89/2005%20Executive%20orders/31execEmergencyEvacuationbyBuses.pdf.

71. State of Louisiana, Executive Department, Executive Order No. KBB 2005-24, *Emergency Occupation of Hotels and Motel Rooms*, September 1, 2005, http://gov.louisiana.gov/assets/docs/24EmergencyHotelOccupation.pdf.

72. Greg Mitchell, "BLOGGING THE HURRICANE, Day 3: Updates All Day from the Scene as the Disaster Spreads," *Editor & Publisher*, August 31, 2005, http://www.editorandpublisher.com/eandp/news/article_display.jsp?vnu_content_id=1001051366.

73. Keith Spera, "Desperation, Death on Road to Safety," *Times-Picayune*, August 31, 2005, http://www.nola.com/weblogs/print.ssf?/mtlogs/nola_Times-Picayune/archives/print075561.html; Gold, "Katrina's Rising Toll," p. 1; Haygood, "'It Was as if All of Us Were Already Pronounced Dead,'" p. A1; Keith O'Brien and Bryan Bender, "Chronology of Errors: How a Disaster Spread," *The Boston Globe*, September 11, 2005, p. A1.

74. Ibid.

75. United States Department of Health and Human Services—Disasters & Emergencies: Hurricanes, "HHS Declares Public Health Emergency for Hurricane Katrina (Determination That a Public Health Emergency Exists)," August 31, 2005, http://www.hhs.gov/emergency/determination.html; David Marks, "Public Health Emergency Declared: Doctors Worried Disease May Strike in Katrina's Aftermath," August 31, 2005, WCBS-TV, New York, http://wcbstv.com/topstories/local_story_243174734.html.

76. "Public Health Emergency Declared in the Gulf Coast," WISTV, August 31, 2005, http://www.wistv.com/Global/story.asp?S=3787389.

77. "Waiting for a Leader," *The New York Times*, September 1, 2005.

78. The White House, "President Outlines Hurricane Katrina Relief Efforts," August 31, 2005, http://www.whitehouse.gov/news/releases/2005/08/20050831-3.html.

79. Brett Martle, "Governor: Everyone Must Leave," *Associated Press*, August 31, 2005, http://apnews.myway.com/article/20050831/D8CAREV00.html.

80. Ibid.

81. Ibid.

82. CBS News, "New Orleans Fights to Stop Looting," August 31, 2005, http://www.cbsnews.com/stories/2005/08/31/katrina/printable808193.shtml.

83. Thomas, "How Bush Blew It."

84. Ibid.

85. O'Brien and Bender, "Chronology of Errors."

86. "Breaking: Condi Rice Spends Salary on Shoes," September 1, 2005, http://www.gawker.com/news/condoleezza-rice/breaking-condi-rice-spends-salary-on-shoes-123467.php; Jo Piazza and Chris Rovzar, Daily Dish, "As South Drowns, Rice Soaks in N.Y.," *New York Daily News*, September 2, 2005; "Condi Rice Leaves NYC High and Dry," September 2, 2005, http://www.gawker.com/news/condoleezza-rice/index.php#breaking-condi-rice-spends-salary-on-shoes-123467.

87. Ibid.; Richard Johnson, "Sightings," Page Six, *The New York Post*, September 2, 2005.

CHAPTER 5

1. Richard Roeper, "Say That Again? 'Things Are Going Relatively Well,'" *Chicago Sun-Times*, September 12, 2005, p. 6.

2. Dan Froomkin, "A Dearth of Answers," Washingtonpost.com, September 1, 2005, http://www.washingtonpost.com/wp-dyn/content/blog/2005/09/01/BL2005090100915.html.

3. The phrase "ambushed by the unexpected" is from a sermon by Rev. Dr. Caesar A.W. Clark of Dallas, Texas.

4. Larry Eichel et al., "Katrina: Failure at Every Turn," *Knight Ridder Newspapers*, September 11, 2005, http://www.philly.com/mld/philly/news/special_packages/hurricane_katrina/12611879.htm.

5. MSNBC staff, "Katrina Forecasters Were Remarkably Accurate; Levee Breaks, Catastrophic Damage Predicted, Contrary to Bush Claims," September 19, 2005, http://www.msnbc.msn.com/id/9369041.

6. Jim Bradshaw, "Forecasters Fear Levees Won't Hold Katrina," *Lafayette Daily Adviser*, August 28, 2005.

7. *The Wiz*, 1975, music and lyrics by Charlie Smalls.

8. Evan Thomas, "How Bush Blew It," *Newsweek*, September 19, 2005, http://www.msnbc.msn.com/id/9287434/.

9. Sidney Blumenthal, "No One Can Say They Didn't See It Coming," Salon.com, August 31, 2005, http://www.salon.com/opinion/blumenthal/2005/08/31/disaster_preparation; Nicole Gaouette, "Katrina's Rising Toll; A Diminished FEMA Scrambles to the Rescue; The agency's standing within the government has been eclipsed by the war on terrorism," *Los Angeles Times*, September 1, 2005, p. 23.

10. Jim Wilson, "New Orleans Is Sinking," *Popular Mechanics*, September 11, 2001.

11. Mark Fischetti, "Drowning New Orleans," *Scientific American*, October 1, 2001.

12. Eric Berger, "Keeping Its Head Above Water: New Orleans Faces Doomsday Scenario," *Houston Chronicle*, December 1, 2001, http://www.chron.com/disp/story.mpl/nation/1153609.html.

13. John McQuaid and Mark Schleifstein, "Washing Away: Special Report from Times-Picayune" (Five-Part Series), June 23–27, 2002.

14. Joel K. Bourne, Jr., "Gone with the Water," *National Geographic*, October 2004, http://magma.nationalgeographic.com/ngm/0410/feature5/?fs=www3.nationalgeographic.com.

15. Nova: Science Now, January 2005, http://www.pbs.org/wgbh/nova/sciencenow/3214/06.html.

16. Chris Mooney, "Thinking Big About Hurricanes: It's time to get serious about saving New Orleans," *The American Prospect*, May 23, 2005, http://www.prospect.org/web/page.ww?section=root&name=ViewWeb&articleId=9754.

17. *Oil Storm*, Directed by James Erskine, written by James Erskine and Caroline Levy, FX Network, June 5, 2005, 8PM EST.

18. Peter Eisler, Jim Drinkard, and Traci Watson, "Engineers Had Warned of a Looming Disaster," *USA TODAY*, September 1, 2005, p. 5A.

19. Will Bunch, "When the Levee Breaks," *Attytood* (Blog), August 30, 2005, http://www.pnionline.com/dnblog/attytood/archives/002331.html.

20. Ibid.; Gaouette, "Katrina's Rising Toll."

21. Bunch, "When the Levee Breaks."

22. Ibid.; Sheila Grissett, "Shifting Federal Budget Erodes Protection from Levees; Because of Cuts, Hurricane Risk Grows," *Times-Picayune*, June 8, 2004, http://nolassf.dev.advance.net/newsstory/levee08.html.

23. Grissett, *Times-Picayune*, June 8, 2004.

24. Bunch, "When the Levee Breaks."

25. Anita Kumar, "One Question Builds: Where Was FEMA?," *St. Petersburg Times*, September 3, 2005.

26. Eisler, Drinkard, and Watson, "Engineers Had Warned of a Looming Disaster," p. 5A.

27. Ibid.

28. Kumar, "One Question Builds."

29. Ibid.

30. Andrew C. Revkin and Christopher Drew, "Intricate Flood Protection Long a Focus of Dispute," *The New York Times*, September 1, 2005, p. 16.

31. Ibid.

32. This is not to suggest that the Army Corps of Engineers is totally blameless for its plight. In fact, some of the choices it made to expend its funds have been called into question in light of the failure of the levees during Katrina. "Before Hurricane Katrina breached a levee on the New Orleans Industrial Canal, the Army Corps of Engineers had already launched a $748 million construction project at that very location. But the project had nothing to do with flood control. The Corps was building a huge new lock for the canal, an effort to accommodate steadily increasing barge traffic. Except that barge traffic on the canal has been steadily declining. In Katrina's wake, Louisiana politicians and other critics have complained about paltry funding for the Army Corps in general and Louisiana projects in particular. But over

the five years of President Bush's administration, Louisiana has received far more money for Corps civil works projects than any other state, about $1.9 billion; California was a distant second with less than $1.4 billion, even though its population is more than seven times as large. Much of that Louisiana money was spent to try to keep low-lying New Orleans dry. But hundreds of millions of dollars have gone to unrelated water projects demanded by the state's congressional delegation and approved by the Corps, often after economic analyses that turned out to be inaccurate." Michael Grunwald, "Money Flowed to Questionable Projects; State Leads in Army Corps Spending, but Millions Had Nothing to Do with Floods," *The Washington Post*, September 8, 2005, p. A01. Although there is a legitimate critique to be made of pork barrel politics that siphon off funds that might otherwise go to worthy causes, this analysis doesn't let the Bush administration off the hook for its choice of sand over water—Iraq over New Orleans—nor does it excuse serious federal inattention to a critical matter of security that would have mandated stricter scrutiny of the actions of the Corps, and far more interest in, and interaction with, its engineers to help protect New Orleans from disaster. Even as critics suggest that no matter how much money was spent, the levees were never intended to withstand a Category 4 hurricane, a strengthened levee system would have considerably upped the chances of preventing, or reducing, damage. The Bush administration not only failed to be fiscally responsible to the Corps, but it failed to be sufficiently concerned with the warnings made by its own Corps, and by FEMA, to act on a predictably disastrous situation.

33. Andrew C. Revkin, "Gazing at Breached Levees, Critics See Years of Missed Opportunities," *The New York Times*, September 2, 2005, p. 15.

34. Cited in Reyben Brody, "The Mayor Needs to Find New Answers: A Former Assistant to N.O. Mayor Ray Nagin Says He Should Embrace Environmental Considerations in Post-Katrina Initiatives," *Independent Weekly*, October 26, 2005, http://indyweek.com/durham/2005-10-19/cover2.html.

35. Louisiana Coastal Conservation and Restoration Task Force and the Wetlands Conservation and Restoration Authority. *Coast 2050: Toward a Sustainable Coastal Louisiana* (Baton Rouge, La.: Louisiana Department of Natural Resources, 1998), p. 1.

36. Ibid., p. 19.

37. Ibid., p. 31.

38. Ibid., p. 40.

39. Bourne, Jr., "Gone with the Water."

40. Robert S. Young and David M. Bush, "Forced Marsh," *The New York Times*, September 27, 2005, p. 25.

41. Ibid.

42. Ibid., p. 41.

43. Mark Schleifstein, "Officials: Coast Is Federal Problem, Too; Plan for Restoration Costs Is Challenged," *The New York Times*, August 27, 2005, p. 3;

"Comment: Katrina Compounded," *The Progressive*, October 2005, http://www.progressive.org/mag_com1005.

44. Susan Milligan, "US Earlier Rebuffed Louisiana on Aid," *The Boston Globe*, September 1, 2005, p. A12.

45. Ibid.

46. "Louisiana's Wetlands," *The New York Times*, February 28, 2004, p. 14.

CHAPTER 6

1. Fox News, "Official: Astrodome," http://www.foxnews.com/story/0,2933,168112,00.html.

2. Ibid.; Julian Borger, "Mayor Issues SOS as Chaos Tightens Its Grip," *The Guardian*, September 2, 2005, http://www.guardian.co.uk/katrina/story/0,16441,1561314,00.html.

3. Borger, "Mayor."

4. Elisabeth Bumiller, "Casualty of Firestorm: Outrage, Bush and FEMA Chief," *The New York Times*, September 10, 2005, p. 11.

5. CNN, American Morning (City of New Orleans Falling Deeper into Chaos and Desperation), September 2, 2005, Transcript: 090201CN.V74.

6. Steve Wieberg and Thomas Frank, "Stadium Makes Visitors as Welcome as It Can," *USA TODAY*, September 1, 2005.

7. Robert E. Pierre and Ann Gerhart, "News of Pandemonium May Have Slowed Aid; Unsubstantiated Reports of Violence Were Confirmed by Some Officials, Spread by News Media," *The Washington Post*, October 5, 2005, p. A08.

8. The White House, Press Conference, "President Asks Bush and Clinton to Assist in Hurricane Relief Efforts, September 1, 2005, http://www.whitehouse.gov/news/releases/2005/09/20050901-3.html.

9. "What Hastert Really Said," *Slate Sidebar*, September 7, 2005, http://www.slate.com/id/2125810/sidebar/2125827/.

10. The White House, "Press Briefing by Scott McClellan," September 1, 2005, http://www.whitehouse.gov/news/releases/2005/09/20050901-2.html; Robert Siegel (Katrina), "U.S. Aid Effort Criticized in New Orleans," *All Things Considered*, September 1, 2005, http://www.npr.org/templates/story/story.php?storyId=4828771.

11. Department of Homeland Security, Press Release, "Press Conference with Officials from the Department of Homeland Security, Justice Department, Defense Department, the National Guard Bureau, U.S. Coast Guard and FEMA," September 1, 2005.

12. ABC, *Nightline*, September 1, 2005.

13. *Times-Picayune*, September 1, 2005, http://www.nola.com/weblogs/print.ssf?/mtlogs/nola_Times-Picayune/archives/print075996.html.

14. The interview with New Orleans mayor Ray Nagin is archived on Air America's Website at http://a901.g.akamai.net/7/901/13186/v002/airamerica.download.akamai.com/13186/aarplace/media/Nagin.mp3.

15. Ibid.

16. Associated Press, "Guard Arrives with Food, Water and Weapons," *Houston Chronicle*, September 2, 2005.

17. Ibid.

18. Greenpeace, "Chemical Plant Explosion in New Orleans," September 2, 2005, http://www.greenpeace.org/usa/news/chemical-plant-explosion-in-ne.

19. Peter Baker, "An Embattled Bush Says 'Results Are Not Acceptable,'" *Washington Post*, September 3, 2005, p. A01.

20. Ibid.

21. Evan Thomas, "How Bush Blew It," *Newsweek*, September 19, 2005, http://www.msnbc.msn.com/id/9287434/print/1/displaymode/1098/.

22. Ibid.

23. Lisa Rosetta, "Frustrated: Fire Crews to Hand Out Flyers for FEMA," *The Salt Lake Tribune*, September 12, 2005, http://www.sltrib.com/utah/ci_3004197.

24. The White House, Press Release, "President Arrives in Alabama, Briefed on Hurricane Katrina," September 2, 2005, http://www.whitehouse.gov/news/releases/2005/09/20050902-2.html.

25. Barker, "An Embattled Bush Says 'Results Are Not Acceptable'" *Washington Post*, September 3, 2005, p. A01; The White House, Press Release, "President Arrives in Alabama."

26. Ibid.; The White House, Press Release, "President Tours Biloxi, Mississippi Hurricane Damaged Neighborhoods," September 2, 2005, http://www.whitehouse.gov/news/releases/2005/09/20050902-6.html.

27. Homeland Security, Press Release, "U.S. Airlines Provide Emergency Airlift for New Orleans Evacuees," September 2, 2005, http://www.dhs.gov/dhspublic/display?content=4782.

28. Associated Press, "Guard Arrives."

29. Ibid.

30. Ibid.

31. Mary Foster (Associated Press Writer), "Guardsmen Evacuate Refugees from Superdome," *Guardian Unlimited*, September 2, 2005.

32. Ibid.

33. Ibid.

34. "Evacuations Resume at Flooded Hospital," CNN.com, September 2, 2005, http://www.cnn.com/2005/HEALTH/09/02/katrina.hospitals/index.html.

35. Salatheia Bryant, Edward Hegstrom, Bill Murphy, and Leigh Hopper, "Officials Open Reliant Center to House up to 11,000 More Evacuees," *The Houston Chronicle*, September 2, 2005.

36. Ibid.

37. The White House, Office of the First Lady, Press Release, "Mrs. Bush Visits Those Affected by Hurricane Katrina," September 2, 2005, http://www.whitehouse.gov/news/releases/2005/09/20050902-7.html.

38. Deb Price, "Black Leaders Blast Government Relief Efforts," *The De-

troit News, September 2, 2005, http://www.detnews.com/2005/nation/0509/02/aut01-302104.htm.

39. Ibid.

40. Ibid.

41. Mike Liddell, "Landrieu Blasts Bush on Katrina Response," *From the Roots* (Community weblog of the Democratic Senatorial Campaign Committee), September 3, 2005, http://www.fromtheroots.org/story/2005/9/3/19542/97952.

42. Michelle Krupa, "Bush Visit Halts Food Delivery," *Times-Picayune*, September 3, 2005.

43. Barker, "An Embattled Bush"; The White House, Press Release, "President Remarks on Hurricane Recovery Efforts," September 2, 2005, http://www.whitehouse.gov/news/releases/2005/09/20050902-8.html.

44. Bush believes he can supply "guns and butter," or fight the war on terror and provide sufficient attention to pressing domestic issues, although such a claim is undercut by the fashion in which the issues related to Katrina, including racial injustice, economic inequality, and poverty, cried out for presidential attention. When Bush was asked at a press conference in Biloxi, Mississippi, about the criticism that the diversion of resources to Iraq has taken away from resources the country needs now, he replied, "I just completely disagree. We've got a job to defend this country and the war on terror, and we've got a job to bring aid and comfort to the people of the Gulf Coast, and we'll do both. We've got plenty of resources to do both. Somebody questioned me the other day about—do we have enough National Guard troops? Of course we do. These governors have got compacts with other states. If they need to call upon another state, the state will send Guard troops. And the people have just got to know, we've got what it takes to do more than one thing, and we'll secure our country from the terrorists, and we'll help rebuild this part of the world." The White House, Press Release, "President Tours Biloxi, Mississippi Hurricane Damaged Neighborhoods."

45. State of Louisiana, Governor Kathleen Babineaux Blanco, "Letter from Governor Blanco to President Bush," September 2, 2005, http://www.gov.state.la.us/index.cfm?md=newsroom&tmp=detail&catID=1&articleID=792&navID=3.

46. The White House, "Press Briefing by Scott McClellan."

47. State of Louisiana, Governor Kathleen Babineaux Blanco, "Letter from Governor Blanco to President Bush."

48. State of Louisiana, Executive Department, Executive Order No. KBB 2005-26, "DECLARATION OF PUBLIC HEALTH EMERGENCY TO SUSPEND OUT-OF-STATE LICENSURE FOR MEDICAL PROFESSIONALS AND PERSONNEL," September 2, 2005, http://gov.louisiana.gov/assets/docs/26Public HealthEmergencyDeclaration.pdf; Executive Order KBB KBB 05-25, "Emergency Evacuation by Buses," September 2, 2005, http://www.state.la.us/osr%5Cother%5Ckbb05-25.htm.

49. Eric Lipton, Christopher Drew, Scott Shane, and David Rhode, "STORM AND CRISIS: Government Assistance; Breakdowns Marked Path from Hurricane to Anarchy," *The New York Times*, September 11, 2005, p. 1.

50. The White House, Press Release, "President Remarks on Hurricane Recovery Efforts."

51. Ibid.

52. Thomas, "How Bush Blew It."

53. Scott Pelley (*60 Minutes* Correspondent), "Katrina Response Sparks Outrage," *(CBS News) 60 Minutes*, September 5, 2005, http://www.cbsnews.com/stories/2005/09/05/60minutes/printable815179.shtml.

54. Ibid.; also see "Convoys Bring Relief to New Orleans," CNN.com, http://edition.cnn.com./2005/US/09/02/katrina.impact, where Nagin says Bush was "very serious" and "very engaging" during his visit to New Orleans. "He was brutally honest. He wanted to know the truth. . . . And we talked turkey. I think we're in a good spot now."

55. Thomas, "How Bush Blew It."

56. Ibid.; for Nagin's comments on Honore: http://a901.g.akamai.net/7/901/13186/v002/airamerica.download.akamai.com/13186/aarplace/media/Nagin.mp3.

57. Thomas, "How Bush Blew It."

58. Ibid.

59. Manuel Roig-Franzia and Spence Hsu, "Many Evacuated, but Thousands Still Waiting," *Washington Post*, September 4, 2005, p. A01.

60. Ibid.

61. Ibid.; Eric Lipton, Eric Schmitt, and Thom Lanker, "Political Issues Snarled Plans for Troop Aid," *The New York Times*, September 9, 2005, p. 1.

62. Ibid.

63. Ibid. The struggle between Bush and Blanco highlights an unintended consequence of the National Response Plan that was drafted after 9/11: that first responders, including civilian police and the National Guard, could be overwhelmed by a disaster or crisis. One of the legacies of Katrina may be a strong debate about the capacity of first responders to address a national crisis, and a rethinking of lines of authority in the face of state and local officials' being placed at a strong disadvantage by disaster or crisis. DHS chief Chertoff has already suggested that active-duty combat troops be trained to take over if first responders are felled. Lipton, Schmitt, and Lanker, "Political Issues Snarled Plans for Troop Aid."

64. Ibid.

65. Roig-Franzia and Hsu, "Many Evacuated."

66. Adam Nagourney and Anne E. Kornblut, "STORM AND CRISIS: The President; White House Enacts a Plan to Ease Political Damage," *New York Times*, September 9, 2005, p. 21.

67. Ibid.

68. "President Sending Additional Troops to Hurricane-Damaged Region"

(Associated Press), *The New York Times*, September 3, 2005, http://www.ny
times.com/2005/09/03/national/nationalspecial/03WIRE-BUSH.html?ex=
1132722000&en=4d58d9e0bf191ccc&ei=5070.

69. Roig-Franzia and Hsu, "Many Evacuated."

70. The White House, Radio Address, "President Addresses Nation, Discusses Hurricane Katrina Relief Efforts," September 3, 2005, http://www.whitehouse.gov/news/releases/2005/09/20050903.html.

71. Nagourney and Kornblutt, "STORM AND CRISIS: The President."

72. Ibid.

73. Ibid.

74. Roig-Franzia and Hsu, "Many Evacuated."

CHAPTER 7

1. Manuel Roig-Franzia and Spence Hsu, "Many Evacuated, but Thousands Still Waiting," *Washington Post*, September 4, 2005, p. A01; "Superdome Evacuation Completed" (Associated Press), MSNBC.COM, http://www.msnbc.msn.com/id/9175611.

2. "Buses Arrive at New Orleans Convention Center" (Associated Press), *News 8 Austin*, September 3, 2005, http://www.news8austin.com/content/your_news/default.asp?ArID=144789so.

3. Roig-Franzia and Hsu, "Many Evacuated"; "Military Claims 42,000 Evacuated," *Herald Sun* (Australia), September 4, 2005.

4. Eric Lipton, Christopher Drew, Scott Shane, and David Rhode, "STORM AND CRISIS: Government Assistance; Breakdowns Marked Path from Hurricane to Anarchy," *The New York Times*, September 11, 2005, p. 1.

5. "Buses Arrive."

6. Roig-Franzia and Hsu, "Many Evacuated."

7. Ibid.

8. "Bush Aides Meet with Black Leaders" (Associated Press), *WJLA ABC News* (Washington, D.C.), September 3, 2005, http://www.wjla.com/news/stories/0905/257278.html.

9. Ibid.

10. Ibid.; Roig-Franzia and Hsu, "Many Evacuated."

11. Saturday, September 3, 2005, "Kanye West: 'George Bush Doesn't Care About Black People'" *Boingboing: a directory of wonderful things*, http://www.boingboing.net/2005/09/03/kanye_west_george_bu.html.

12. "Reaction to Katrina Split on Racial Lines," CNN.com, September 13, 2005, http://www.cnn.com/2005/US/09/12/katrina.race.poll/.

13. "Kanye West."

14. Scott Shane, "At Hearing, States and National Guard Make Appeals for Aid," *The New York Times*, September 29, 2005, p. 30.

15. "The Katrina Exit; Tending to a Home Tragedy Is Reason to Leave Iraq," *Pittsburgh Post-Gazette*, September 9, 2005, p. B–6. Although I agree

with the criticism of the war in Iraq, I agree with Christopher Hitchens that the moral appeal of my position need not rest on a zero-sum social concern, so that to pay attention to one issue cancels out concern for another. In fact, it may even be morally repugnant to suggest a selfish, narcissistic concern for one's own kin and country while others who suffer in the world are left to their own fate because there is only so much concern to go around. As Hitchens writes, such logic goes, "We should get out and leave them to their own devices. We need the stuff at home, goddamn it. This has all the charm and beauty of John Kerry saying that we ought not to be opening firehouses in Baghdad while closing them in the United States. It also has all the easy appeal of a zero-sum, provincial, isolationist mentality." See Hitchens, "Don't blame Iraq for the mess: More should have been done for New Orleans, but the U.S. didn't lack troops," *Ottawa Citizen*, September 7, 2005, p. A15. What Hitchens misses, however, is that critical political attention can be attenuated by concentration on (foreign or domestic) matters seen as more pressing, and important, than other equally significant matters. Bush's obsession with fighting terror has robbed him of the capacity to pay attention to the civil liberties and social justice that, ostensibly, are part of the reasons the troops are in Iraq to begin with. In short, it need not be an either/or proposition, or a zero-sum game, that rules the distribution of political attention and social concern, but it is usually very difficult for politicians preoccupied with defending a particular policy track and agenda in war to sufficiently account for resource sharing back home. Thus, we avoid the ugly moral myopia to which Hitchens points—one that rests on a carefully cultivated, and exclusive, self-concern—while underscoring the need to take inventory of social justice and relations with others on our terrain. Thus, when black folk asked (in World War II, Vietnam, the Gulf War) what sense it made to protect freedoms for others on foreign soil that we couldn't enjoy back home, it wasn't an argument against foreign folk enjoying, for instance, democracy or justice. It was simply a critique of such injustices at home, and a plea to partake of the same recognition and social goods that others away from home might enjoy because of their efforts.

16. Shane, "At Hearing, States and National Guard Make Appeals for Aid."

17. Scott Shane and Tom Shanker, "When Storm Hit, National Guard Was Deluged Too," *The New York Times*, September 28, 2005, p. 1.

18. "Troops Told 'Shoot to Kill' in New Orleans," *ABC News Online*, September 2, 2005, http://www.abc.net.au/news/newsitems/200509/s1451906.htm.

19. "Order Slowly Returns to New Orleans as Rescue Drive Redoubled" (AFP), *Political News*, September 3, 2005, http://www.political-news.org/breaking/15243/order-slowly-returns-to-new-orleans-as-rescue-drive-redoubled.html.

20. "Lt. Gen. Honore a 'John Wayne Dude,'" CNN.com, September 3, 2005, http://www.cnn.com/2005/US/09/02/honore.profile; Kevin Chappell,

"The Aftermath of Hurricane Katrina: And the Man Who's Helping Put Things Back Together," *Ebony*, November 2005, pp. 284–287.

21. Roig-Franzia and Hsu, "Many Evacuated."

22. Ibid.

23. Ibid.

24. Homeland Security, Press Release, "Highlights of United States Government Response to the Aftermath of Hurricane Katrina," September 4, 2005, http://www.dhs.gov/dhspublic/display?content=4784. The DHS document claimed that 17,000 lives were saved, 35,000 citizens were evacuated, and 499 shelters had been put up to house 135,000 people; that 35,000 National Guard personnel were on site, joined by 4,000 members of the U.S. Coast Guard; that there were 5,000 FEMA responders; and that 4.8 million meals ready to eat (MREs) and 11 million liters of water were distributed. (Brigadier General Mark Graham of U.S. Northern Command said elsewhere that 35,000 people had been evacuated from the city in 788 bus journeys and 55 airlifts.) DHS bragged of plans to evacuate 10,000 people a day, which began on Saturday, in the "largest emergency domestic airlift of people in U.S. history." The agency claimed that "this is the largest and most comprehensive National Guard response to a natural disaster." (The previous record was reached in 1989, when 32,000 California Guardsmen were called into service during the Loma Prieta earthquake.) But it would take more than press releases to relieve the impression that the federal government's forces were ill equipped to provide disaster relief.

25. FEMA announced that "one hundred percent of evacuees housed in the New Orleans Superdome and Convention Center have been evacuated" (FEMA, Press Release, "Hurricane Katrina Response and Recovery Update," September 4, 2005, http://www.fema.gov/news/newsrelease.fema?id=18602). FEMA also broke down the numbers and locations of the 222,400 evacuees: 6,000 went to Alabama, 1,000 to D.C., 1,400 to Florida, 900 to Georgia, 60,000 to other parts of Louisiana, 16,000 to Mississippi, 100 to Tennessee, and 137,000 to Texas. FEMA's numbers on shelters, 563, and the people housed in them, 151,409, were higher than those cited by DHS. FEMA said that a twelve-car Amtrak train would make two daily round trips between New Orleans and Lafayette, Louisiana, to evacuate 650 passengers to various destinations on each trip. In its release, FEMA noted that 100 million MREs had been shipped by the Department of Defense to shelters and that more than 170,000 meals were being served to affected areas daily. There were also 29 Disaster Medical Teams (DMAT), 5 Disaster Mortuary Operation Response Teams (DMORT), 2 Veterinary Assistant Teams (VMAT), and 1 Mental Health Team in place in Louisiana, while Mississippi had 10 DMATs, 5 DMORTs, and 1 Mental Health Team. Besides the more than 30,000 National Guard troops on the ground, FEMA noted the additional 12,730 Active Duty troops and military personnel who had been deployed. FEMA bragged that 15,665 people had been saved by the Coast Guard, more than three times the number of folk

saved in 2004. Finally, FEMA had dispatched 5,877 personnel to the field, including 1,811 National Disaster Medical System (NDMS) medical professionals and 1,777 Urban Search and Rescue (US&R) staff.

26. Jeanne Meserve, "E-Mails Show FEMA Infighting, Frustration," CNN.com, October 18, 2005, http://www.cnn.com/2005/POLITICS/10/18/fema.memos/index.html.

27. Lipton et al., "STORM AND CRISIS."

28. Ibid.

29. Ibid.

30. Andrew Martin and Andrew Zajac, "Offer of Buses Fell Between the Cracks," *Chicago Tribune*, September 23, 2005, http://www.chicagotribune.com/news/nationworld/chi-0509230350sep23,1,1130161.story?coll=chi-newsnationworld-hed.

31. Ibid.

32. Ibid.

33. Mark Benjamin, "Communications Breakdown," Salon.com, September 9, 2005, http://www.salon.com/news/feature/2005/09/09/comm_meltdown.

34. Stephen J. Hedges, "Craft with Food, Water, Doctors Needed Orders," *Chicago Tribune*, September 4, 2005, http://www.chicagotribune.com/news/nationworld/chi-0509040369sep04,1,4144825.story?ctrack=1&cset=true.

35. http://news.globalfreepress.com/movs/katrina/BBC_Katrina.mpg. Kelly was obviously spoken to about his forthright comments and implicit criticism of the federal government, and the president. He issued an email correction to his comments: "USNORTHCOM was prepositioned for response to the hurricane, but as per the National Response Plan, we support the lead federal agency in disaster relief—in this case, FEMA. The simple description of the process is the state requests federal assistance from FEMA which in turn may request assistance from the military upon approval by the president or Secretary of Defense. Having worked the hurricanes from last year as well as Dennis this year, we knew that FEMA would make requests of the military—primarily in the areas of transportation, communications, logistics, and medicine. Thus we began staging such assets and waited for the storm to hit. The biggest hurdles to responding to the storm were the storm itself—couldn't begin really helping until it passed—and damage assessment—figuring out which roads were passable, where communications and power were out, etc. Military helos began damage assessment and SAR on Tuesday. Thus we had permission to operate as soon as it was possible. We even brought in night SAR helos to continue the mission on Tuesday night. The President and Secretary of Defense did authorize us to act right away and are not to blame on this end. Yes, we have to wait for authorization, but it was given in a timely manner." Kevin Drum, "Political Animal," *Washington Monthly*, September 5, 2005, http://www.washingtonmonthly.com/archives/individual/2005_09/007054.php.

36. Bill Conroy, "U.S. Customs' Hurricane-Relief Blackhawks Pulling Press

Duty," *The Narcosphere*, September 1, 2005, http://www.narcoshere.narco news.com.

37. Ibid.

38. Nancy Imperiale, "Airboaters Stalled by FEMA," *Florida Sun-Sentinel*, September 2, 2005, http://www.sun-sentinel.com/news/local/florida/orl-cane boats0205sep02,0,4766048.story?coll=sfla-news-florida.

39. Ibid.

40. Ann Rodgers, "Homeland Security Won't Let Red Cross Deliver Food," *Pittsburgh Post-Gazette*, September 3, 2005, http://www.post-gazette.com/ pg/05246/565143.stm.

41. (Tribune staff reports) "Daley 'Shocked' at Federal Snub of Offers to Help," *Chicago Tribune*, September 2, 2005, http://www.chicagotribune.com/ news/local/chi-050902daley,1,2011979.story?coll=chi-news-hed.

42. Shannon Sollinger, "Loudoun Relief Crew Turned Away," *Loudoun Times-Mirror* (Virginia), September 2, 2005, http://www.zwire.com/site/tab1. cfm?newsid=15144436&BRD=2553&PAG=461&dept_id=506035&rfi=6.

43. Jill Zarend-Kubatko, "Many Ways to Aid Victims," *Tri Valley Central*, September 2, 2005, http://www.zwire.com/site/news.cfm?newsid=15147862 &BRD.

44. Pelican, Daily Kos (Blog), "Just to Give You a Sense of Just How Badly FEMA Has F*cked Up," September 3, 2005, http://www.dailykos.com; Scott Shane, "STORM AND CRISIS: The Fallout; After Failures, Officials Play Blame Game," *The New York Times*, September 5, 2005, p. 1; Claudia Kemmer (Associated Press), "German Plane with 15 Tons of Aid Turned Back from U.S.," *Star-Tribune (Minnesota)*, September 10, 2005, http://www.startribune .com/stories/125/5607363.html; "Jefferson Parish Sheriff Harry Lee Comman- deers Sam's Wal-Mart Stores," *Times-Picayune*, September 11, 2005, http:// www.nola.com/weblogs/print.ssf?/mtlogs/nola_Times-Picayune/archives/ print078842.html; Lisa Rosetta, "Frustrated: Fire Crews to Hand Out Flyers for FEMA," *The Salt Lake Tribune*, September 12, 2005, http://www.sltrib. com/utah/ci_3004197.

45. Rosetta, "Frustrated."

46. Laurie Smith Anderson, "Doctor Says FEMA Ordered Him to Stop Treating Hurricane Victims," *2theadvocate News*, September 16, 2005, http:// www.2theadvocate.com/stories/091605/new_doctorordered001.shtml.

47. Ibid.

48. Ibid.

49. Transcript for September 4, *Meet the Press*, September 4, 2005, http:// www.msnbc.msn.com/id/9179790.

50. Ibid.

51. E&P Staff, "An Angry 'Times-Picayune' Calls for Firing of FEMA Chief, and Others, in Open Letter to President Bush," *Editor & Publisher*, September 4, 2005, http://editorandpublisher.com/eandp/news/article_display.jsp?vnu_ content_id=1001054586.

52. Ibid.

CHAPTER 8

1. Elisabeth Bumiller and Clyde Haberman, "Bush Makes Return Visit; Two Levees Secured," *The New York Times*, September 6, 2005, p. 1; KOMO Staff and News Services, "President Bush Tours Gulf States Again," *KOMOTV*, September 5, 2005, http://www.komotv.com/news/story.asp?ID=38987.

2. Bumiller and Haberman, "Bush Makes Return Visit"; "Repairs Complete on 17th Street Levee," KRON4, September 5, 2005, http://www.kron4.com/Global/story.asp?S=3808657.

3. Bumiller and Haberman, "Bush Makes Return Visit."

4. KOMO Staff, "President Bush Tours Gulf States Again." Blanco later tried to downplay her difference with the president. "We'd like to stop the voices out there trying to create a divide. We're all in this together." See Will Lester (Associated Press writer), "Bush Says He'll Find Out What Went Wrong," *San Francisco Gate*, September 6, 2005, http://www.sfgate.com/cgi-bin/article.cgi?file=/n/a/2005/09/06/national/w083222D53.DTL.

5. Bumiller and Haberman, "Bush Makes Return Visit."

6. Ibid.; Lester, "Bush Says He'll Find Out."

7. E&P Staff, "Barbara Bush: Things Working Out 'Very Well' for Poor Evacuees from New Orleans," *Editor & Publisher*, September 5, 2005, http://editorandpublisher.com/eandp/news/article_display.jsp?vnu_content_id=1001054719.

8. Ibid.

9. Naomi Klein, "The Rise of Disaster Capitalism," *The Nation*, May 2, 2005, http://www.thenation.com/doc/20050502/klein.

10. Ibid.

11. Lolita C. Baldor, "Halliburton Subsidiary Taps Contract for Repairs," *Washington Post*, September 5, 2005, p. A20. The deal was first announced on September 1, 2005, on the Halliburton Watch Website. See "Halliburton Gets Katrina Contract, Hires Former FEMA Director," *Halliburton Watch*, September 1, 2005, http://www.halliburtonwatch.org/news/hurricane_katrina.html.

12. Baldor, "Halliburton Subsidiary."

13. "Halliburton Gets Katrina Contract."

14. Ibid.

15. "Halliburton Donates More than $1 Million to Hurricane Relief," Press Statement, Halliburton Co., September 20, 2005.

16. Eric Lipton and Ron Nixon, "Many Contracts for Storm Work Raise Questions," *The New York Times*, September 26, 2005, p. 1; Jamie Wilson Washington, "Katrina Relief Contracts Come Under Investigation," *The Guardian* (London), September 27, 2005, p. 15.

17. Lipton and Nixon, "Many Contracts."

18. Ibid.; Oliver Morgan, "Congress Probes Hurricane Clean-Up Contracts," *The Observer*, September 11, 2005, http://observer.guardian.co.uk/business/story/0,6903,1567081,00.html.

19. Angie C. Marek, "Minorities Miss Out on Contracts," *U.S. News & World Report*, October 6, 2005.

20. Hope Yen, "U.S. Pledges to Boost Minority Contracts" (Associated Press), Blackenterprise.com, October 10, 2005, http://www.blackenterprise.com/yb.

21. Hope Yen (Associated Press), "Minority Firms Getting Few Contracts," *Sacramento Bee*, October 5, 2005, http://64.233.161.104/search?q=cache: og6aMWuOrB4J:www.sacbee.com/24hour/jobs/story/2782597p-11393901c. html+Hope+Yen,+Minority+Firms+Getting+Few+Katrina+Contracts&hl= en.

22. Latif Lewis, "Black Firms Seek Contracts after Katrina," Blackenterprise.com, September 2005.

23. Yen, "Minority Firms."

24. "Sens. Clinton, Mikulski Call for FEMA Overhaul," NBC4 (Los Angeles), September 6, 2005, http://www.nbc4.tv/news/4941092/detail.html; Lester, "Bush Says He'll Find Out."

25. The White House, "Press Briefing by Scott McClellan," September 7, 2005, http://www.whitehouse.gov/news/releases/2005/09/20050907-2.html; "GOP Leaders Agree to Joint Katrina Hearings," CNN.com, September 8, 2005, http://edition.cnn.com/2005/POLITICS/09/07/katrina.congress.

26. Richard W. Stevenson and Anne E. Kornblut, "STORM AND CRISIS: The Emergency Agency; Director of FEMA Stripped of Role as Relief Leader," *The New York Times*, September 10, 2005, p. 1.

27. Ibid.

28. Ibid.; Lara Jakes Jordan (Associated Press), "FEMA Director Brown Relieved of Hurricane Responsibilities," *San Diego Union-Tribune*, September 9, 2005, http://www.signonsandiego.com/news/nation/katrina/20050909-1105-katrina-brown.html.

29. Helen Dewar and Dana Milbank, "Cheney Dismisses Critic with Obscenity," *Washington Post*, June 25, 2004, p. A04.

30. "Bush Gets Ground Tour of Katrina Damage," CNN.com, September 12, 2005, http://www.cnn.com/2005/US/09/12/katrina.impact; Richard W. Stevenson, "STORM AND CRISIS: The Emergency Agency; After Days of Criticism, Emergency Director Resigns," *The New York Times*, September 13, 2005, p. 26.

CHAPTER 9

1. Peter Ortiz, "Deportation Fears Keep Latinos from Seeking Katrina Aid," DiversityInc.com, September 9, 2005, http://www.diversityinc.com.

2. Ibid.

3. C. Stone Brown, "Katrina's Forgotten Victims: Native American Tribes," DiversityInc.com, September 9, 2005, http://www.diversityinc.com.

4. Ibid.

5. Anita Johnson, Thenmozhi Soundararajan, and Jeff Chang, "Frustration

and Survival in the Superdome," *AlterNet*, September 16, 2005, http://www.alternet.org/katrina/25564/.

6. Matt Aupzo (Associated Press), "Katrina Threatens to Wipe Out Many Gulf Coast Shrimpers," *Environmental News Network*, September 15, 2005, http://www.enn.com/biz.html?id=1041.

7. Johnson, Soundararajan, and Chang, "Frustration and Survival."

8. As historian Barbara Fields argued nearly a quarter century ago, "Class and race are concepts of a different order; they do not occupy the same analytical space, and thus cannot constitute explanatory alternatives to each other." For Fields, "class refers to a material circumstance: the inequality of human beings from the standpoint of social power," while race, "on the other hand, is a purely ideological notion." Fields says that once "ideology is stripped away, nothing remains except an abstraction which, while meaningful to a statistician, could scarcely have inspired all the mischief that race has caused during its malevolent historical career." She concludes that "because class and race are not equivalent concepts, it is erroneous to offer them as alternatives to each other." Barbara Fields, "Ideology and Race in American History," in J. Morgan Kousser and James M. McPherson, editors, *Region, Race, and Reconstruction: Essays in Honor of C. Vann Woodward* (New York/Oxford: Oxford University Press, 1982), pp. 143–177. I am not seeking to substitute one for the other, but simply to highlight how the interaction of two strong variables produces material effects on the black poor.

9. Alan Berube and Steven Raphael, "Access to Cars in New Orleans," Brookings Institution, September 15, 2005, http://www.brookings.edu/metro/20050915_katrinacarstables.pdf.

10. Ibid.

11. For an exploration of what I term the *Afristocracy*, my extended response to Cosby, and my engagement with the issues broached in his infamous remarks, see my *Is Bill Cosby Right? Or Has the Black Middle Class Lost Its Mind?* (New York: Basic Civitas Books, 2005).

12. Cynthia Tucker, "Katrina Exposes Our Callous Treatment of the Poor," *The Atlanta Journal-Constitution*, September 6, 2005, http://www.uexpress.com/asiseeit/?uc_full_date=20050906.

13. Ibid.

14. Cynthia Tucker, "Bill Cosby's Pointed Remarks May Spark Much-Needed Debate," *As I See It*, Uexpress.com, May 26, 2004, http://www.uexpress.com/asiseeit/index.html?uc_full_date=20040526.

15. Ibid.

16. Cynthia Tucker, "Bill Cosby's Plain-Spokenness Comes Not a Moment Too Soon," *As I See It*, Uexpress.com, September 25, 2004, http://www.uexpress.com/asiseeit/index.html?uc_full_date=20040925.

17. Ibid.

18. Jesse Washington (Associated Press), "Katrina Inspires Generosity of Black Americans," MSNBC.com, September 9, 2005, http://www.msnbc.

msn.com/id/9260569; Kelefa Sanneh, "Rapping for a Hometown in Hurricane Crisis," *The New York Times*, September 19, 2005, p. E1.

19. Sanneh, "Rapping for a Hometown in Hurricane Crisis"; Desiree Cooper, "Outrage, Caring Mix in Katrina Response," *Detroit Free Press*, September 15, 2005, http://64.233.161.104/search?q=cache:iP3L7ti52aAJ:www.freep.com/news/metro/cooper15e_20050915.htm+Outrage,+Caring+Mix+in+Katrina+Response&hl=en; Nekesa Mumbi Moody (Associated Press Music Writer), "Danny Glover and Harry Belafonte Criticize Bush Administration for Slow Katrina Response," BlackNews.com, September 29, 2005, http://www.blacknews.com/pr/katrinajazz101.html; Duff Wilson, "Sports Business; In Katrina Relief, Some Leagues Are Digging Deeper," *The New York Times*, September 23, 2005, p. D4; Remmie Fresh, "Kanye, Common, Mos Def, Talib Help Kevin Powell with Relief Effort," ALLHIPHOPNEWS.com, September 8, 2005, http://www.allhiphop.com/hiphopnews/?ID=4805.

20. Martin Luther King, Jr., "A Time to Break Silence," in James Melvin Washington, editor, *A Testament of Hope: The Essential Writings and Speeches of Martin Luther King, Jr.* (New York: HarperCollins Publishers, 1991, reprint), p. 241.

21. Josh Tyrangiel, "Why You Can't Ignore Kanye," *Time*, August 29, 2005, p. 54.

22. "Carlson Attacks Kanye over Bush Racism Claims," Contactmusic.com, September 9, 2005, http://www.contactmusic.com/new/xmlfeed.nsf/mndweb pages/carlson%20attacks%20kanye%20over%20bush%20racism%20claims.

23. Lawrence N. Powell, "New Orleans: An American Pompeii?" September 2005, pp. 2–3. Paper in author's possession.

24. "Master P Questions Kanye's Telethon Rant," Contactmusic.com, September 9, 2005, http://www.contactmusic.com/new/xmlfeed.nsf/mndweb pages/master%20p%20questions%20kanyes%20telethon%20rant.

25. "Kanye West Stands by Critique of President Bush at $2 Bill Show," MTVNEWS.com, September 12, 2005, http://www.mtv.com/news/articles/1509309/20050912/story.jhtml.

26. Ibid.

27. "T.I., David Banner Get Behind Kanye's Bush Comments," MTVNEWS.com, http://www.mtv.com/news/articles/1509000/20050906/story.jhtml.

28. Ibid.

29. Ibid.

30. Vanessa Satten, "Still Lives Through," *XXL*, December 2005, pp. 112, 114.

31. Ibid.

32. Dave Zirin, "Etan Thomas Rises to the Occasion," *The Nation*, September 28, 2005, http://www.thenation.com/doc/20050926/zirin.

33. Ibid. See Etan Thomas, *More Than an Athlete: Poems by Etan Thomas* (Atlanta: Moore Black Press, 2005).

34. For an explanation of Bob Moses's philosophy of civil rights and education, see Robert P. Moses and Charles E. Cobb, Jr., *Radical Equations: Civil*

Rights from Mississippi to the Algebra Project (Boston: Beacon Press, reprint, 2002).

35. "Black People Loot, White People Find?" *Boingboing: A Directory of Wonderful Things*, August 30, 2005, http://www.boingboing.net/2005/08/30/black_people_loot_wh.html.

36. Ibid.

37. Satten, "Still Lives Through."

38. Ibid.

39. Jordan Flaherty, "Notes from Inside New Orleans," *New Orleans Independent Media Center*, September 2, 2005, http://neworleans.indymedia.org/news/2005/09/4043.php.

40. Susannah Rosenblatt and James Rainey, "Katrina Takes a Toll on Truth, News Accuracy," *Los Angeles Times*, September 27, 2005, p. A16; Brian Thevenot and Gordon Russell, "Rape. Murder. Gunfights. For Three Anguished Days the World's Headlines Blared that the Superdome and Convention Center Had Descended into Anarchy," *The Times-Picayune*, September 26, 2005, p. A01.

41. Thevenot and Russell, "Rape. Murder. Gunfights."

42. Rosenblatt and Rainey, "Katrina Takes a Toll."

43. Ibid.

44. Ibid.

45. Thevenot and Russell, "Rape. Murder. Gunfights."

46. Ibid.

47. Ibid.

48. Ibid.

49. Rosenblatt and Rainey, "Katrina Takes a Toll."

CHAPTER 10

1. "Rabbi: Storm Was God's Punishment," *St. Petersburg Times*, September 10, 2005, p. 5A.

2. "Al-Quaida Hails U.S. Deaths," *The Toronto Sun*, September 15, 2005, p. 7.

3. Selwyn Crawford, "Storms as Wrath of God?" *The Dallas Morning News*, October 5, 2005, http://www.dallasnews.com/sharedcontent/dws/dn/religion/stories/DN-wrath_01rel.ART.State.Edition1.22187b9f.html.

4. Ibid.

5. Ibid.

6. This is from a synopsis of Boone's appearance on Pat Robertson's *700 Club* show on the program's Website, cited in Eric Deggans, "Add to Katrina's Toll Race-Tinged Rhetoric," *St. Petersburg Times*, September 14, 2005, p. 6A.

7. Crawford, "In Disasters"; Jim Rensen, "Hurricane News in Brief," *The Philadelphia Inquirer*, September 1, 2005, http://www.philly.com/mld/inquirer/news/nation/12530586.htm; "Franklin Graham Sees 'Revival' for New Orleans" (Associated Press), CNN.com, October 4, 2005, http://www.ccn.com/2005/US/10/14/katrina.graham.ap/index.html; "Religious Conserva-

tives Claim Katrina Was God's Omen, Punishment for United States," *Media Matters for America*, October 11, 2005, http://mediamatters.org.

8. Deggans, "Add to Katrina's Toll."

9. Ibid.

10. Ibid.

11. I am not arguing that all conservative Christians hold the view that only sinners suffer. I am suggesting, however, that many conservative Christians view suffering as the most direct and visible confirmation of sin in a person's life. Thus, fewer conservative Christians offer insightful theological reflections on the character of suffering than would otherwise be the case if they probed beyond the reflexive tendencies of asserting tragedy as the concomitant of infidelity to the faith, or as the sure symptom of fatal departures from the path of righteousness.

12. See Harold Kushner's provocative treatment of the subject, *When Bad Things Happen to Good People* (New York: Anchor Books, reprint, 2004).

13. Fr. Thomas Rosica, "Where Was God in This Crisis?" *The Toronto Sun*, September 11, 2005, p. C6.

14. "Commentary: Hurricane Katrina," *Religion & Ethics Newsweekly*, Episode 901, September 2, 2005.

15. Ibid.

16. Ibid.

17. Ibid.

18. "Feature: The Five Cantors," *Religion & Ethics Newsweekly*, Episode 540, June 7, 2002. LaBelle was responding to a Catholic bishop's statement about sexual abuse among clergy in the Catholic Church. LaBelle avowed that "I am disappointed that the policy does not hold the bishops themselves, where appropriate, to some censure for very unhealthy and inappropriate behavior (in Boston, for example). That may happen in executive sessions, however. The policy's structure might need to be more specific in setting up a way to censure bishops or major superiors who misbehave themselves." Later, LaBelle suggests that the "various discussions about celibacy, homosexuality, married clergy, and ordination of women have done little but blur the issues," hinting that while he is sensitive to some victims, i.e., the youth abused by the clergy, he is equally insensitive to others victimized by a different class of issues. Although LaBelle suggests that such issues "should be addressed, at another time and place," they are "not essentially related to this issue." Of course, given the fact that the church had long failed to address the issue of clergy exploitation of children and youth until its hand was forced, it is likely that the other "distracting" issues will likewise be avoided until the Catholic Church is forced to confront them. In any regard, the major point is that LaBelle failed in this context on a nationally televised program devoted to ethics in religious communities to suggest that the clergy's behavior exhibited "original sin." In this light, one must draw the conclusion that LaBelle is more offended by the behavior of the black hurricane survivors in New Or-

leans, whose offenses turned out to be largely exaggerated, than he is by the demonstrable and grave injustices of fellow clergy in the Catholic Church.

19. "Commentary: Hurricane Katrina."

20. Leibniz explored theodicy in a book published in 1710, entitled *Essais de Théodicée sur la bonté de Dieu, la liberté de l'homme et l'origine du mal,* thus beginning for Western philosophy and religious thought a new phase in the question of evil.

21. Edward Rothstein, "Seeking Justice, of Gods or the Politicians," *The New York Times,* September 8, 2005, p. 1.

22. Ibid.

23. Ibid.

24. Ibid.

25. Ibid.

26. Ibid.

27. Peter Steinfels, "The Scarcely Heard Question Is How God Could Have Allowed the Catastrophe to Occur," *The New York Times,* September 10, 2005, p. 15.

28. Ibid.

29. Ibid.

30. Ibid.

31. See my take on pride in *Pride: The Seven Deadly Sins* (New York: Oxford University Press, 2006).

32. Martin Luther King, Jr., "I Have a Dream," in James Melvin Washington, editor, *Testament of Hope: The Essential Writings and Speeches of Martin Luther King, Jr.* (San Francisco: HarperSanFrancisco, reprint, 1991), p. 219.

33. Christopher Cooper, "Old-Line Families Escape Worst of Flood and Plot the Future," *The Wall Street Journal,* September 8, 2005, p. A1.

34. James Carroll, "Church, State, and Katrina," *The Boston Globe,* September 12, 2005, p. A15.

EPILOGUE

1. Brennen Jensen and Elizabeth Schwinn, "Donations for Hurricane Relief Exceed $2-Billion, but Costs Soar," *The Chronicle of Philanthropy,* November 2005, http://www.philanthropy.com/free/update/2005/11/2005110302.htm.

2. Kevin Drum, "Chronology," *Washington Monthly* (Political Animal), September 1, 2005, http://www.washingtonmonthly.com/archives/individual/2005_09/007023.php.

3. Yoji Cole, "DiversityInc Exclusive: FEMA's Almost All-White Leadership Plagued by Discrimination Complaints," DiversityInc.com, September 20, 2005, http://www.diversityinc.com; Yoji Cole, "Can FEMA Relate to Rita Victims? Bias Complaints Higher than Other Federal Agencies," DiversityInc.com, September 23, 2005, http://www.diversityinc.com.

4. Naomi Klein, "GOP Opportunity Zone," *The Nation*, September 23, 2005, http://www.thenation.com/doc/20050926/klein.

5. Naomi Klein, "Let the People Rebuild New Orleans," *The Nation*, September 26, 2005, http://www.thenation.com/doc/20050926/klein.

6. Jensen and Schwinn, "Donations."

7. "Katrina Aftermath," *Religion & Ethics Newsweekly*, Episode no. 902, September 9, 2005, http://www.pbs.org/wnet/religionandethics/week902/p-newsfeature.html.

8. Even when they are identified, the haphazard way in which the remains of the 8/29 victims are treated reflects a far different approach to this disaster than to the terrorist attacks of 9/11. Consider the story reported about some victims in New Orleans by the *New York Times*. "The death certificate for Norman Parr, 69, said he died in New Orleans, while Carol Parr, 59, was said to have perished on Fable Drive, but at the wrong address. Mr. Parr's certificate lists his death as 'Hurricane Katrina Related' but also adds that it was due to 'cardiovascular disease' and 'decomposition.' Likewise, Ms. Parr's certificate cited decomposition as a cause of death, though it also noted she had drowned. And when Douglas Arceneaux Jr. went to collect the wallet and other personal effects that had been used to identify his parents, Douglas, 69, and Betty, 65, the workers at St. Gabriel said they had been lost. As families finally begin to receive the bodies of their relatives from St. Gabriel, many have found them accompanied by documents that, instead of shedding light on their deaths, point to enormous sloppiness in recordkeeping and procedures at the morgue. Some have complained of bodies far more decomposed when they came out than when they went in; others that evacuees who died in the company of their families were taken to St. Gabriel without notice and kept there for weeks. Moreover, as of Friday not a single DNA sample from victims had been matched against samples submitted by families over the past two months, said Dr. Louis Cataldie, the state emergency medical director. Dr. Cataldie said that was because federal officials had not yet approved a DNA testing contract with a laboratory. And the director of the federal mortuary team at the Find Family Call Center, responsible for communicating with the families of victims, was arrested last week on charges that he had solicited sex in a public park in Baton Rouge. The disarray has tormented families who had been seeking reliable official information on how their relatives died. Many were already upset by news reports about victims that have received prominent attention here, including unproved allegations of mercy killings in New Orleans hospitals during the flood and the cremation of some bodies in the northwestern parish of Caddo before their families could locate them." Shaila Dewan, "Bungled Records of Storm Deaths Renew Anguish," *The New York Times*, November 13, 2005, p. 1.

AFTERWORD

1. Dan Barry and Adam Nossiter, "Mardi Gras Set for City Stripped of All but Pride," *New York Times*, February 17, 2006, p. 1.

2. Cynthia Willard-Lewis, interview with author, 2005.

3. Steven Hahn, *A Nation Under Our Feet: Black Political Struggles in the Rural South from Slavery to the Great Migration* (Cambridge, Mass.: The Belknap Press of Harvard University Press, 2003), pp. 456–457.

4. Jesse Jackson, interview with author, 2005.

5. James N. Gregory, *The Southern Diaspora: How the Great Migrations of Black and White Southerners Transformed America* (Chapel Hill: The University of North Carolina Press, 2005), p. 28.

ACKNOWLEDGMENTS

As usual, I am thankful to the late Liz Maguire for her intellectual companionship, strong friendship, and especially her brilliant editorial vision. I am grateful as well to Chris Greenberg for his superb help. I am thankful to Christine E. Marra, Anna Kaltenbach, Nancy Hall, and Donna Riggs for their excellent craft and inspired care for the manuscript.

I thank Paul Farber, my assistant, for his great research help and his marvelous work in keeping everything in order. I am grateful as well to James Peterson (a wonderful brother) and Salamishah Tillet (a triple threat), brilliant young scholars whose work and life are an inspiration to me.

I am also grateful to my Department chairs at the University of Pennsylvania—Ann Matter and Tukufu Zuberi—who provide a great atmosphere for teaching and writing. I am grateful to all the folk who help me at Penn as well: Valerie Walker, Gale Garrison, Carol Davis, Onyx Finney, Marie Hudson, and Cheryl Graham-Seay. I am grateful to Vanesse Lloyd-Sgambati for her expert media help. I am grateful as well to Robert and Benjamin Bynum (and to Zoe and Sherry too), for their incredible food, serious elegance, soulful atmosphere—and great book signings—at Zanzibar Blue.

I send a loving shout out to all my dear New Orleans friends, especially Winston, Wendy and Blair Burns, Brandon Odoms, Renee

McHenry, Wyane Encalarde, and Mia X, who withstood Katrina and proved they are strong and soulful survivors. I also send love to the brilliant and beautiful journalist Suzanne Malveaux, whose moving report from New Orleans brought tears to so many eyes.

I am grateful to all the amazing Katrina survivors from New Orleans who sat for interviews: Roslyn and Dwayne Woodfox, Lennard Noble, James Thomas II, DeWitt Galman, Christopher Gardner, Brenda Collins, Girard Walker, Oliver and Brenda Harris, Antoine and Dale Barriere, Michelle Jackson, Frank Jones, Andrew Morton, Dorothy Spells, Garvin Garvey, Celwynn Napoleon, Sherry Browning, Eva Haskins, Shirley Mitchell Morris, Melanie (16-years-old), Sam Jones, Steve Grayson, Cynthia Willard-Lewis, Joycelyn Moses, Jennifer Robertson, Michelle Keifer, Theresa Morris, Alvin Chambliss, Darlene Mathieu, Darnell Herrington, Lizell Brooks, Irma Regis, Nadine Jarmon, and Ronald Chisom. I am grateful to Harry Belafonte, Jesse Jackson, Gina Charbonnet, Scott Synder, David Phears, Marilyn Taylor, Chris Weaver, Susan Hudson Wallace, Mark Warner, Jaya Mejia (thanks for the list), and D. Z. Cofield for their interviews, and for their strong work on behalf of the Katrina survivors.

I am thankful for the love and support of my wonderful friends: Susan Taylor (Queen, you allowed me the greatest experience of New Orleans through your generosity and love) and Khephra Burns (Smooth); Stan and Barbara Perkins; Karen Lloyd and Coach Joe Hoskins; Linda Johnson Rice and Mel Farr (Superstar); Andriette Earl and Kashka; Marc Morial and Michelle Miller; Iyanla Vanzant; and of course, Soyini Madison.

Finally, I am thankful for the love and support of my family: my mother, Addie Mae Dyson, and my brothers Anthony, Everette, Jr., Gregory and Brian, and to my children Michael II, Maisha, and Mwata. And finally, to Marcia, whose love for, and commitment to, Katrina survivors has occupied nearly every waking hour of her life since the storm descended, this book is a gesture of our refusal to allow the story of Katrina's victims and survivors to be drowned by the floods of amnesia or swept away by the winds of neglect.

INDEX